LIVERPOOL SHOPFRONTS

THROUGH TIME

Daniel K. Longman

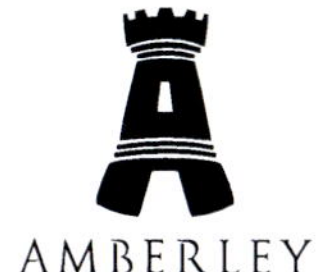

AMBERLEY

First published 2026

Amberley Publishing
The Hill, Stroud
Gloucestershire, GL5 4EP

www.amberley-books.com

ISBN 978 1 3981 2139 3 (print)
ISBN 978 1 3981 2140 9 (ebook)

British Library Cataloguing in Publication Data.
A catalogue record for this book is available from
the British Library.

Typeset in 10pt on 13pt Celeste.
Origination by Amberley Publishing.
Printed in the UK.

Appointed GPSR EU Representative:
Easy Access System Europe Oü, 16879218
Address: Mustamäe tee 50, 10621, Tallinn, Estonia
Contact Details: gpsr.requests@easproject.com,
+358 40 500 3575

Introduction

The High Street as we know it is a relatively recent phenomenon. The name can relate to any area of a town or city where the most important shops and businesses can be found. It is not always a formal designation, but sometimes the High Street is indeed on High Street. Here in Liverpool, Church Street is considered by most to be the principal shopping street of the city; it is named after St Peter's Church which was built there in 1700. In those days, Church Street had only a handful of houses, a concept entirely at odds with the vibrant and urbanised thoroughfare we know today.

Further back in medieval times most of what was consumed was produced, gathered or bartered as and when needed. Additional goods could be found at markets and fairs where people could buy and sell all manner of items from common livestock and crops, to exotic spices and luxurious jewellery. Liverpool's right to hold markets dates from 1207 when King John granted the people in the vicinity of 'Liuerpul' a Royal Charter to become a recognised town and hold a weekly market.

The charter also encouraged people to put down roots in this sleepy settlement by the river and offered free burgages (smallholdings) to whoever did so. The advantages of being a burgess in a borough such as Liverpool were substantial. Holders were required to pay an initial rent of one shilling per year but were free of the other expenses and costs normally associated with tenure to a local lord, as well as freedom from certain dues on trade. As such, the charter grafted a new trading class onto a small and isolated populace whose lives were otherwise engaged in farming, fishing and pastoral pastimes.

As the years went by the burgess class cried out for greater freedoms and in 1229 King Henry III granted an improved Charter which was fundamentally effective for the next four centuries. This included freedom from tolls throughout the kingdom and the right to establish merchant guilds. For those less fortunate, manorial rights lay with the powerful Molyneux family, local gentry from whom the Corporation finally leased these valuable privileges in 1672. These were later purchased in perpetuity in 1773.

The city continued to thrive and by 1800 it counted approximately 80,000 souls among its inhabitants. Liverpool's main outdoor market had grown around St George's Church, where the Victoria Monument now stands. The formal opening of St John's Market followed in 1822, adding to others to be found around the town selling such staples as fish, fruit, vegetables and hay, to name but a few. Services could now be commonly sourced, with many trades and professions operating in this expanding community, building, repairing and altering all manner of items as shopping became a familiar pursuit.

As the town grew even bigger, many of the important streets we recognise today began to take form, each shaped by a revolutionary change that saw thousands move from rural life to city living. An increasing number of dedicated shops began to appear on an ever more urban landscape, some with rather simple and primitive appearances, but others with incredibly picturesque facades with rich decoration and sumptuous detail.

By the close of the nineteenth century, the High Street had become a universal fixture in every town and city up and down the country, and in the now city of Liverpool, nearly 700,000 residents called this place home. It is these people who you may well spot when perusing through this book.

The pages within feature just a small number of shopfronts from across the ages as seen from in and around the city in earlier times. These are contrasted with their more recently depicted equivalents; however, it has not been possible to include every image I would have liked or examples from every suburb within the city limits. Perhaps more may follow in another edition featuring yet more illustrations of commercial premises from times gone by.

In compiling this book, it has been disappointing but not surprising to see a general decline in the appearance of our retail spaces over the years. The Victorians and Edwardians undoubtedly took great pride in designing their shopfronts and we are lucky that a number of them still survive. That said, so many others have been lost through a redundancy of purpose, optimistic but shortsighted design decisions, or worst still completely obliterated through enemy action in the Second World War.

We may not realise it, but we too are responsible. We are living through a time of great change, an unstoppable digital revolution which is having a palpable and detrimental effect on our high streets. E-commerce is driving many retailers out of business as society's demand for convenience and affordability takes precedence over what is fast becoming nostalgia. The future of our high streets and the shops that create them is unknown. What is certain however is that if today's retailers wish to survive the next 100 years, then they and we will need to adapt, and decide what we want and expect from our town centres as we continue our progress on into the twenty-first century.

Daniel K. Longman MBE

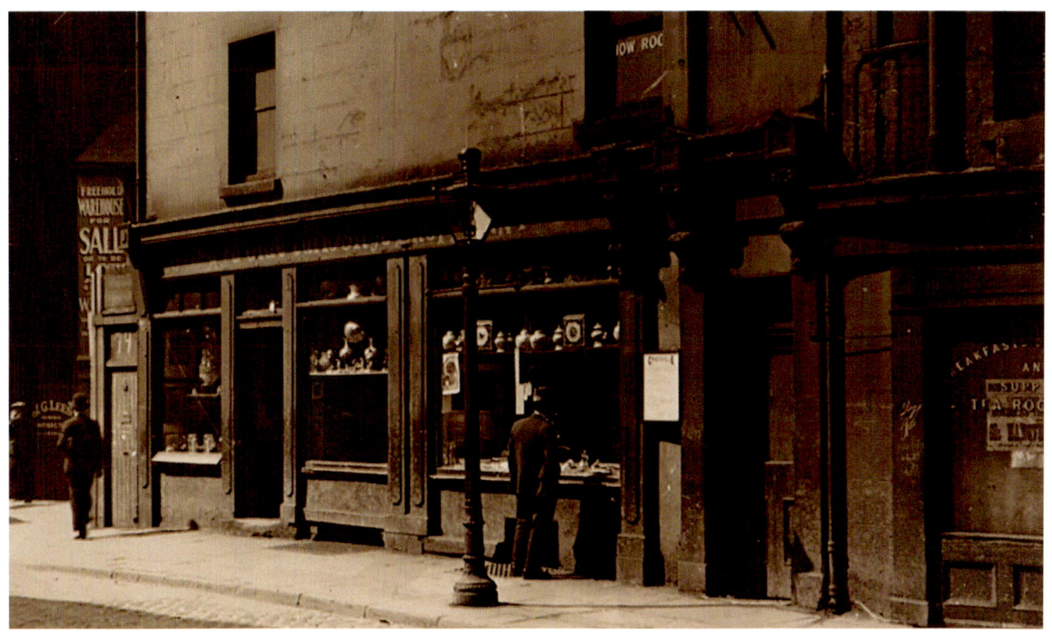

The Olde Curiosity Shop, Hanover Street

Above: A figure peers through the window of the olde curiosity shop that once stood on Hanover Street. This was an antique emporium containing numerous nostalgic items and vintage paraphernalia housed within a simple Victorian premises complete with its own showroom on the upper level. The ground floor featured large glass windows to showcase the very best stock with a series of ornate scroll pilasters framing the view.

Below: A distinctly modern design known as the Bling Building now occupies the site with a multistorey zinc glazing grid across its entire elevation, punctuated by bevelled window details to the upper levels. Constructed as part of the Liverpool One masterplan, the building was designed by architect Piers Gough and was officially completed in 2008. It is home to a bar with hotel rooms above.

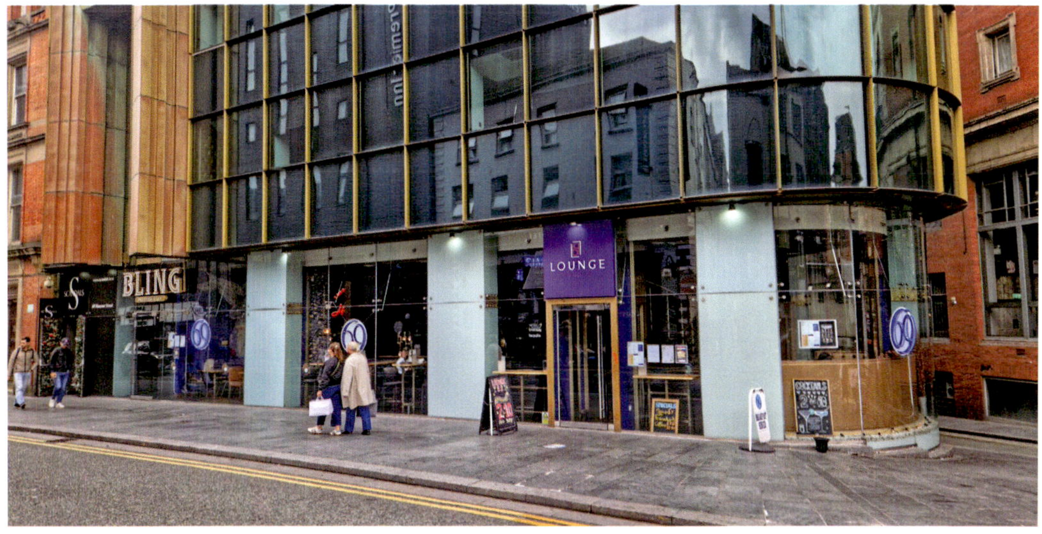

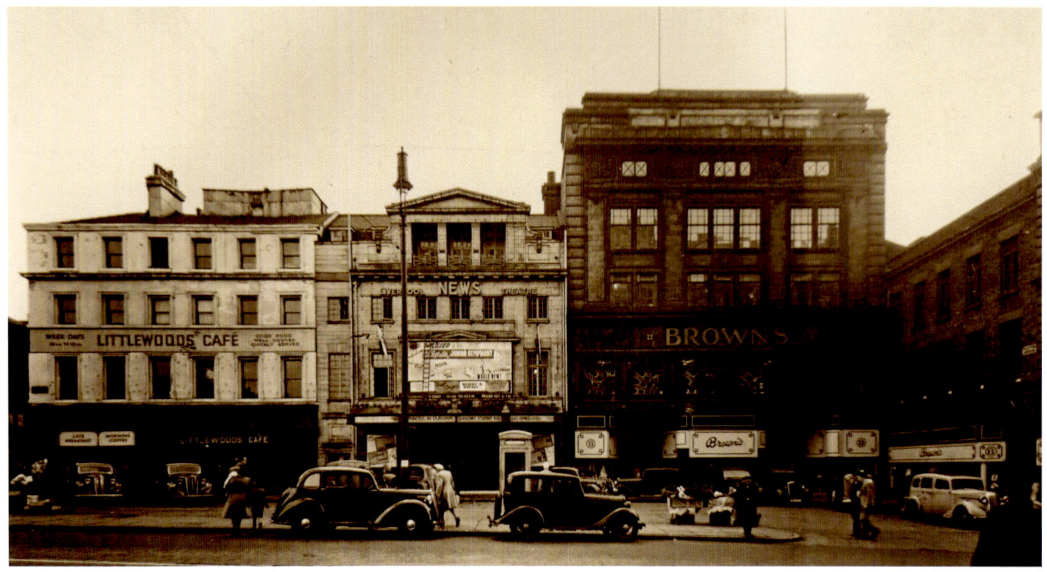

Clayton Square

Above: This view of Clayton Square reveals more of the piecemeal nature of its development with the Victorian four-storey structure of the former Waterloo Hotel occupied by a Littlewoods Cafe. Alongside was the classically inspired News Theatre built in 1912. Nearby a branch of Browns Department Store towered over the square since the 1920s, with Art Deco decorations adding interest to its magnificent facade.

Below: The old buildings of Clayton Square were swept away in a 1980s scheme of development which gave birth to the Clayton Square Shopping Centre. The plan was inspired by Liverpool's industrious past, with enormous brick-faced warehouse-style buildings, with window arches and banding detail beneath mansard-style rooftops. At its centre remains a huge glazed walkway enclosing the majority of Cases Street.

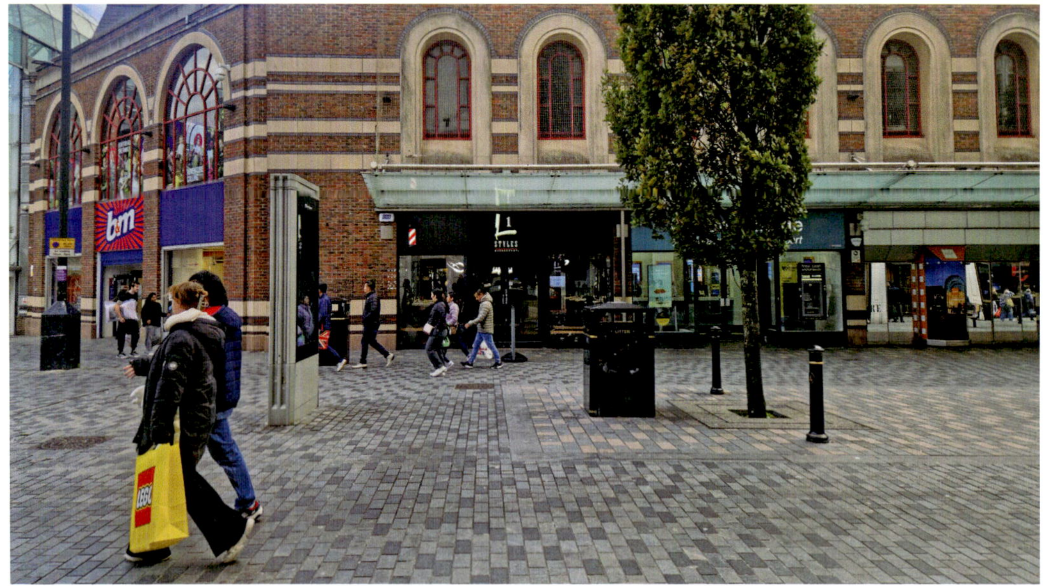

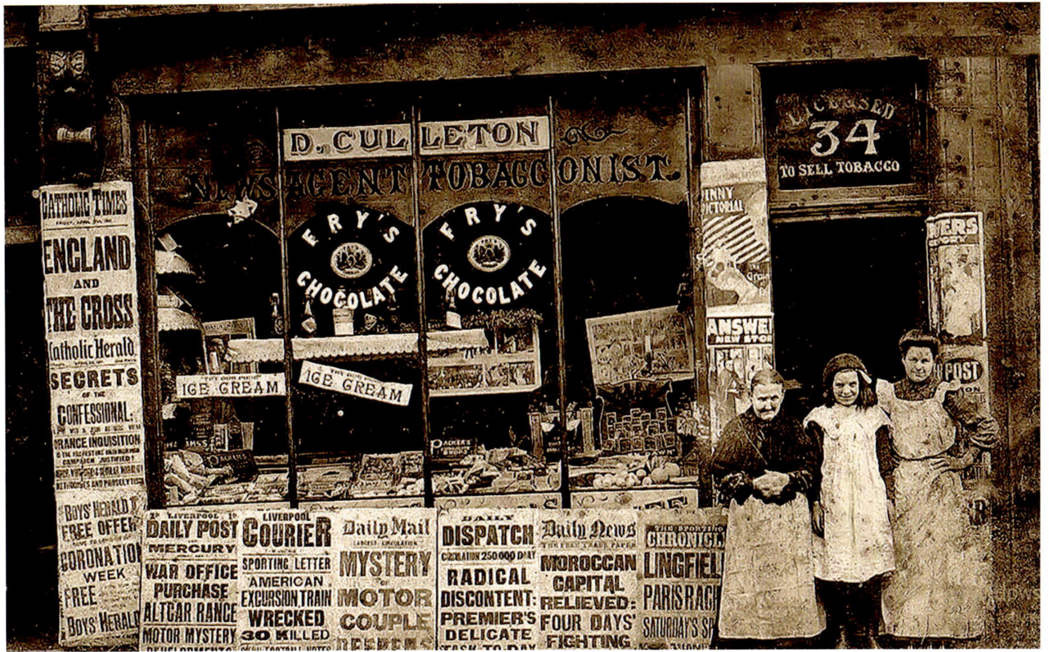

No. 34 Hopwood Street

Above: Denis Culleton's newsagent and tobacco shop stood at No. 34 Hopwood Street, then the perfect place to discover all the latest headlines. The shopfront consisted of a simple square window divided by glazing bars that housed stock, in addition to providing space for advertising tempting pleasures such as chocolate and ice cream.

Below: This is now a part of the city unrecognisable to former times with the old Victorian properties demolished many years ago. Today this part of Hopwood Street is now known as Bangor Street and is the site of numerous late twentieth-century domestic dwellings and a pub known as the Britannia, a far cry from the rows of back-to-back terraces that once covered the cityscape.

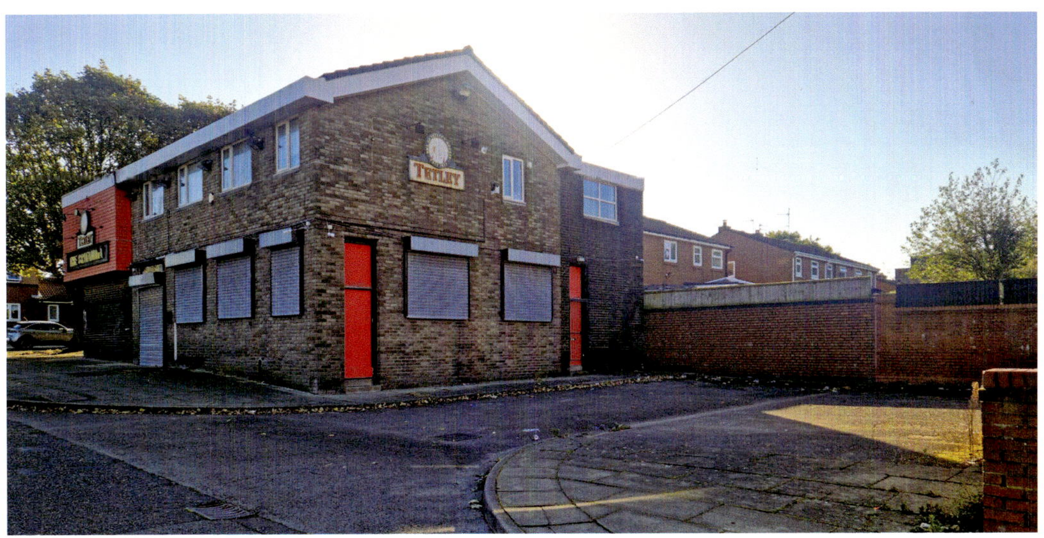

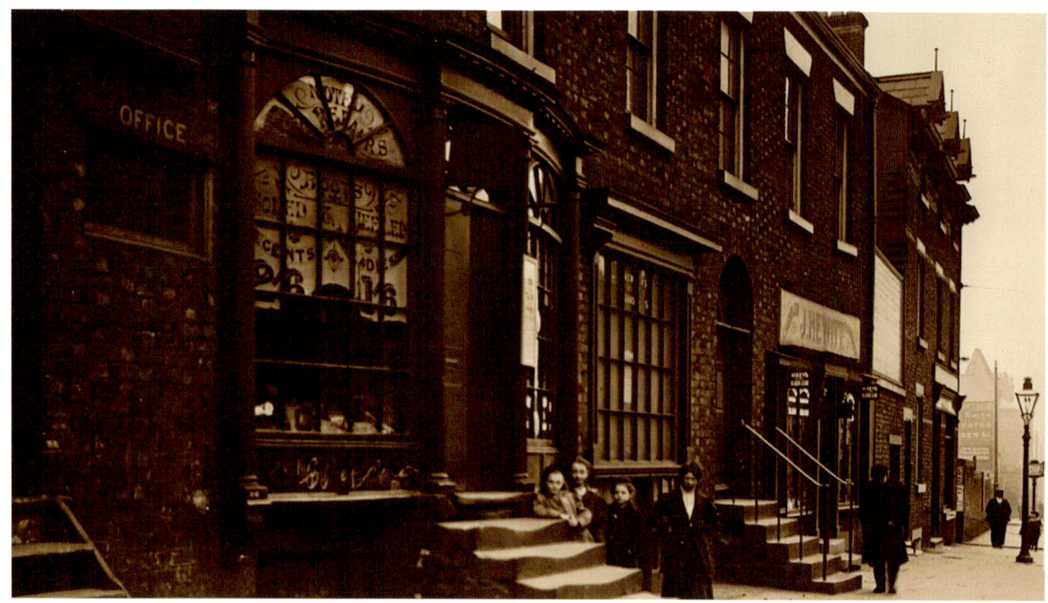

No. 102 High Street

Above: Dating from the late eighteenth century, this wonderful Georgian building featured a set of well-worn stone steps leading to a bowed shopfront complete with Doric pilasters and fanlights over multiple examples of paned glass. At the time of this photograph taken in 1905, the premises was in use as a unisex shoe repair shop.

Below: This historic property at No. 102 High Street still survives and is likely to be the oldest shopfront in Liverpool. The address has been home to a wood-turning enterprise since the 1980s but with little change to its outward appearance. The shop and the wider terrace of which it forms a part is now Grade II* listed.

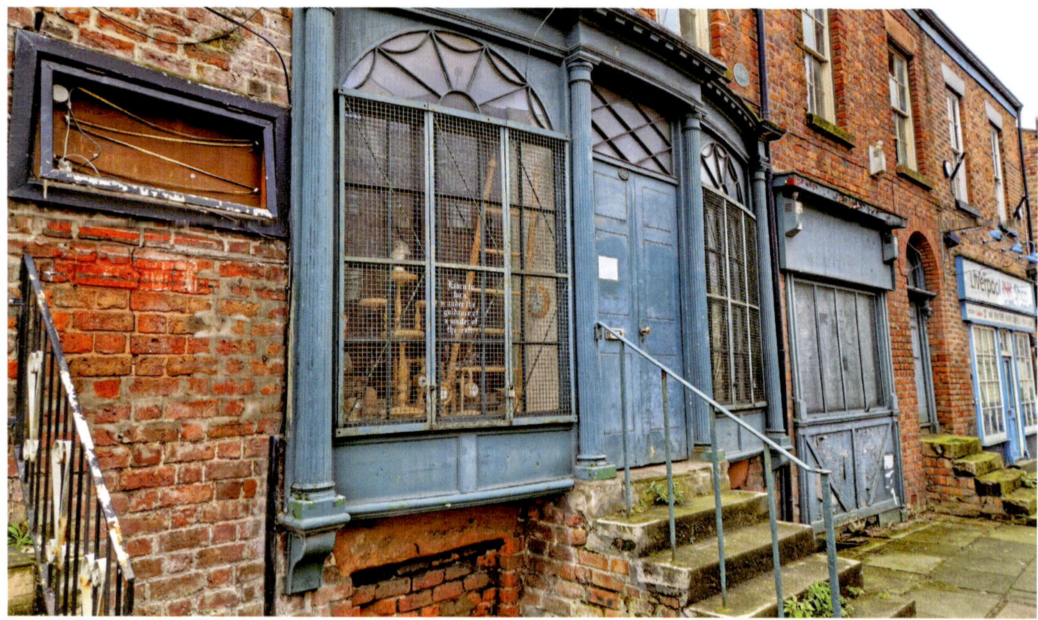

The Futurist, Lime Street

Right above: This cinema first opened its doors as The Lime Street Picture House in 1912 and was finished in a luxurious classical design by Chadwick & Watson. The structure was saturated with detail beneath an imposing pediment, architectural columns, balconies, a variety of window designs and extravagant festoons all upon a white terracotta facade.

Right below: The cinema was renamed The Futurist in 1920 and remained active for sixty years. However, in 2016 the buildings here were demolished after a long period of vacancy and deterioration. In their place, an immense retail, hotel and accommodation complex was constructed with a supermarket across the ground floor. An abundance of glazing now borders Lime Street, with etched panels above featuring what once was.

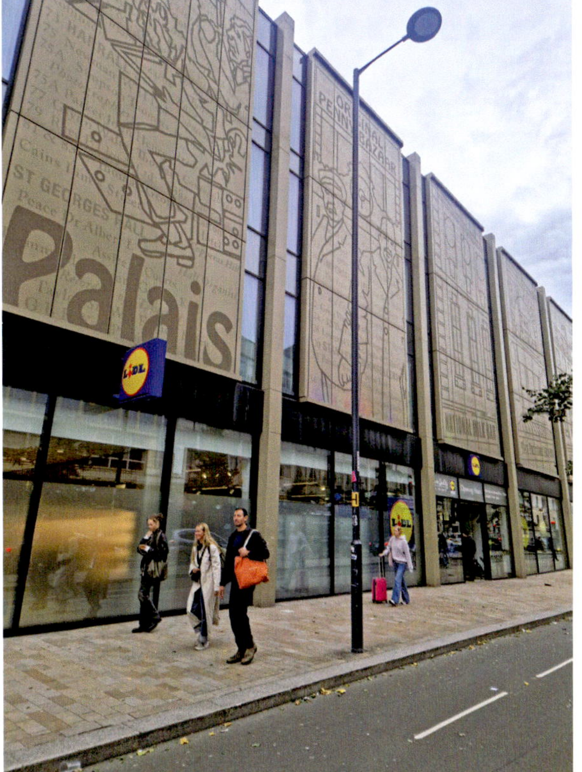

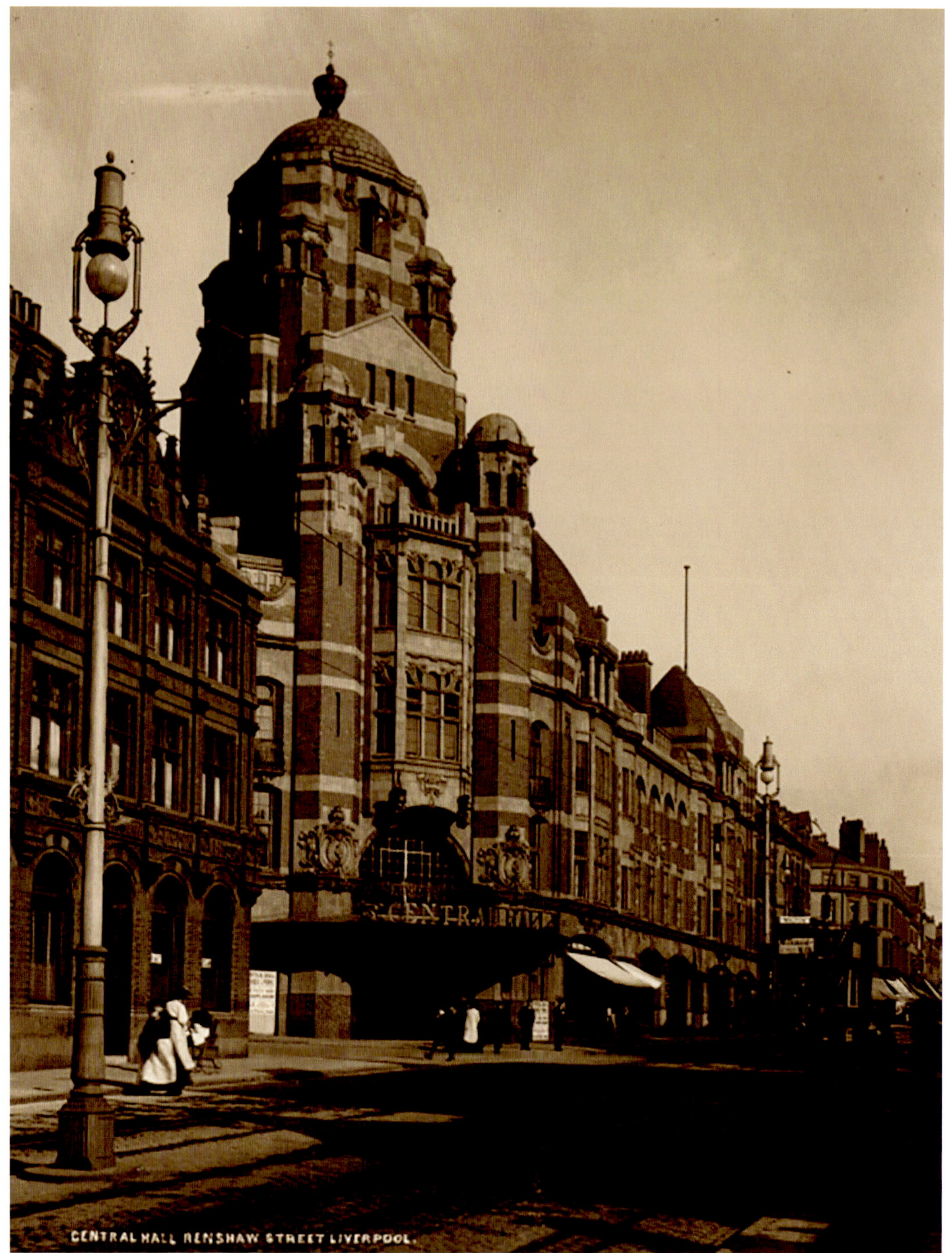

Central Hall, Renshaw Street

This Art Nouveau masterpiece dates to 1905 and was built as a Methodist chapel. However, its design purposely steered away from overtly religious iconography, and instead resembles more of a large department store or theatre. At ground level shops were sublet, each benefiting from having large glass window displays directly out onto the street.

10

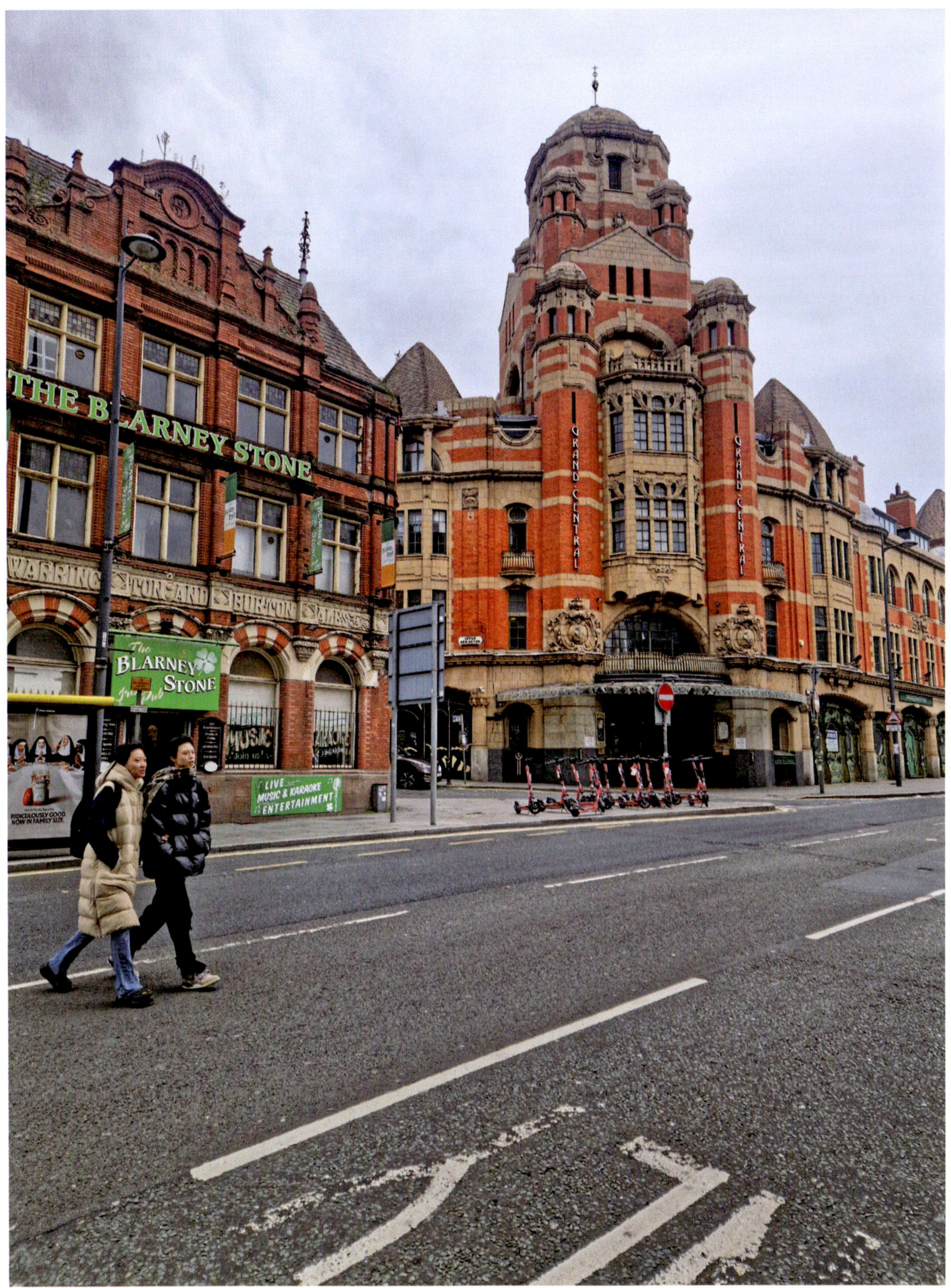

The monumental building is no longer used for worship and after many years as a residence to a comprehensive mix of retailers, it is now predominantly enjoyed as a live music venue known as The Dome. The former shops facing the highway within this Grade II listed building have since been converted into drinking establishments.

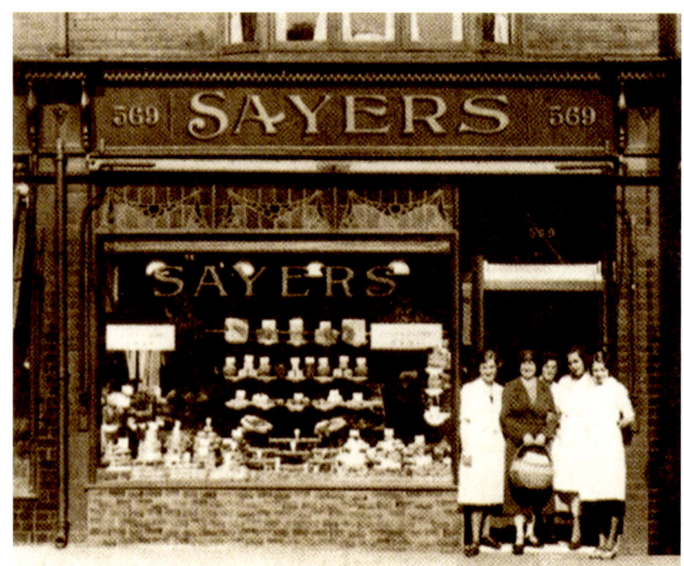

No. 569 Prescot Road

Above: A party of ladies stand in the doorway of No. 569 Prescot Road. This was the home of Sayers bakers and from where their very first goods were sold in the year 1912. By the time this 1920s image was taken, the building boasted a large plate-glass window to show off their range of tasty delicacies, with stained festoon glass above and a simple but effective sign for Sayers across the fascia.

Below: The famous bakery brand no longer occupies the original Sayers site, and the shopfront has since been adapted to front a beauty salon. It is sadly devoid of the architectural niceties and particulars which could once be admired here and now offers a somewhat less interesting facade with which to entice new customers.

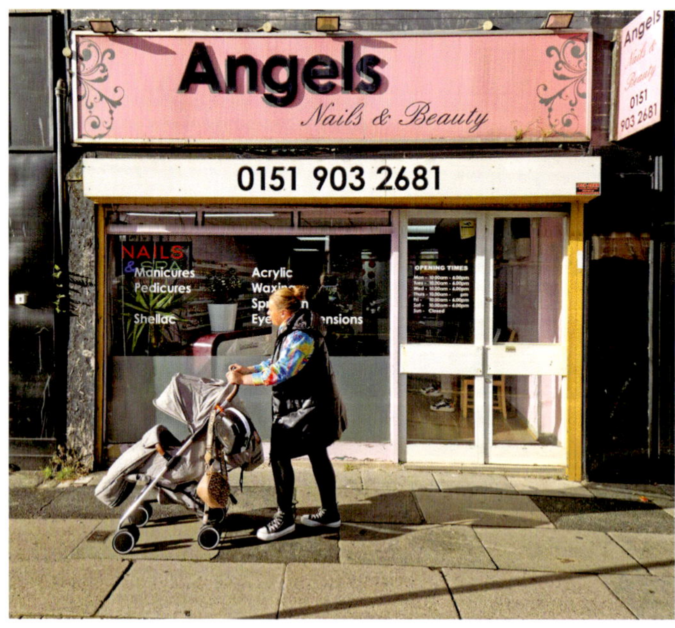

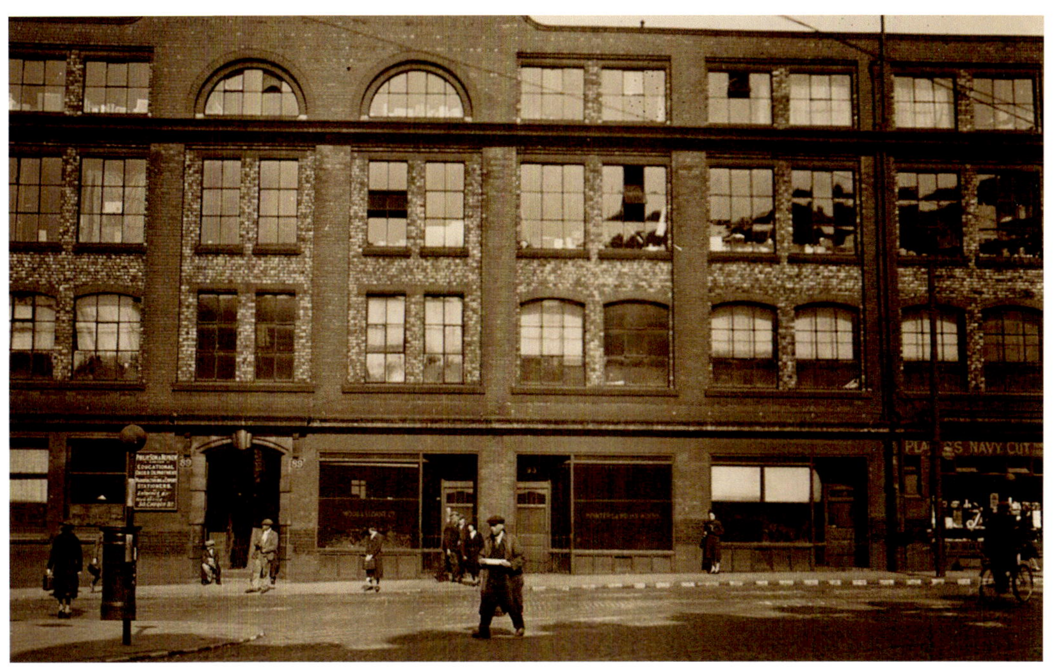

Wood and Sloane, Paradise Street

Above: The premises of Wood and Sloane were seen here in Paradise Street in 1939. The business specialised in printing and binding in this large industrial building which featured various casement windows set within a brick and stone elevation. At ground level, individual units with matching recessed doors could be seen behind metal security gates.

Below: Nothing remains of the former building, with much of Paradise Street being flattened during the horrors of the Blitz. Now situated just yards from the modern development of Liverpool One, this site has been utilised for city centre living and features a mix of semi-detached houses and bungalows originally laid out in the 1980s.

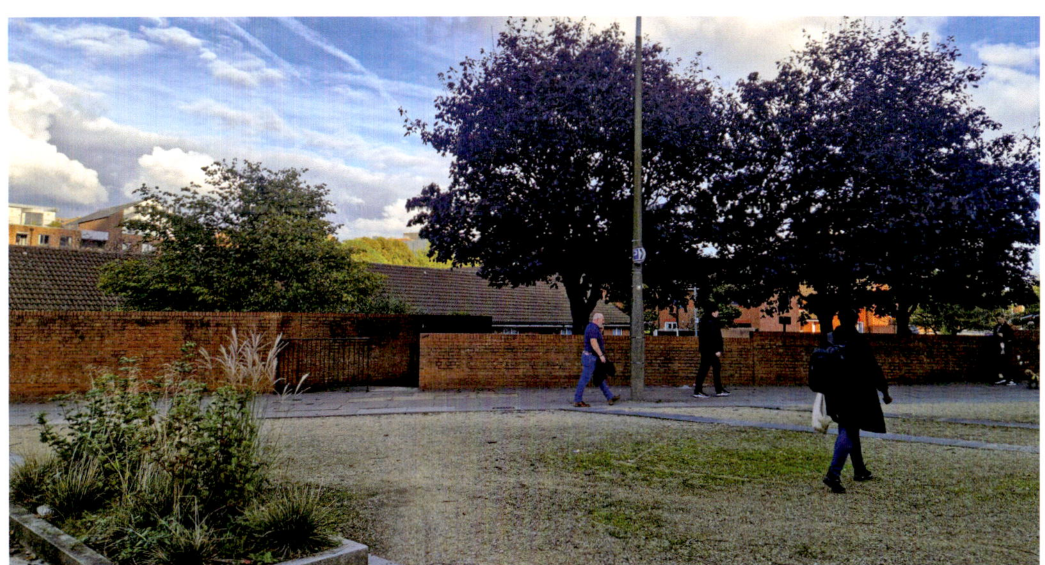

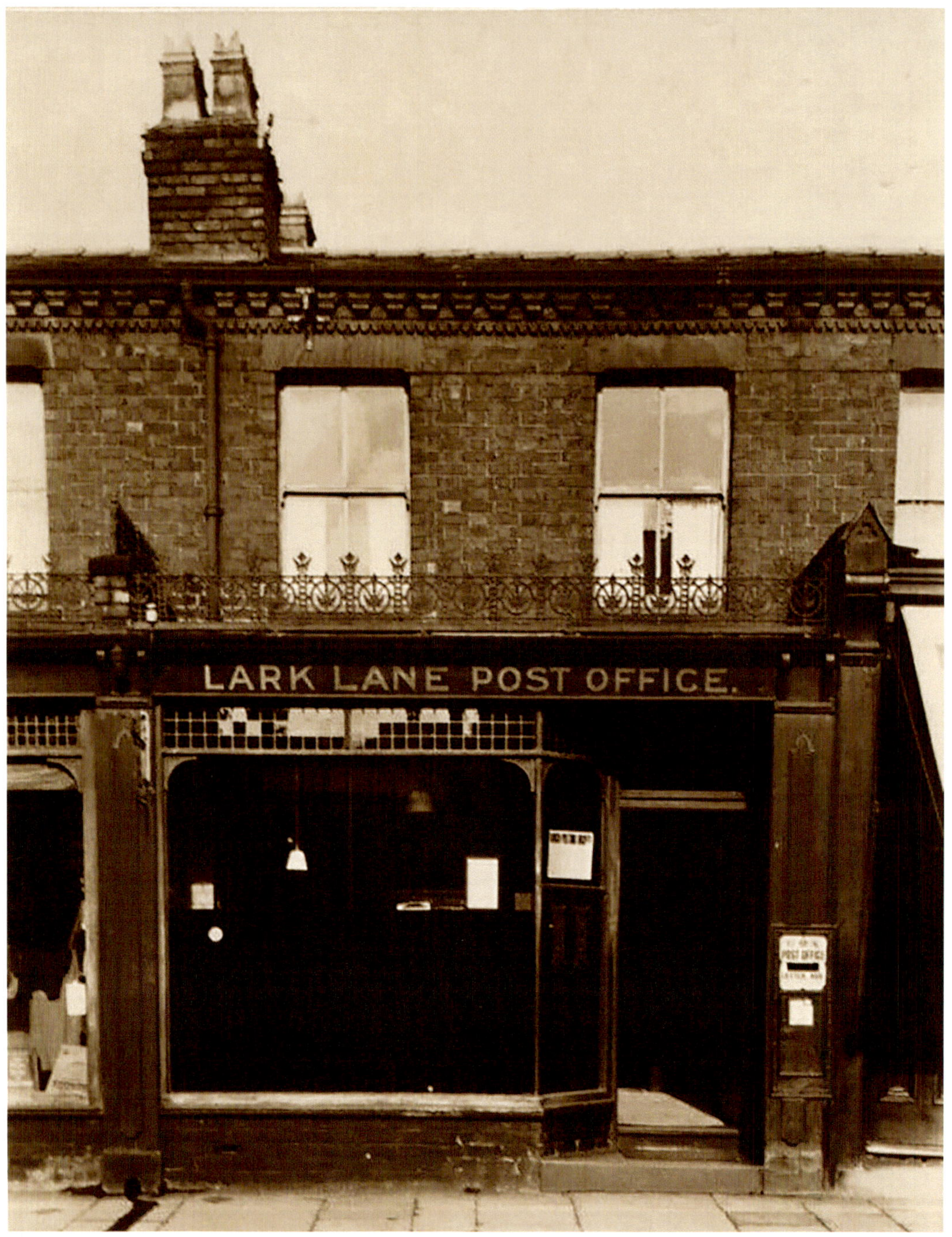

Lark Lane Post Office

The eponymous Lark Lane Post Office once stood at No. 77 and provided postal and other services across the city and beyond. As such it had little need to advertise and on the contrary, its window display had been blocked out for customer privacy. A small postbox had been set into the largely unembellished shopfront pilasters whilst its decorative window panels appear to have seen better days.

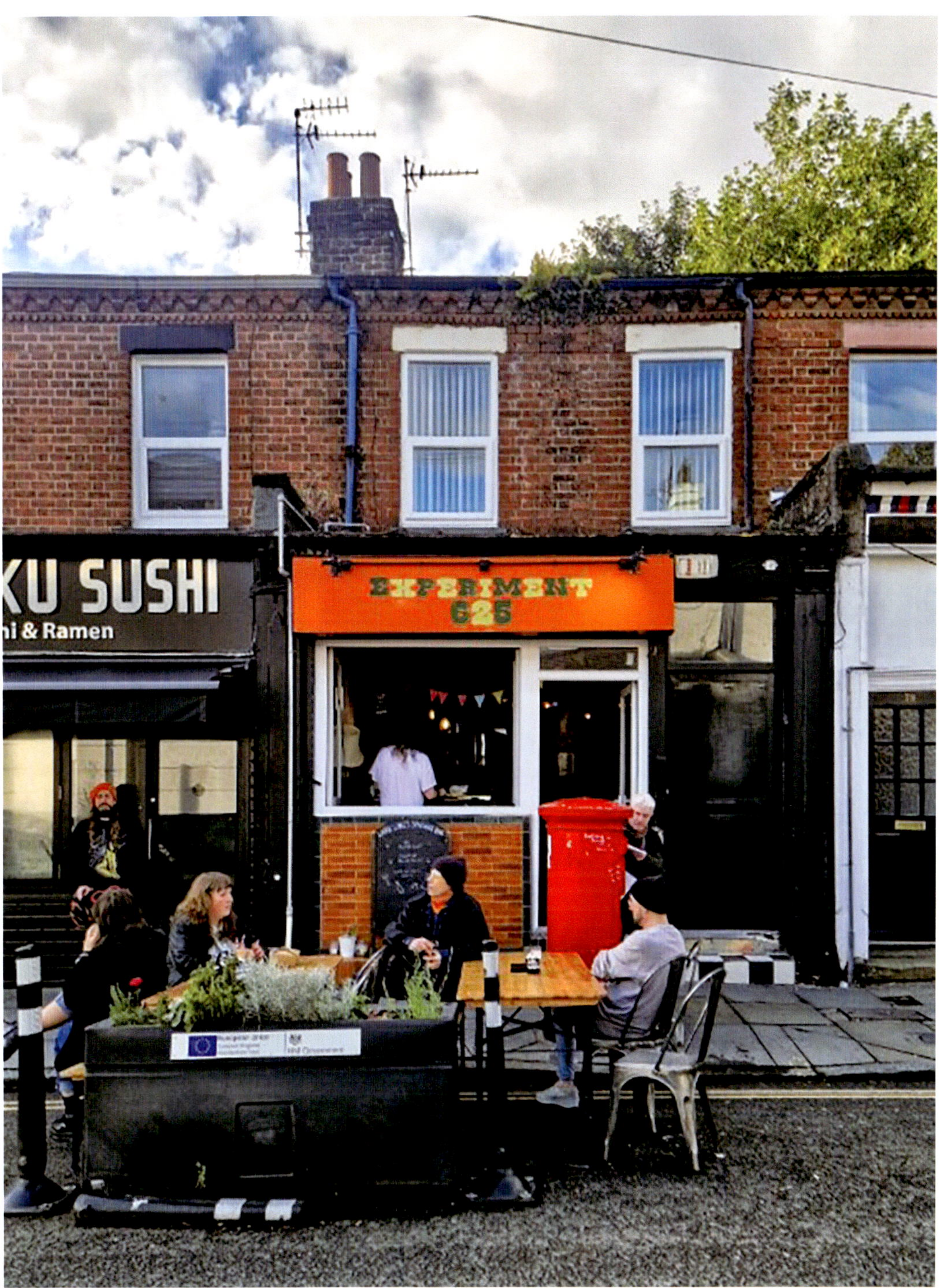

In recent years many businesses have chosen the vibrant hub of Lark Lane to make a profit, resulting in alterations to most of the buildings here. The entrance to the former post office has been relocated with private access provided to the flat above. Downstairs is now in use as a bar but an old red postbox remains on the pavement.

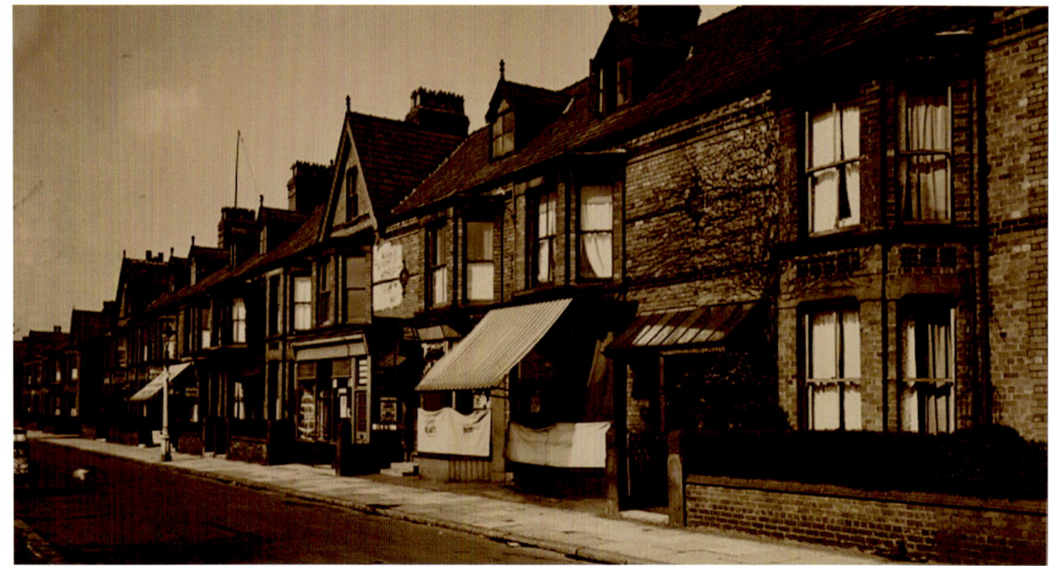

Penny Lane

Above: The residential properties here in the famous Penny Lane were constructed in the late nineteenth century in response to improved transport links to this formerly rural part of the city. Some were later converted for commercial use, with the bay windows adapted and awnings added to cater for this move to business.

Below: The buildings here have returned to residential use but some recall clues of their earlier commercial adaptations. The square ground floor of No. 89 projects out from the building line, but its former display window has been filled with more domestic fenestration. Low boundary walls have also been built for properties nearby that have lost their awnings and signage in a bid for a more homely aesthetic.

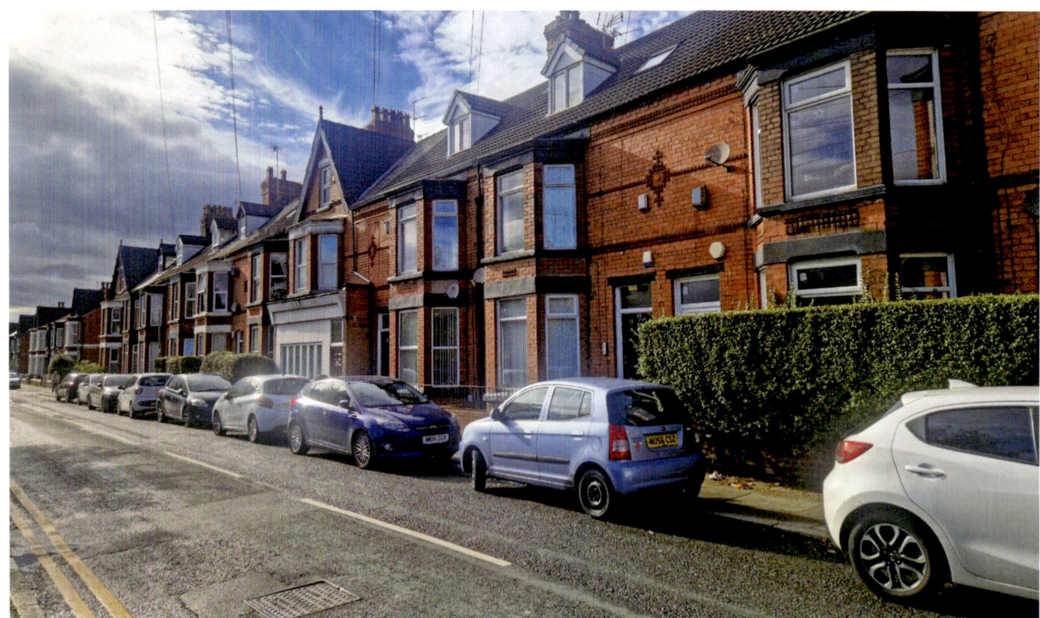

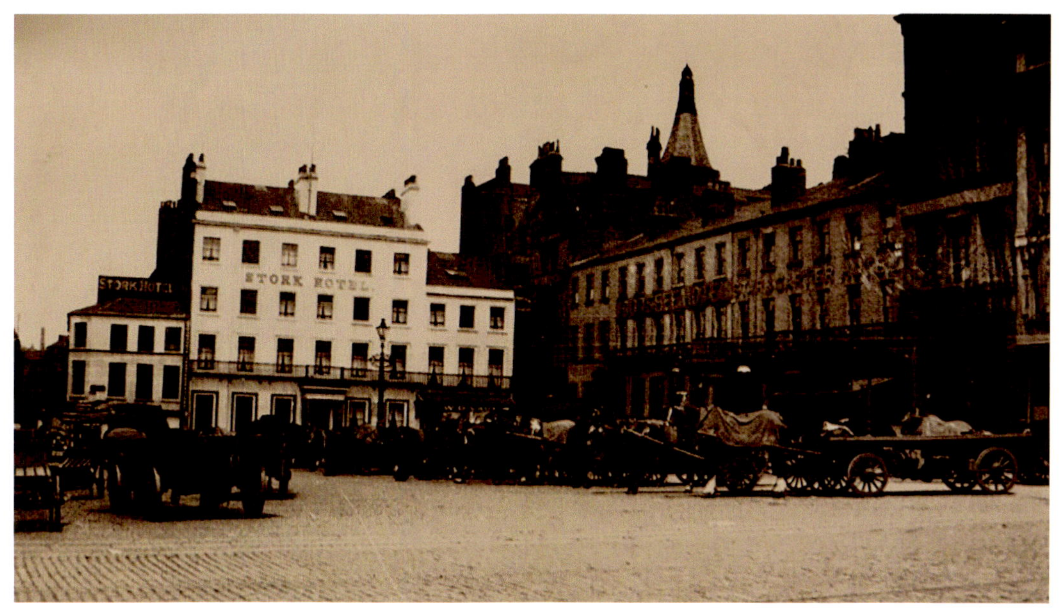

Queen Square

Above: Queen Square was originally laid out in the eighteenth century featuring a mix of dwellings and commercial premises catering to the many who came to this busy port. It grew to become a thriving open market, overlooked by the early Victorian Stork Hotel. At ground level, various shopfronts faced the square in a rich array of architectural styles.

Below: By the 1990s the Queen Square traders had departed and the land on which they earned a living was repurposed as an uninspiring car park. However, the square was redeveloped the same decade and is now home to several restaurants and a hotel along with access to a multistorey car park, finished in a design inspired by the buildings that once stood here.

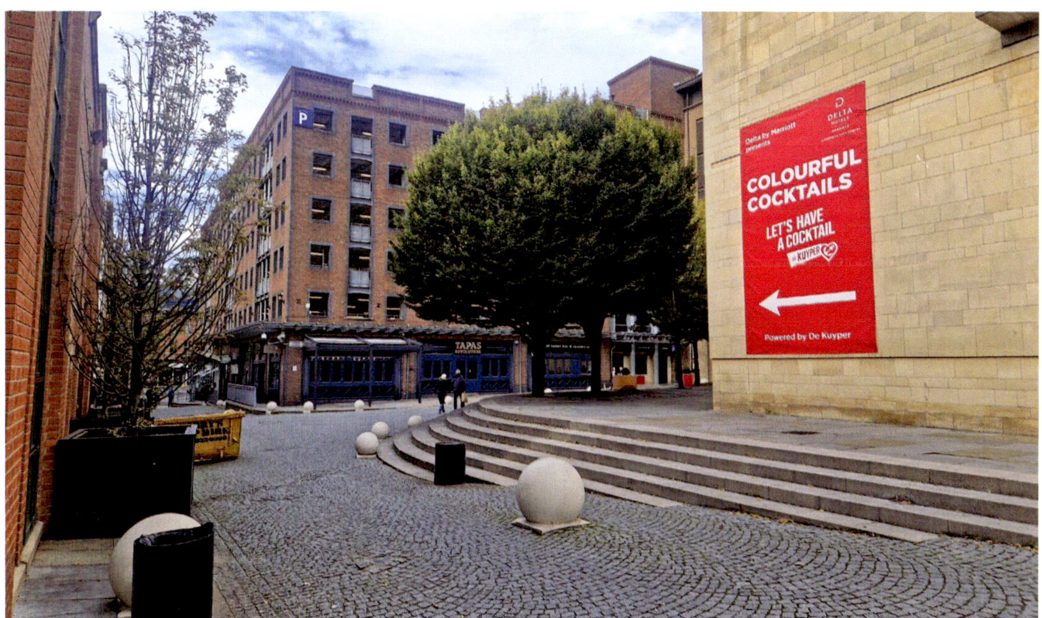

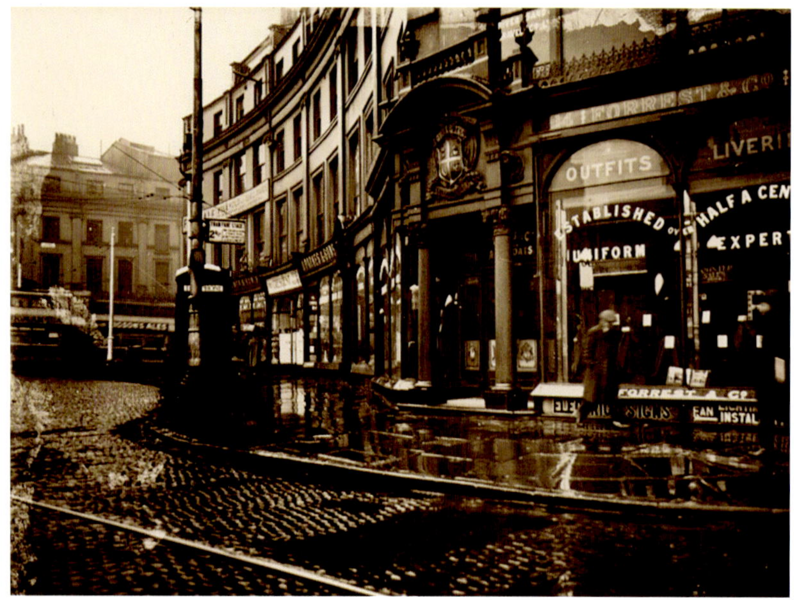

St George's Crescent

Above: The grand appearance of St George's Crescent is seen here in the 1920s. This sweeping curve offered shopkeepers a splendid address to sell their wares, including the fashionable tailors of Forrest and Co. The building featured large windows, recessed doorways and classical influences such as mighty marble columns and mascarons set into the impressive frontage.

Below: This part of the city fell victim to heavy bombing during the Second World War with many of its buildings razed to the ground. St George's Crescent was one such casualty, and this half facing Lord Street and Derby Square was reconstructed as Merchants Court in 1957. Fronted with Portland stone and green marble columns, the property provides office accommodation.

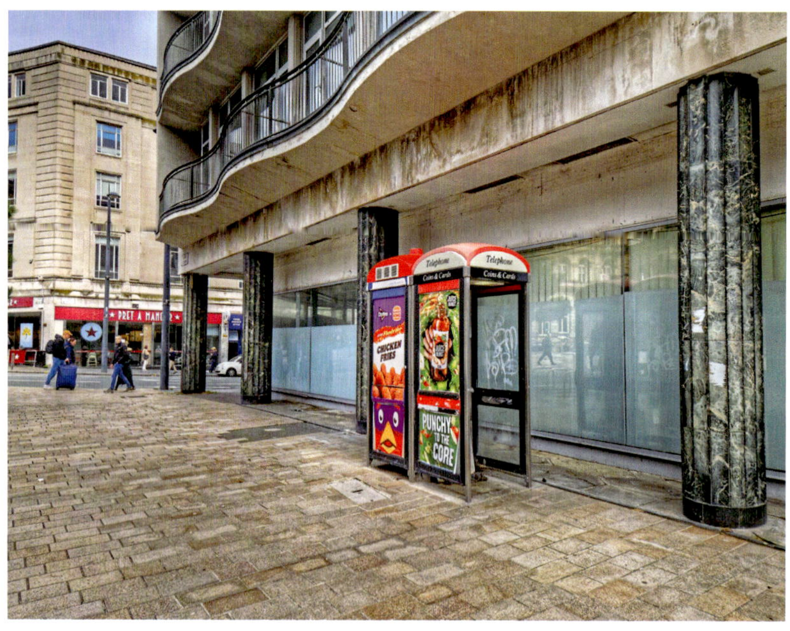

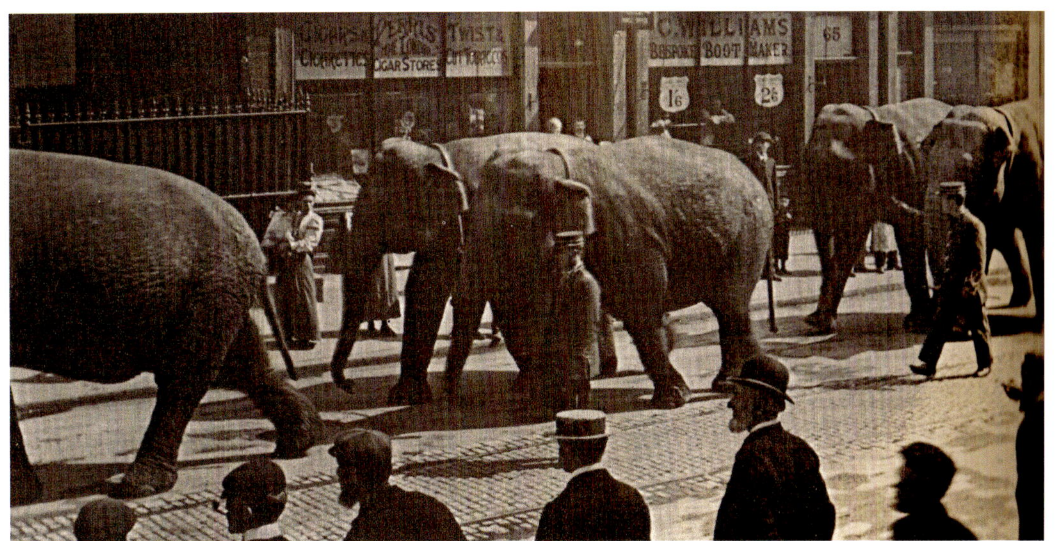

Oxford Street

Above: An unusual scene as a herd of circus elephants passes the premises of John Perris's tobacco shop and Charles William's boot and shoemakers. These shops stood alongside a public house, all part of a small and ordinary two-storey terrace. The shops featured matching designs of tripartite windows and simple rectangular doorways with similar styles of promotion upon the glass.

Below: Only the Oxford Pub remains but even its future is uncertain having been last put to use as a corner shop some time ago. The rest of the terrace was demolished in the 1960s, leaving this fragment of Oxford Street undeveloped. The land currently offers a welcome green space within this otherwise built-up part of the city, the postcode featuring various housing blocks and institutions connected with the University of Liverpool.

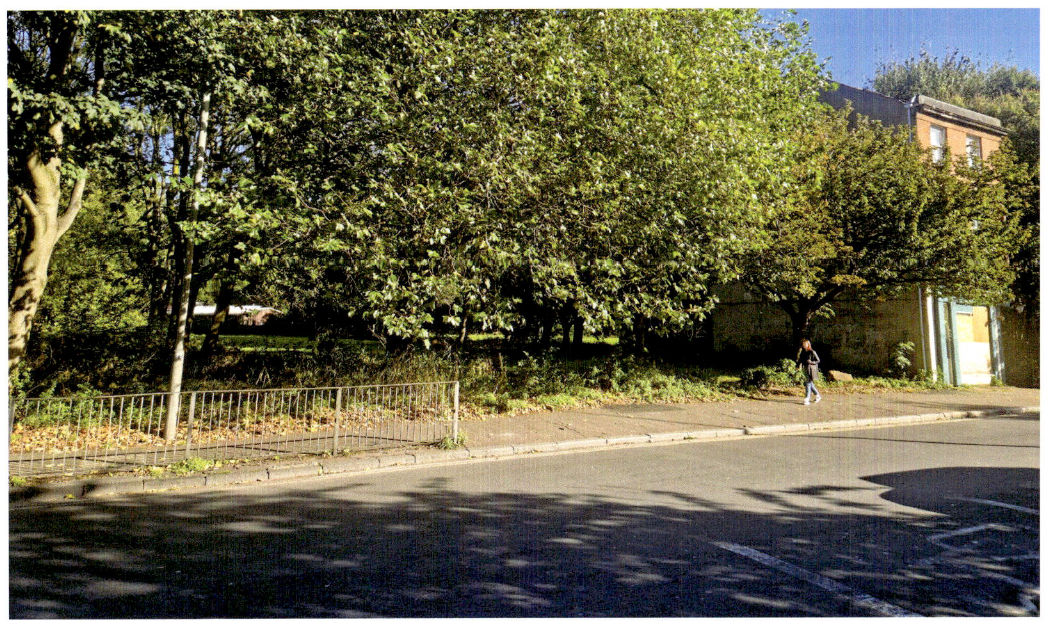

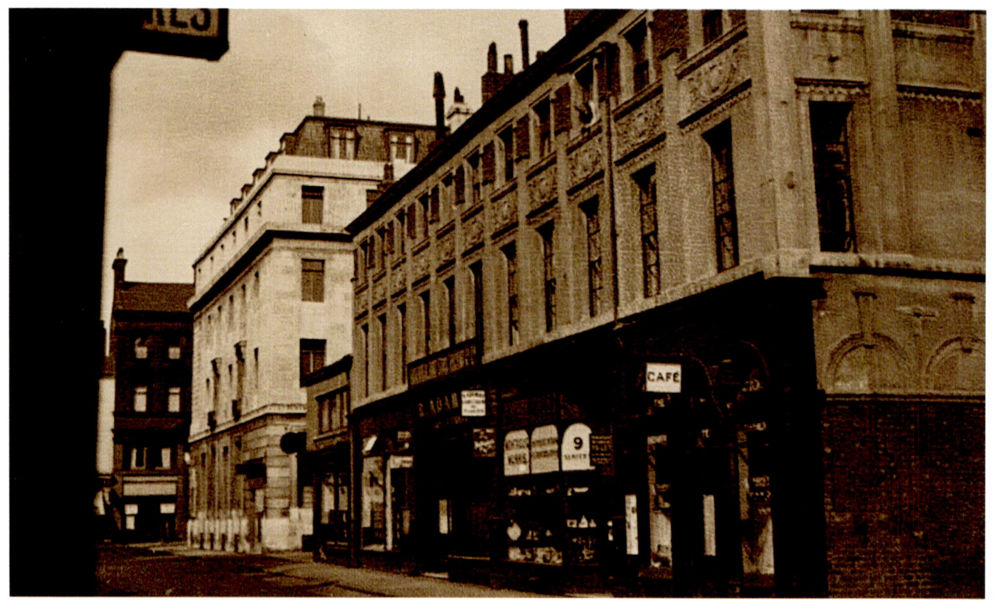

Slater Street

Above: A blend of different shopfronts faced out onto Slater Street with a mix of tripartite arches and recessed designs, with particular embellishment applied to the upper levels adding an additional element of elegance to this commercial terrace. Up ahead stood the sizable stone-clad home of Lloyds Bank, constructed in 1927, which towered over its smaller older neighbours in this lively shopping district.

Below: A trio of rectangular windows have been inserted into the Fleet Street elevation along with the placement of unsightly signage, but the basic design of this corner property remains. Adjoining units however have been reduced to a repetitive rendered row and the upper-storey decoration that had previously graced the principal elevation has been consigned to history.

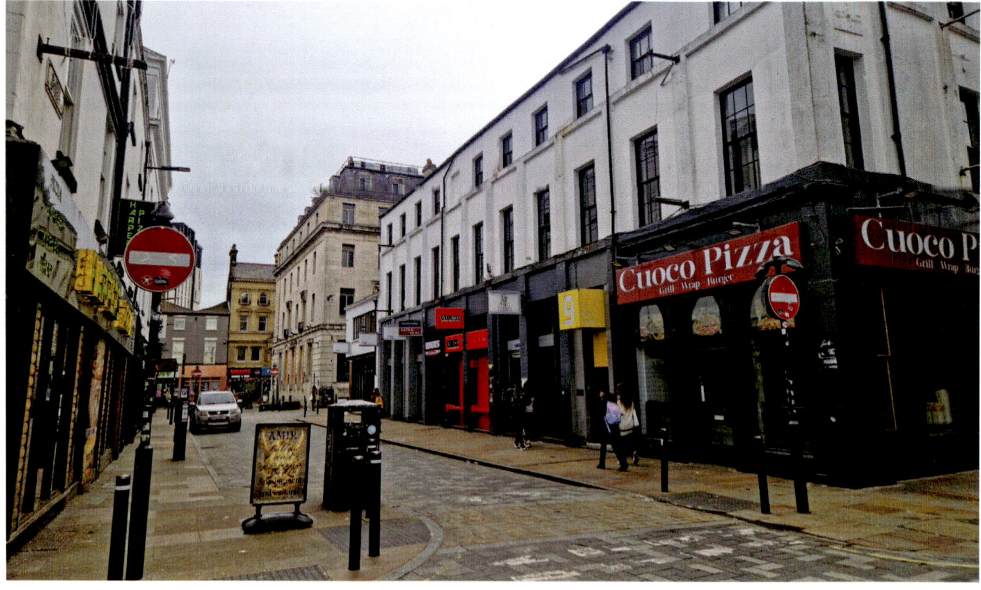

Right: A shopkeeper stands proudly in the doorway of No. 100A Picton Road in the 1920s. Mr Fletcher had taken full advantage of his large window display which can be seen full of goods across multiple shelves. Tobacco and chocolate appear to have featured heavily in advertising which adorned the majority of this otherwise simple and unpretentious Victorian building.

Below: The old shopfront has since been unceremoniously removed and the former opening bricked up in adapting the building for residential use. A pair of plastic windows have taken the place of the once charming timber-framed window display, with very little left of the lamented traditional architectural designs of old.

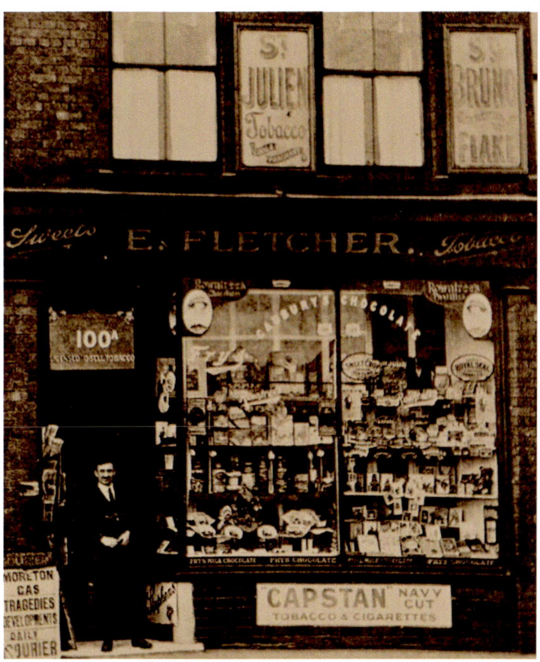

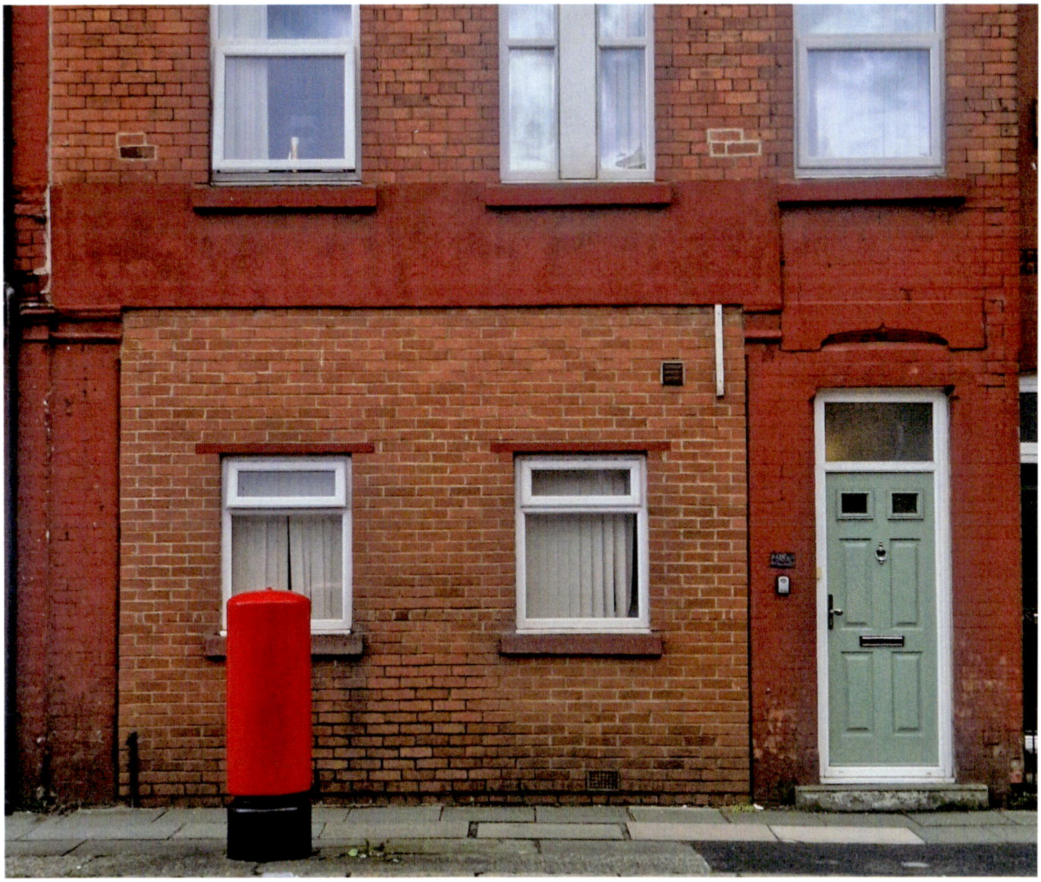

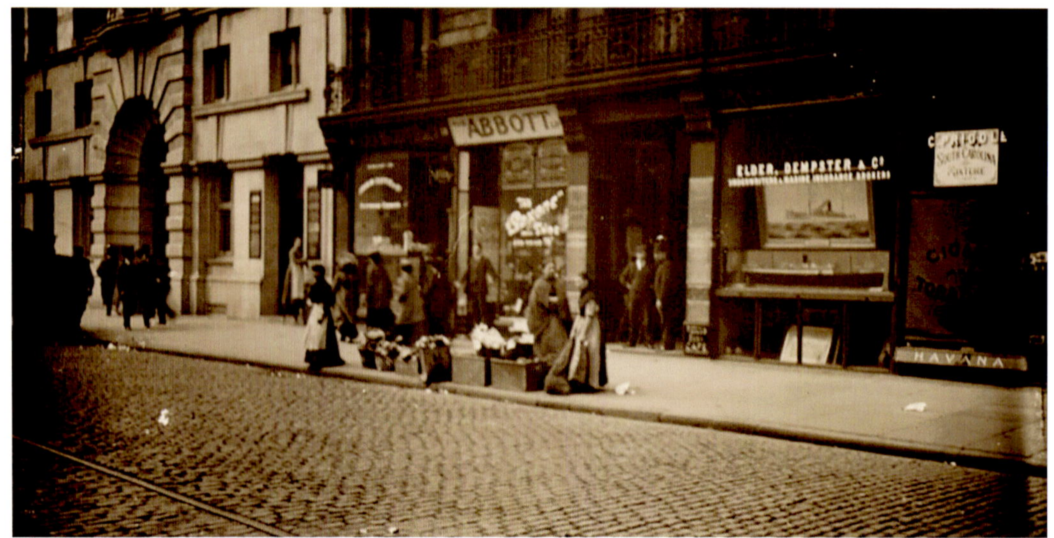

Castle Street

Above: One of Liverpool's most elaborate neighbourhoods, Castle Street is home to a number of the city's most impressive buildings. This early twentieth-century view shows a scene outside Nos 10–18 with a mixture of traditional glazed-timber shopfronts beneath a row of ornate iron railings. Trading continued out on the street with the presence of flower women selling from baskets at the roadside.

Below: The old shops around here have taken on a more hedonistic atmosphere with the majority transformed into bars and eateries. As part of these changes, many of the buildings have unfortunately been tarnished by oversized facias and the loss of original glazing arrangements, with many businesses also exploiting the street for outdoor seating and pavement cafes in better weather.

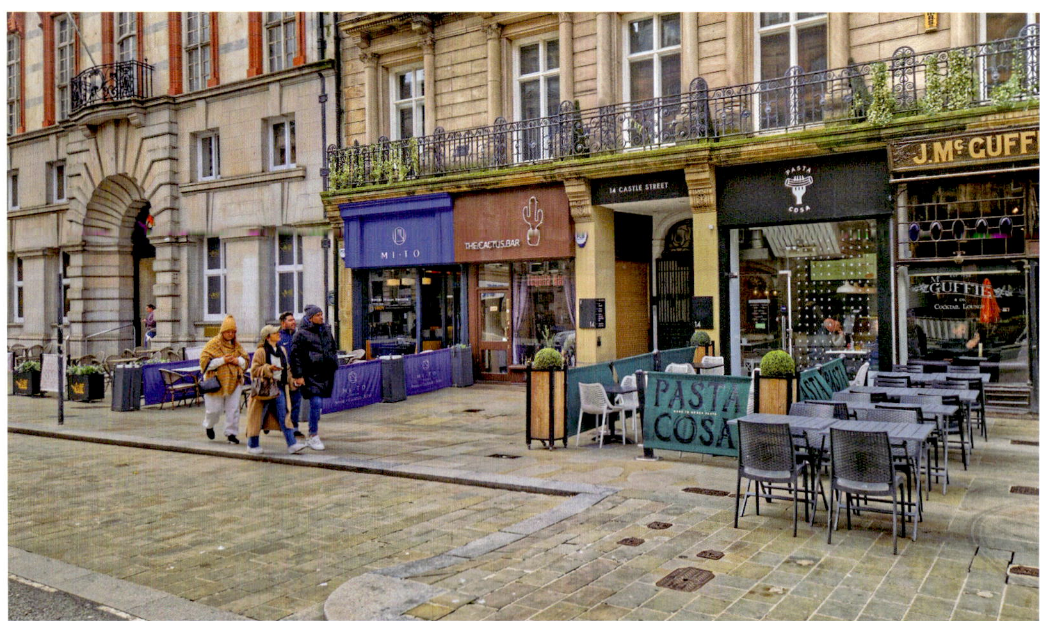

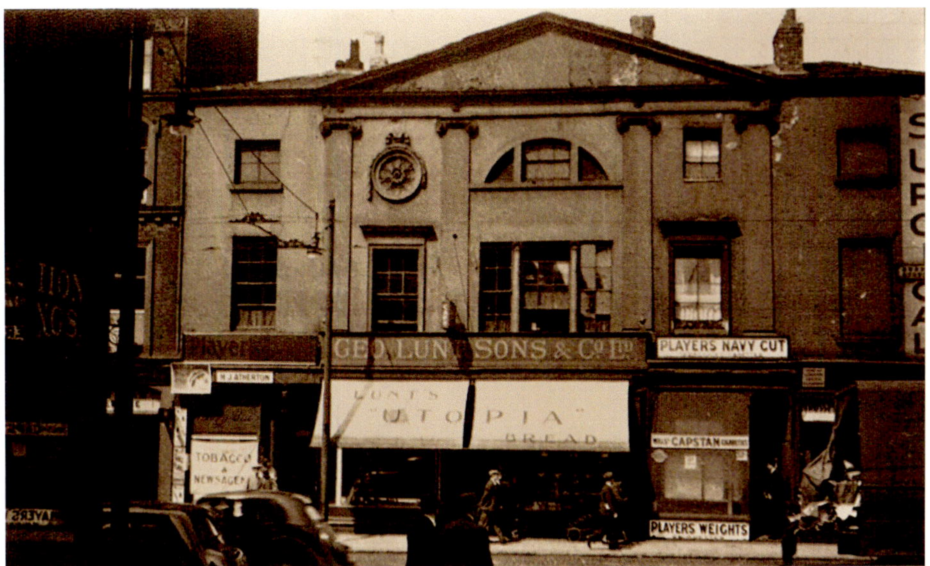

Berry Street

Above: This substantial property was originally constructed as both a residential and commercial premises by John Warmsley in the early nineteenth century. Finished in an exuberant style, it was designed with symmetrical columns, Ionic pilasters and a swagged patera for added flare above a row of individual shop units.

Below: The shopfronts have been removed and the ground floor opened up to become a Chinese restaurant with large windows set between a series of hefty pilasters and the placement of 3D signage. An off-licence next door has covered their shopfront in plastic advertising panels which somewhat detracts from the more nuanced surviving architectural features above.

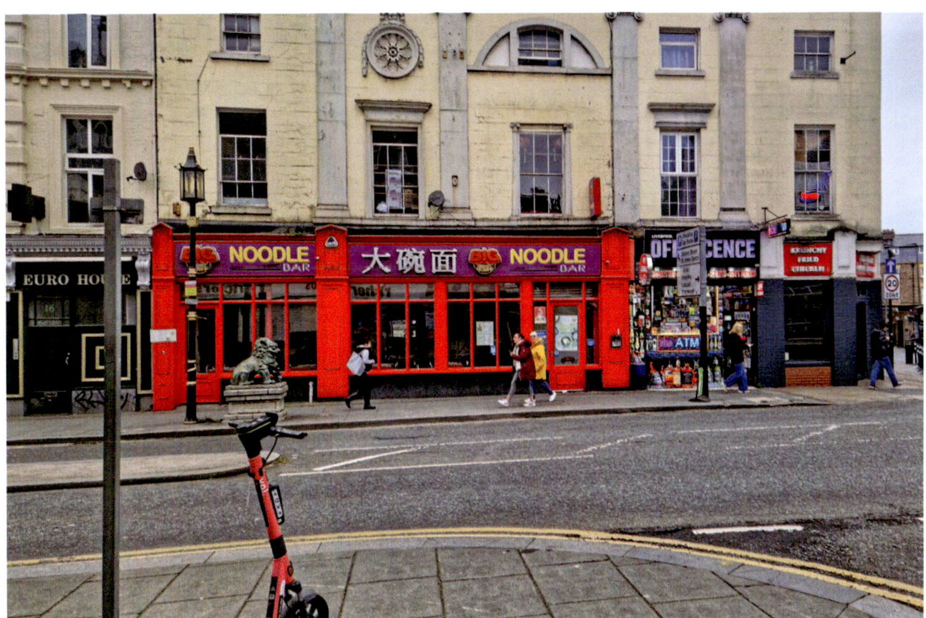

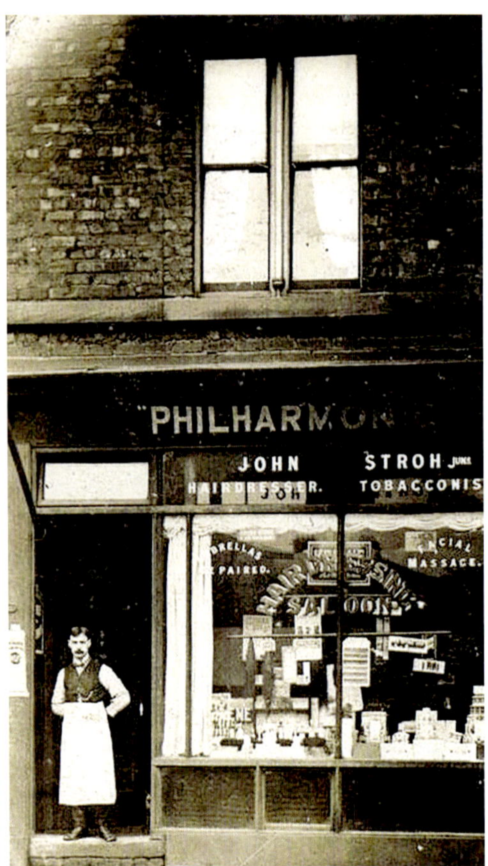

No. 11 Falkner Street

Left above: Master hairdresser John Stroh can be seen standing in the doorway of his terraced timber shopfront at No. 11 Falkner Street. In earlier times this had been an academy of music, but by the early twentieth century the ground floor had become a barbering saloon complete with advertisements of services offered upon the glazing, and various products displayed behind.

Left below: A delightful shopfront remains at this address, but the shop itself no longer exists. It now serves only to offer an outlook for diners of the restaurant which occupies much of the terrace. In addition to a sage green makeover and installation of decorative panelling, a retractable awning has been added over the fascia, with seating provided on the pavement outdoors.

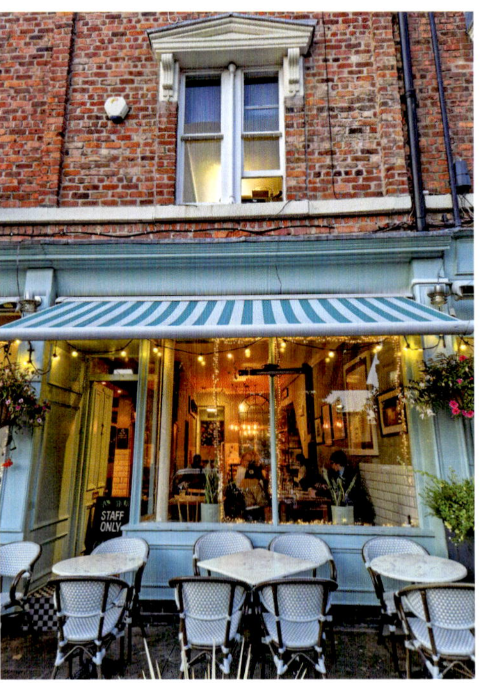

No. 52 Bold Street

Right above: No. 52 Bold Street was originally built as a Victorian concert hall in 1853 but within a decade the property was converted for retail use. The alterations saw the installation of new and necessary additions, but it also retained many of its original architectural delights such as hood mould windows, rusticated voussoirs, classical balustrades and a richly carved frieze and cornice across the upper floor.

Right below: This Grade II listed property is now in use as a bar with a set of decorative red columns on show across the Bold Street facade. Windows formerly facing Concert Street have been obscured with advertisements promoting the venue within; however, the important architectural details which contribute to the significance of the building can still clearly be appreciated.

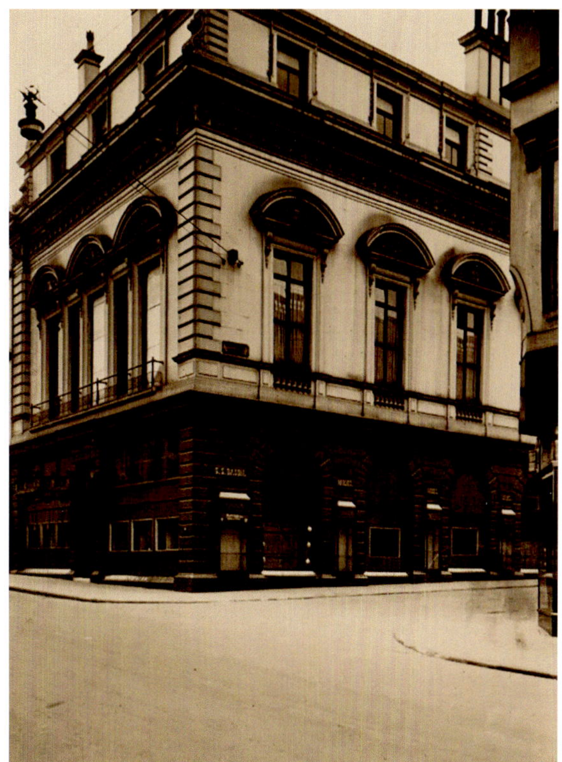

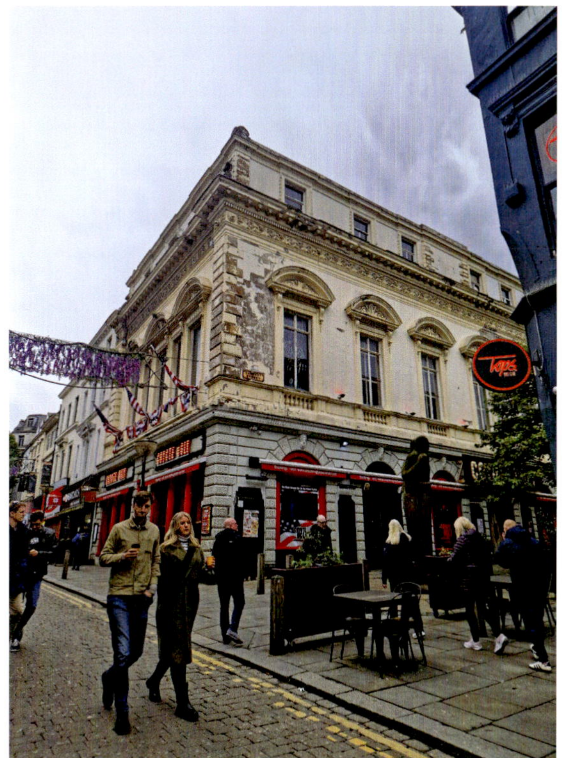

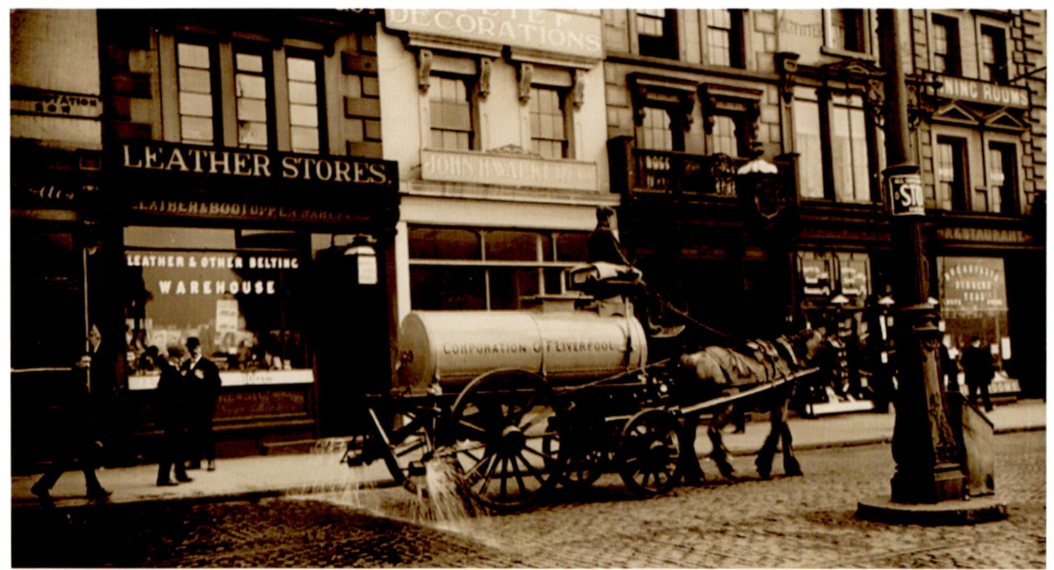

Commutation Row

Above: Cleaning the setts along Commutation Row, this corporation worker passed by a mix of beautiful shopfronts including that of John Matthews who specialised in leather goods from his three-storey warehouse. It featured somewhat minimalist windows between projecting quoins and signage. Further along with its splendid timber entrance and lantern, the Court House public house offered a sophisticated welcome.

Below: The historic Commutation Row and its miscellaneous range of shopfronts was torn down in the 1990s having stood derelict for some time. Calls to save this part of Liverpool's history went unheeded and plans for offices and flats were approved for the site, built to the designs of architecture firm Geoffrey Reid Associates in the year 2000.

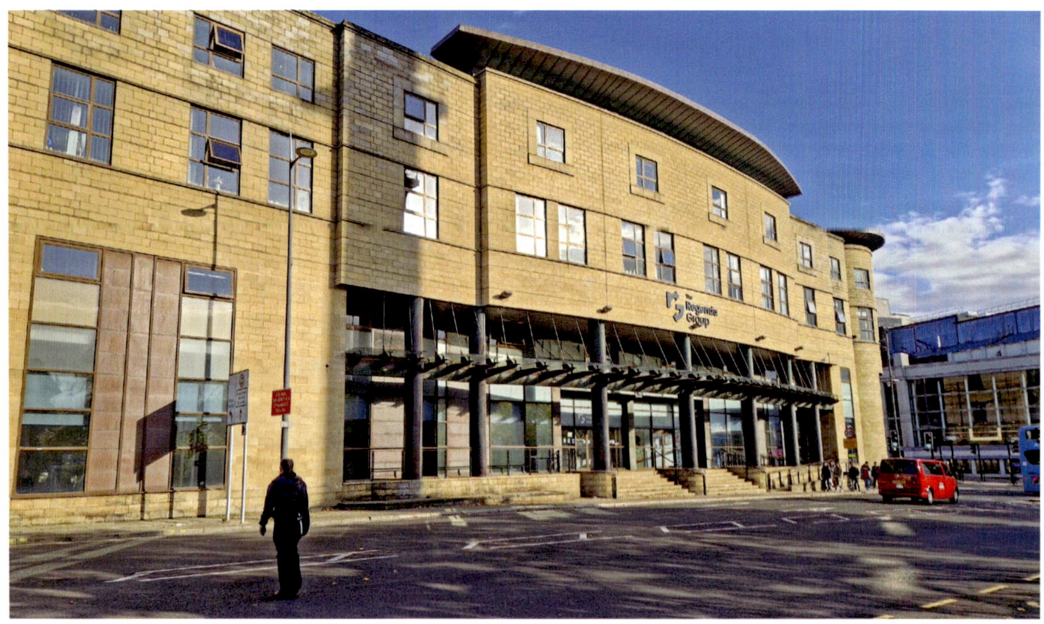

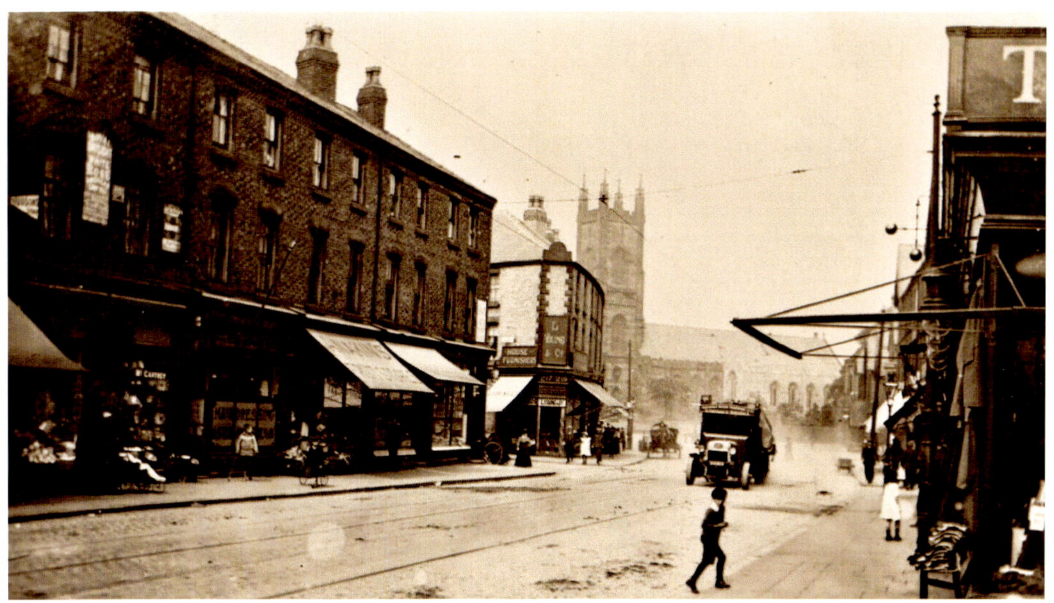

County Road

Above: The tower of St Mary's Church loomed over Walton's County Road and its commercial collectives in this busy Edwardian view. A brick-built terrace offered matching retail spaces to traders with awnings out over the pavement. A similar pattern of construction was built opposite, whilst the premises of L. Young & Co. offered an ideal space for advertisements framed perfectly by stone quoins.

Below: This area of the city and its surrounding buildings are still very recognisable despite most shopfronts needing some repair and occupation. As well as losing their traditional timber surrounds, metal roller shutters have been added to the majority of the stores here in the name of security, along with various styles of bulky plastic facias.

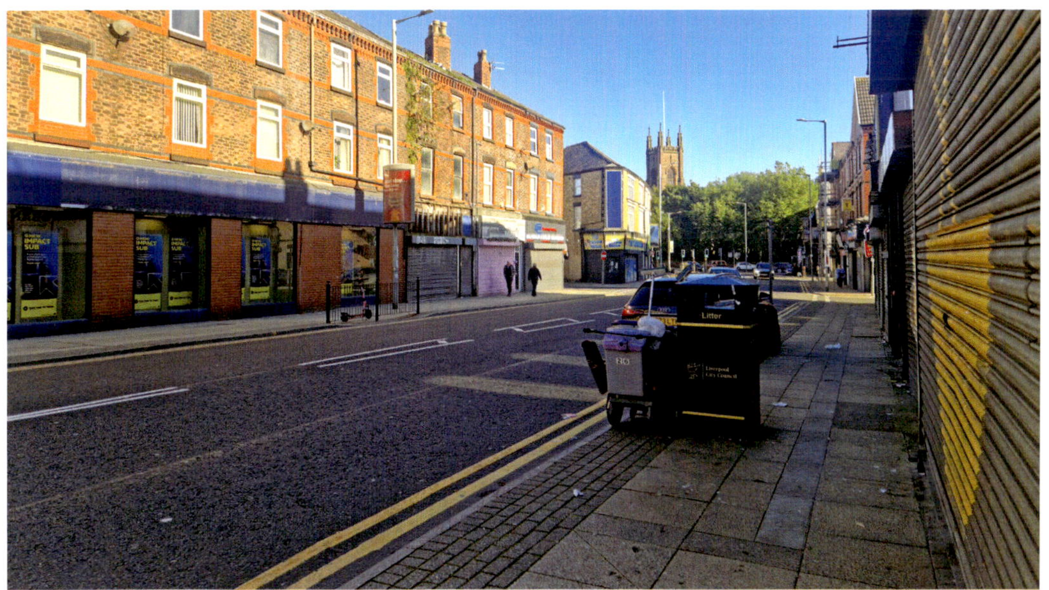

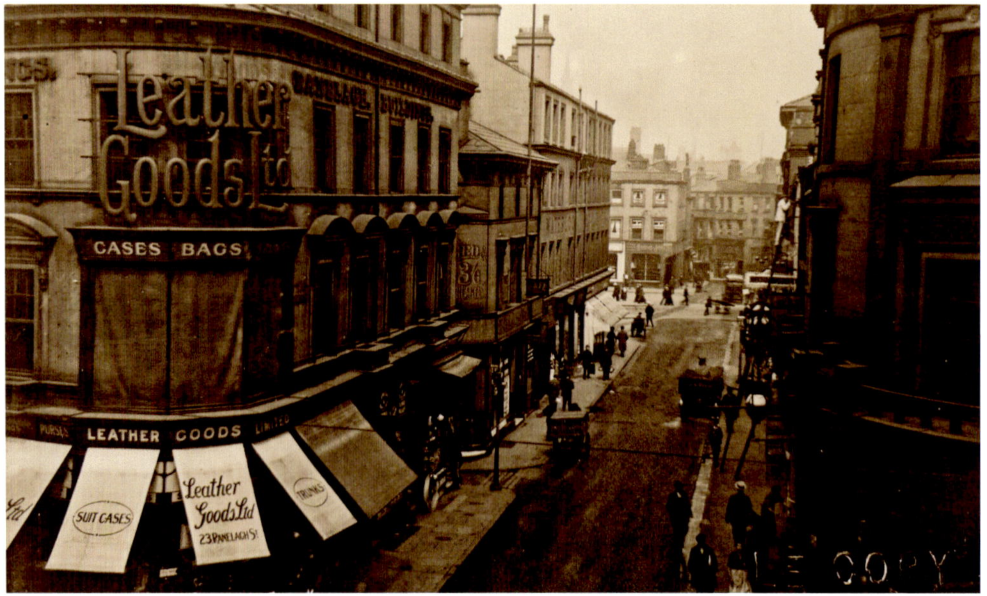

Cases Street

Above: The awnings of Ranelagh Buildings are seen garnished with goods sold by the Leather Goods Ltd, the prodigious sign of which was fixed high on the upper level. Far less conspicuous businesses stood alongside, including a café and bed and breakfast which offered its room rates on its exterior wall. The various buildings of Clayton Square could be seen in the distance along with a brave decorator carrying on his work.

Below: A very different perspective now as the enormous glazed enclosure of Clayton Square houses half the street. A branch of the coffee chain Starbucks occupies the ground floor of Ranelagh Buildings, but many of its former neighbours have been demolished. Across the way, a singular shopfront has survived, sandwiched between two historic pubs.

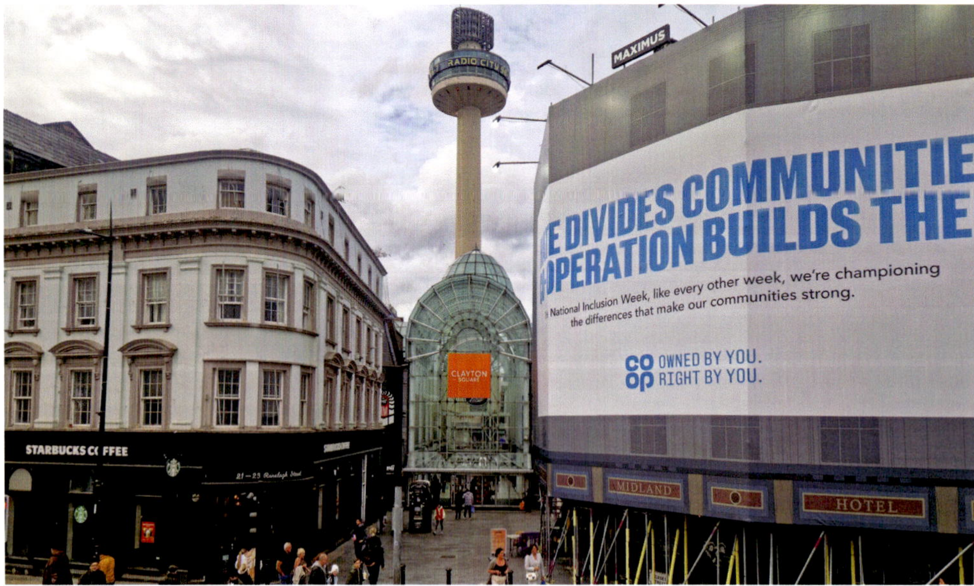

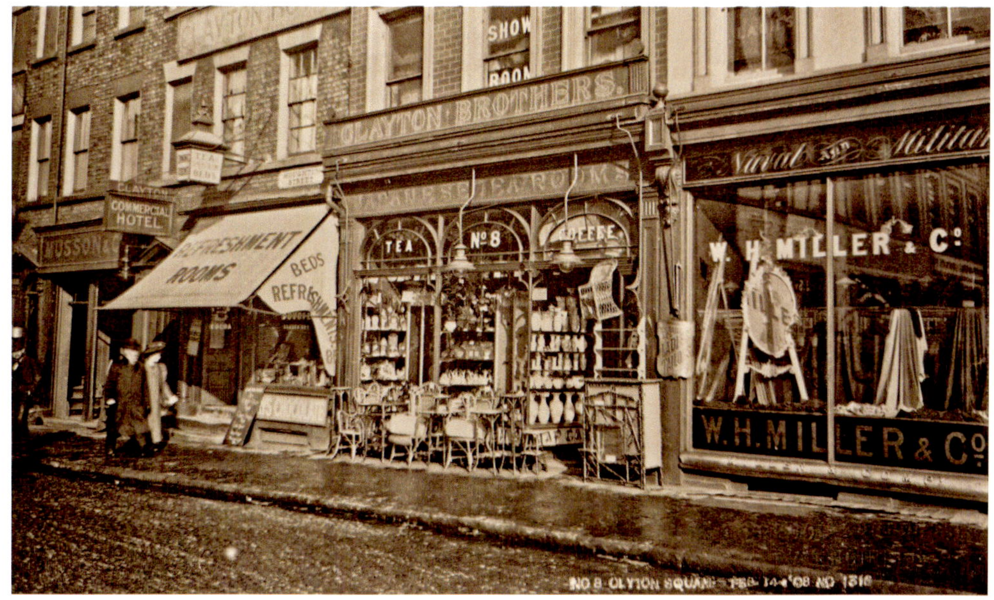

No. 8 Clayton Square

Above: This image depicts the view across Clayton Square with its unusual Japanese tearooms which traded from No. 8. The premises also sold a range of Eastern curios, furniture, clothing, vases, and of course tea. The Clayton Commercial Hotel with its projecting advertisement lantern stood alongside at No. 7, whilst the upmarket shop of W. H. Miller tailors and naval and military outfitters and Co. occupied No. 9.

Below: The development of St John's shopping precinct in 1969 signalled the end of these aged buildings and the arrival of a new and exciting era of commerce. Constructed across 72,000 sq. ft, this immense revolutionary wonder allowed shoppers to purchase their goods all under one roof, free from the risk of traffic and the whims of the weather.

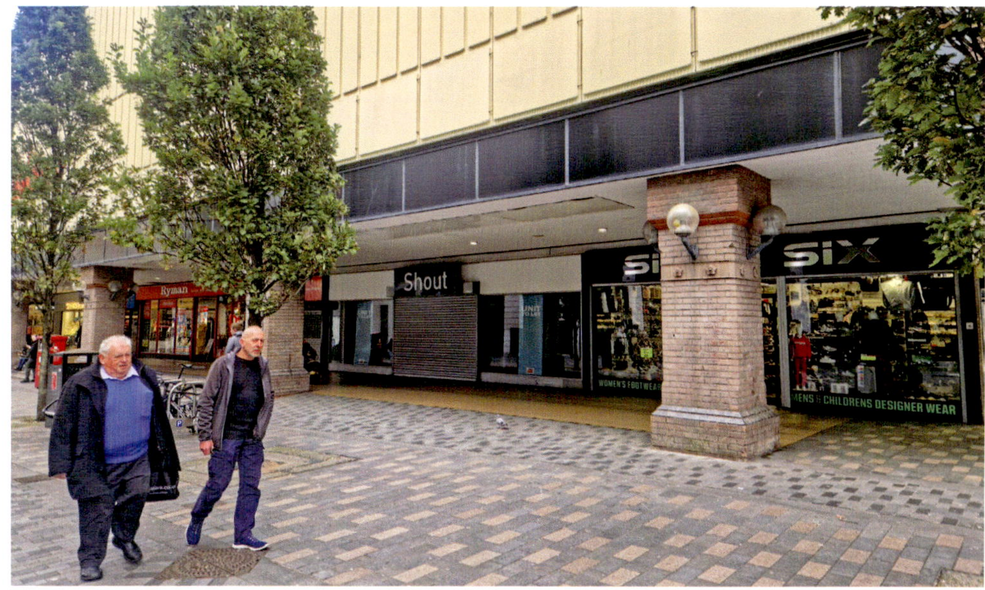

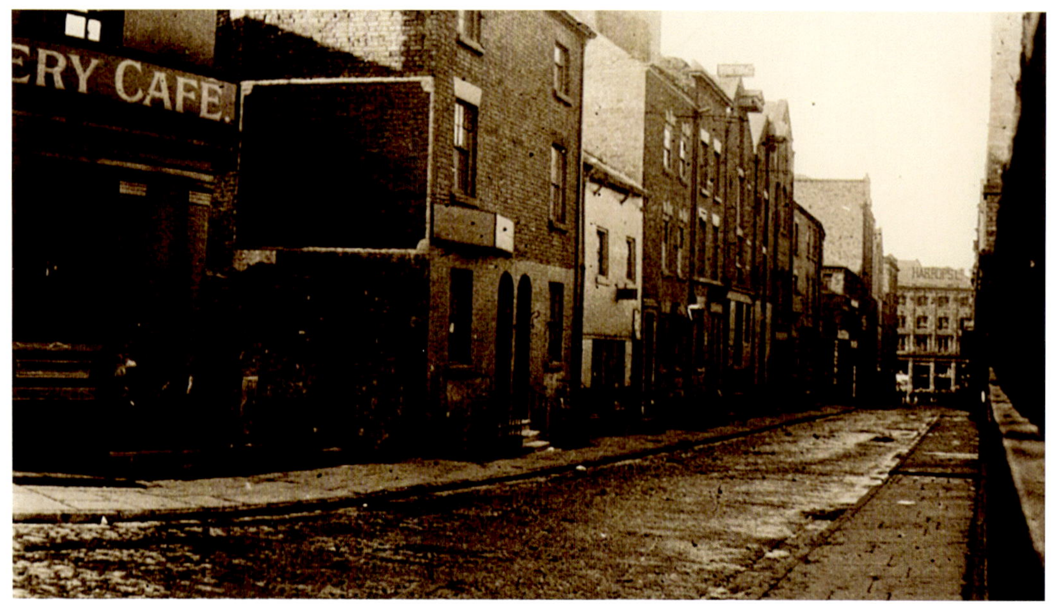

College Lane

Above: Modest housing, pubs and warehouses once lined College Lane, as seen from the perspective of Hanover Street in the early 1900s. In the distance, a large sign for Harrops furniture store could be seen looming down over shoppers in Paradise Street, whilst a more low-key advertisement awaited placement upon a cleaned and prepared brick wall.

Below: The scene today is a mix of the old and new with rather recent developments constructed as part of the Liverpool One project juxtaposed with more historic designs. These older buildings however have been modified for current requirements with new shopfronts, doors and glazing inserted into old multistorey warehouses that still border the street.

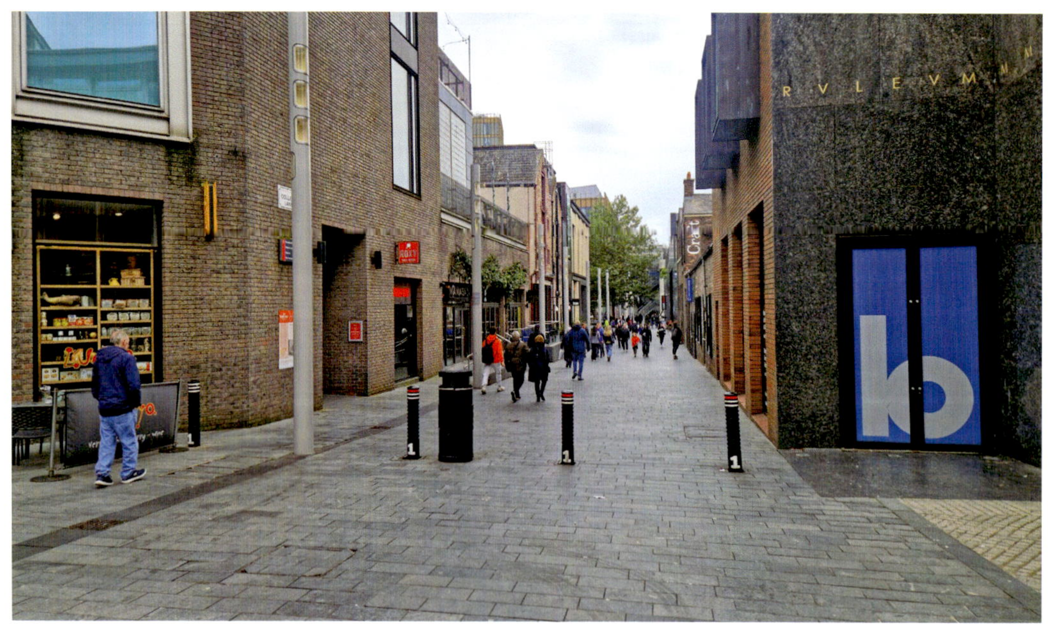

Nos 85–89 Bold Street

Right above: Nos 85–89 Bold Street are seen here in the middle of the Second World War. The department store of Blackler's had opened a temporary premises as their main store in Great Charlotte Street had been obliterated. Alongside, large lettering for chemists Clay & Abraham sat above a decorative arched window arrangement; however, that of their neighbour appears to have been prudently secured against possible bomb damage.

Right below: These addresses look very different with much of their detail and interest washed away with the passage of time, with only No. 85 offering a glimpse of a once prevalent style and design. The use of these properties has also altered with a specialist seafood restaurant, a hair salon and an eponymous coffee shop now trading from these respective buildings.

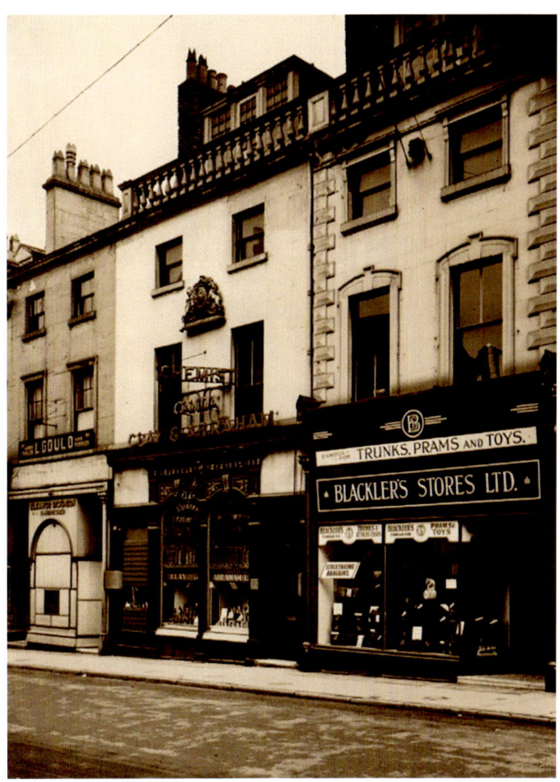

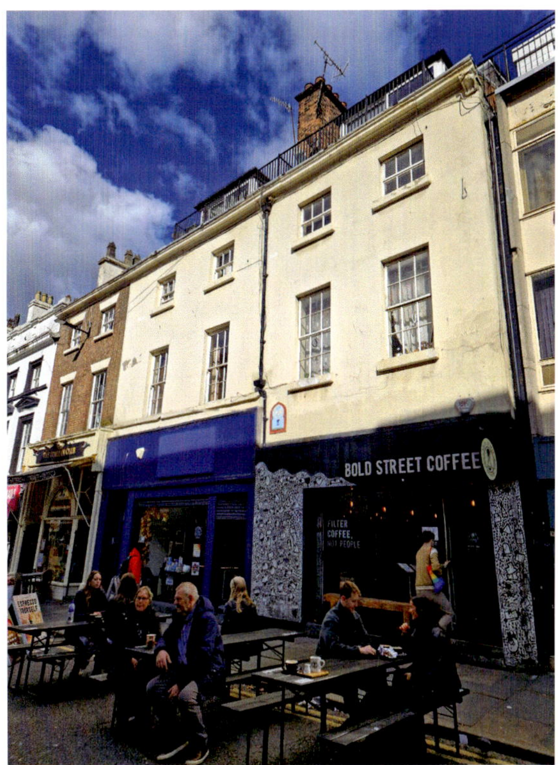

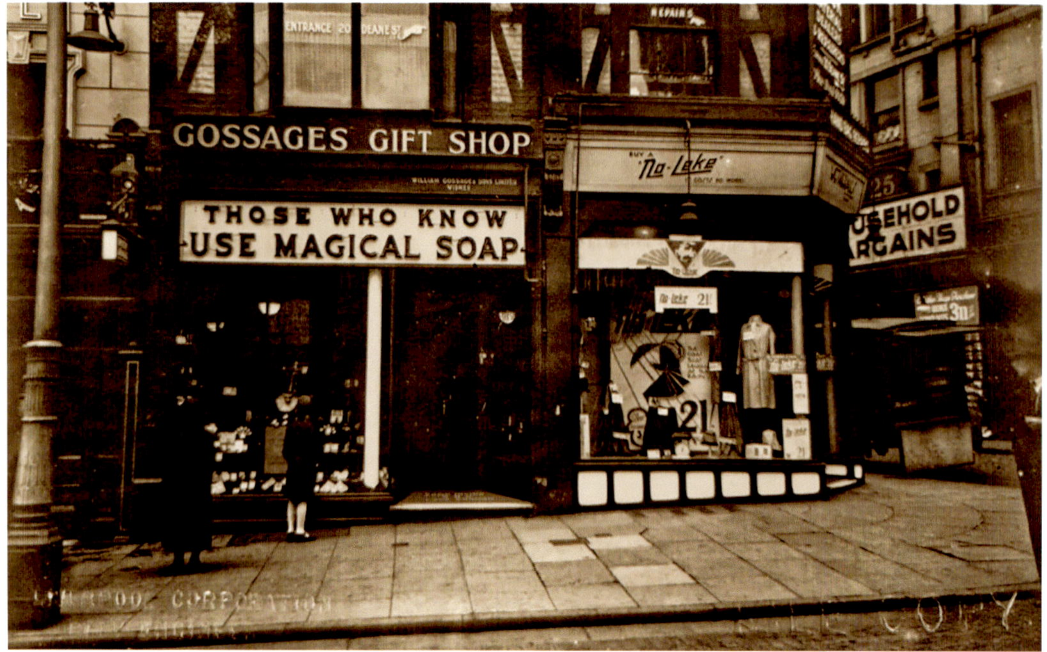

Gossages, Ranelagh Street

Above: The half-timbered facade of Gossage's Gift Shop with its principal fascia board designed to tease customers in with promises of magical soap. A Christian Science Reading Room advertised its nearby premises from the first-floor glazing whilst next door, the waterproof garments of Wetheralls could be admired through the window display at the corner of Deane Street.

Below: Major infrastructure changes saw the buildings here replaced in the mid-twentieth century which also saw the loss of Deane Street itself. Today this part of the city is home to an Irish bar with rooms above, along with a second bar next door also designed with a common Celtic theme. This now stands on the site of the long-lost road to Elliot Street.

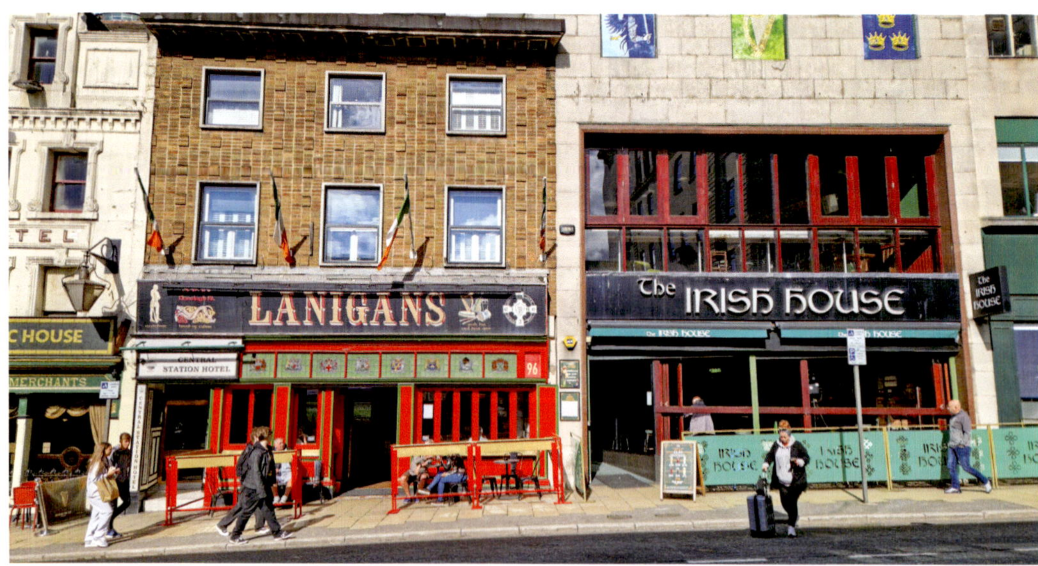

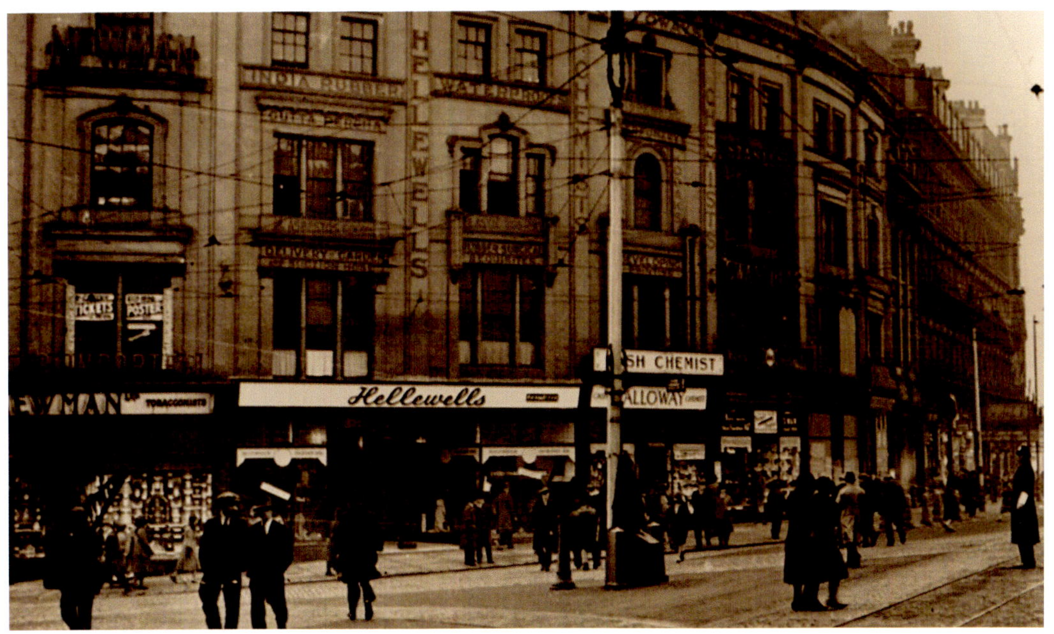

Lime Street

Above: A magnificent array of shopfronts could once be discovered at the junction of Lime Street and Ranelagh Street as an impressive classical edifice towered over shoppers below. The repetitive pattern of units graced the curve of the ground floor as various styles of advertising added to the interest of this landmark high-rise construction.

Below: An analogous view today reveals how post-war development has taken shape on this corner, with a markedly brutalist approach to this important city centre junction. A bar known as the Celtic Corner occupies the majority of the ground floor, faced in a pseudo timber effect, large frosted windows and ostentatious branding above.

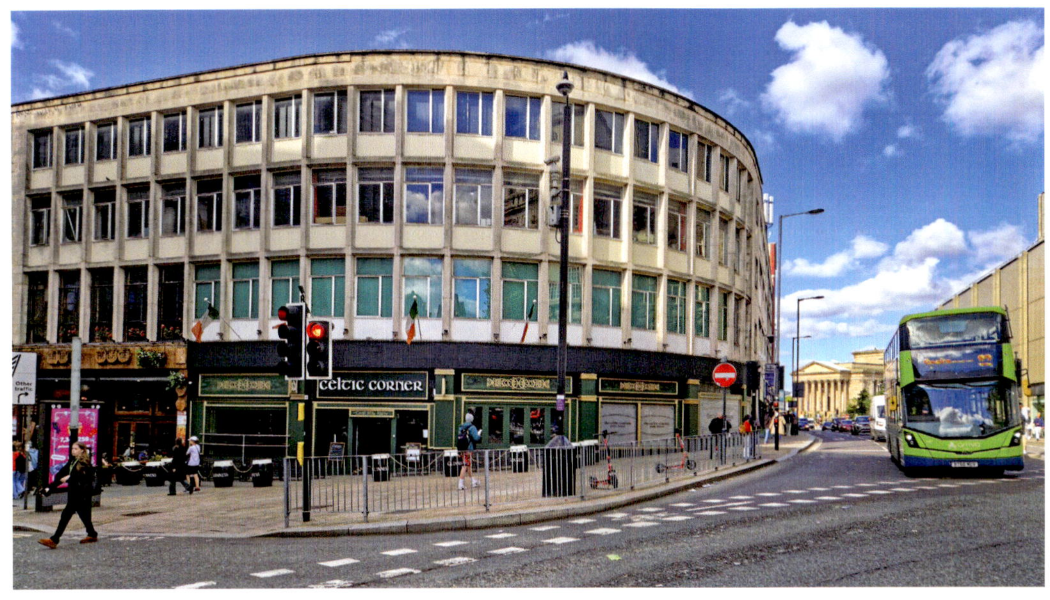

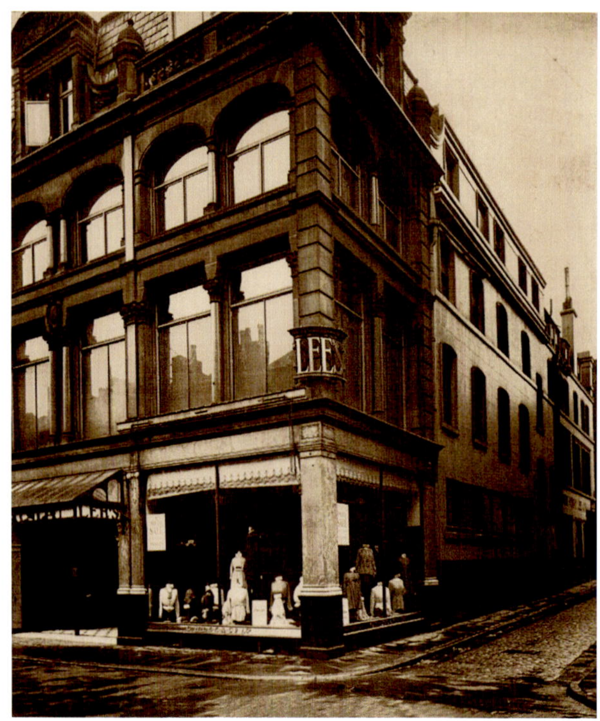

George Henry Lee, Basnett Street

Left above: A view of the George Henry Lee building at the corner of Basnett Street and Leigh Street reveals an insight into the fashions of the 1930s. The sartorial display was framed by marble pilasters and plate-glass windows. Above, more marble could be found in rows of classical columns alongside motifs and a dated cartouche, with a delicate canopy offering patrons shelter from the rain.

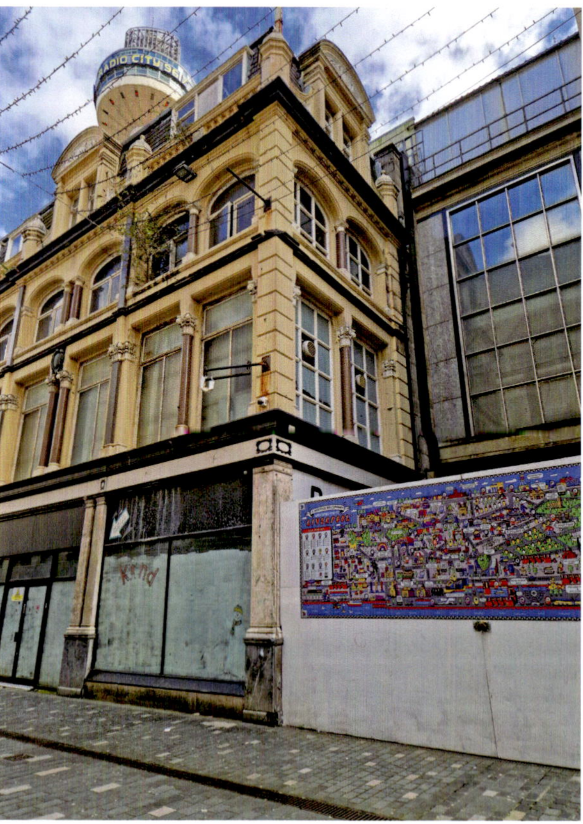

Left below: The business no longer trades and today the vast ground floor stands vacant. However, the building remains highly legible with its important architectural features still intact. A major change to Leigh Street has seen this section of the passage closed off, with access now reserved for the commercial buildings of nearby Church Street and Parker Street.

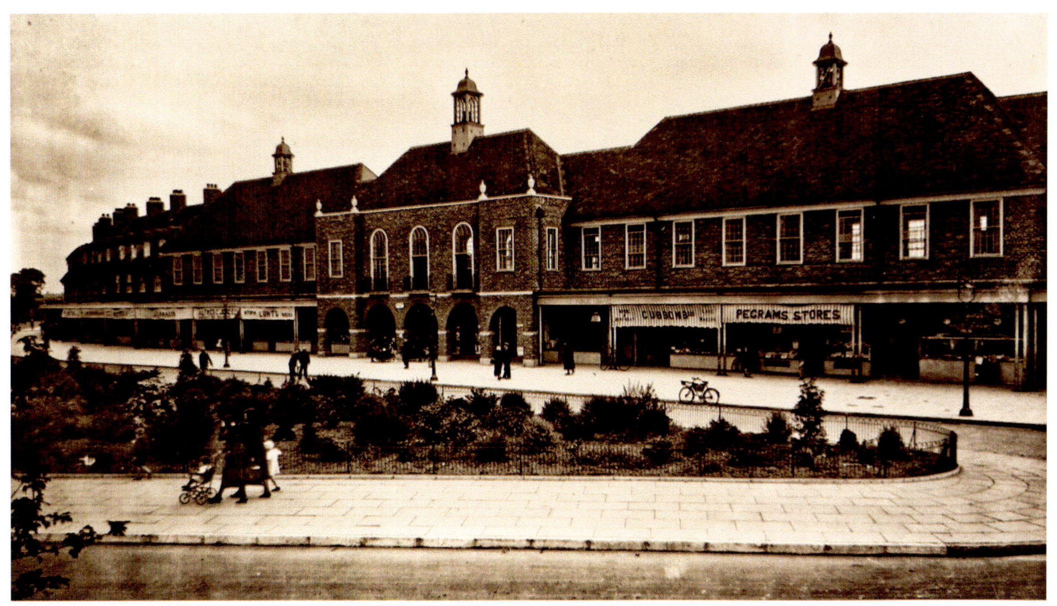

Dovecot Place

Above: The 1930s brought with it a handsome crescent known as Dovecot Place. This fine example of civic architecture provided a home to a variety of ground-floor shops. Each store was set back from the road beneath a long covered walkway, with a quintet of projecting brick arches positioned at the building's core. The design allowed for ample room for shopkeepers who also took advantage of additional advertising space across the verandah, such as fabric banners.

Below: Dovecot Place continues as a significant example of local contemporary twentieth-century design and remains a retail destination for the surrounding community. Nevertheless, there have been some unsympathetic design choices applied to some of the individual units including metallic external roller shutters, harming the overall visual cohesion that was originally intended for the site.

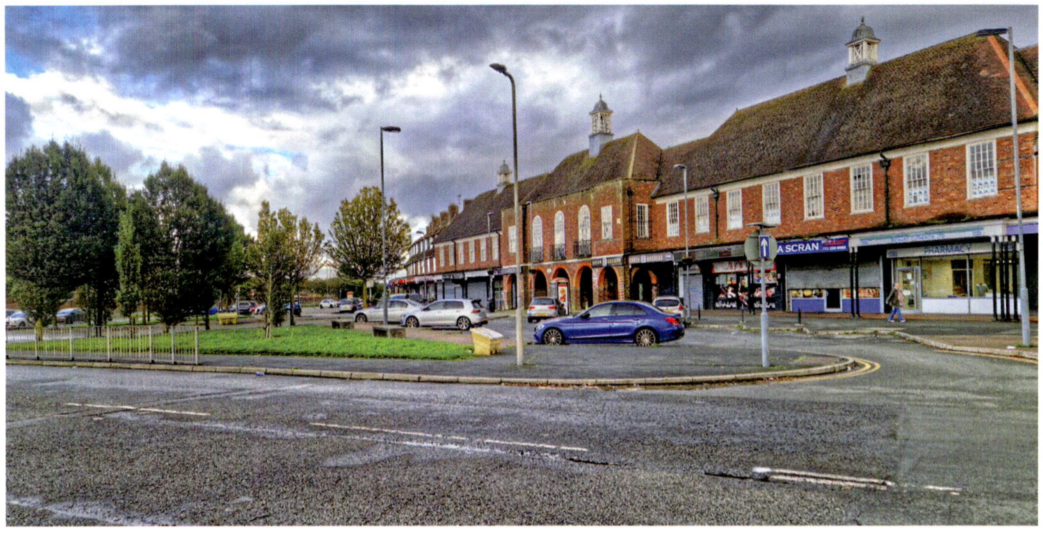

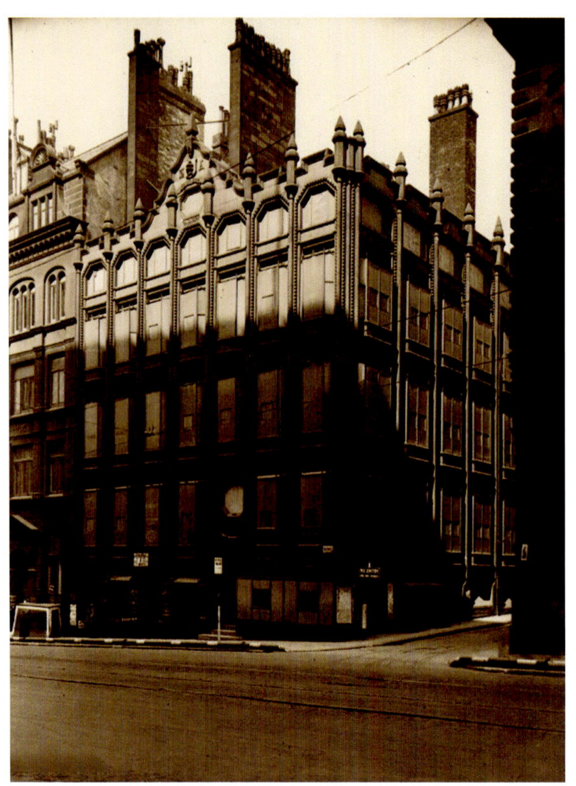

Oriel Chambers, Water Street

Left above: Oriel Chambers was primarily built as offices in 1864 but the designs included lettable units at street level. The building has been described as a pioneer in the use of expressed cast-iron construction and the first in the UK to feature a glass curtain wall. Depicted here secured during the Second World War, Beale and Hiller stationers printers along with the tobacconist Turmeaus Ltd can be seen occupying the ground floor facing onto Water Street.

Left below: A Grade I listed designation has been applied to Oriel Chambers, the highest of all grades, demonstrating the national importance of this building's historic and architectural significance. It is no surprise to see very little change to the building over the years, with a coffee shop trading from one of the ground-floor units and other professions operating within.

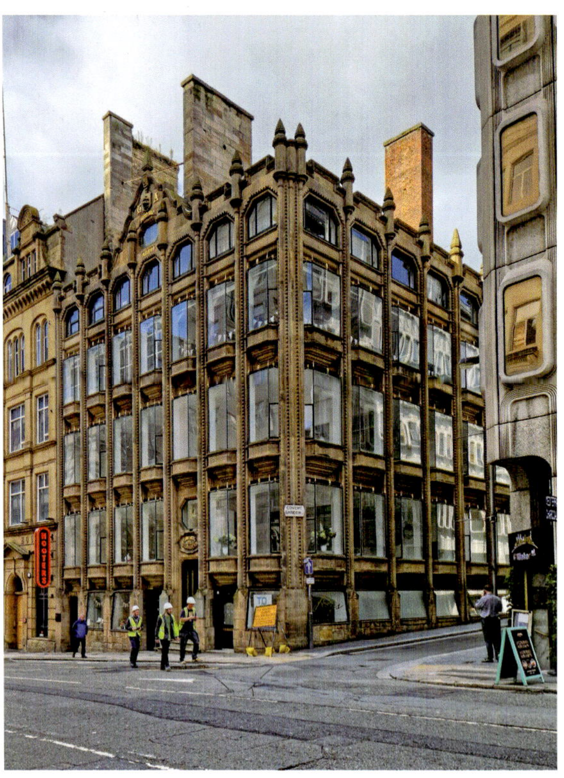

St Andrews School, Slater Street

Right above: This view shows what was St Andrews School at the corner of Slater Street and Fleet Street. The building was erected in 1818 to teach up to 270 children paid for by charitable subscription, with a building next door to sell religious literature and offer accommodation for charities. By the time of this twentieth-century photograph, the handsome chapel-like building was home to R. Jackson & Sons art supplies.

Right below: There has been some alteration to the old school which is now home to a bar and short stay apartments. Modern touches include a new colour palette, signage, lighting, but its bubble facade finish is questionable. The building remains as one of the more characterful constructions in the neighbourhood which has seen many of its properties adapted into bars and nightclubs.

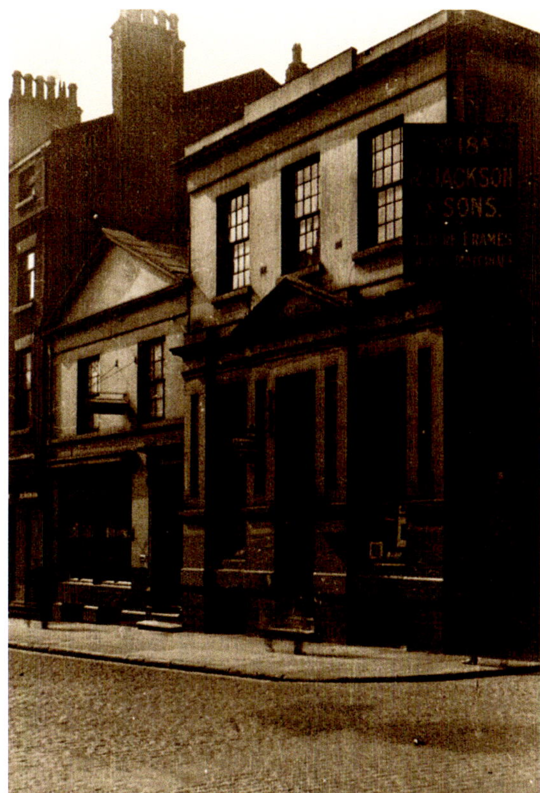

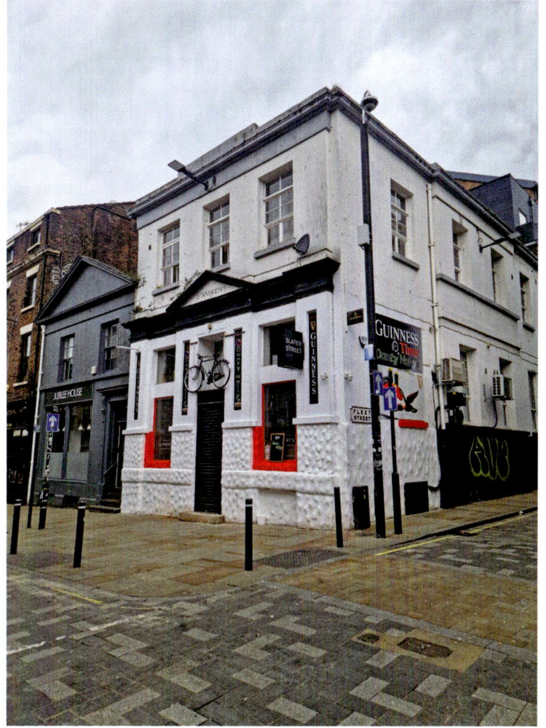

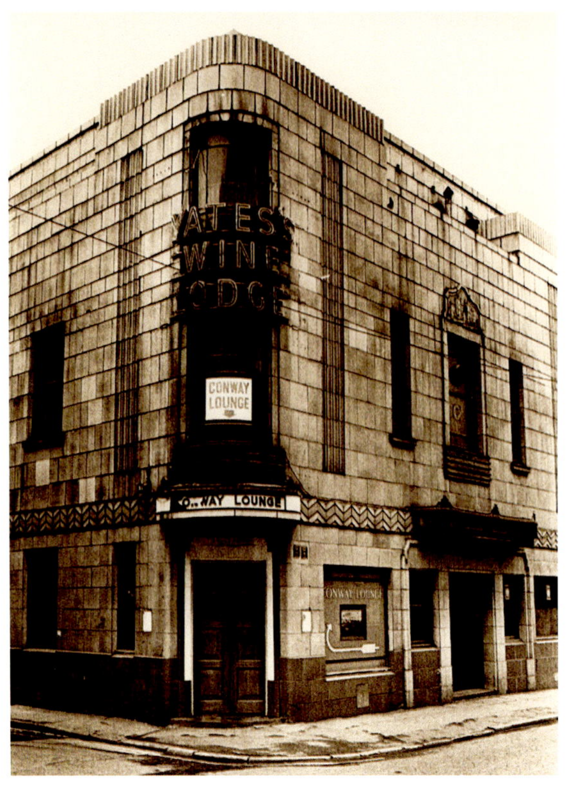

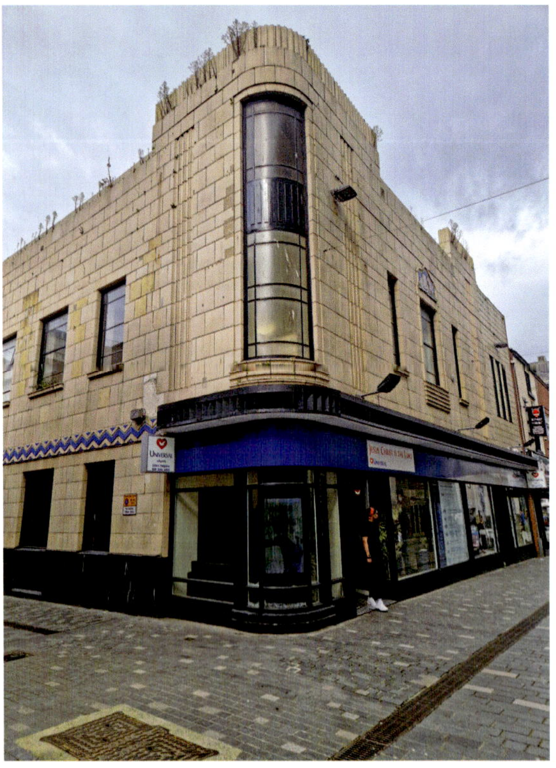

Yates, Tarleton Street

Left above: The pub chain Yates was founded in 1884 and remains Britain's oldest pub chain. The Conway Lounge, as the sizable signage confirmed, was a branch of Yates in Tarleton Street and boasted a liberal mix of Art Deco features, most strikingly through its curved design, Crittall windows and patterned decoration. A depiction of Conway Castle adorned the facade in memory of an earlier pub at this site, demolished in approximately 1937.

Left below: The building still stands; however, the frontage itself has been amended to suit a change to retail use with the insertion of a new shopfront. The corner door has gone and instead, a curved-glass window occupies the return, whilst the former recessed entrance has given way to display windows and the unfortunate loss of attractive decorative detail above.

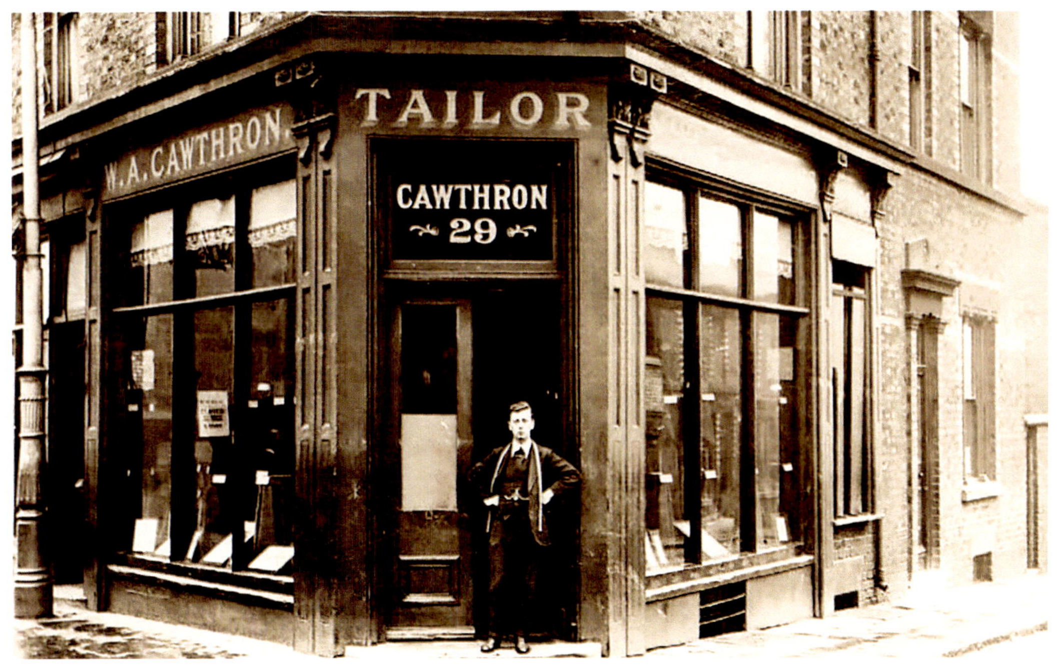

No. 29 Walton Road

Above: A man who can only be presumed to be William Albert Cawthron stood proudly in the doorway of his shop in Walton Road. The merchant tailor occupied the corner premises which featured a robust set of pilasters with a series of windows and doors in perfect proportion. Extra detail could be found in scroll brackets with elegant hand-painted signage carefully applied above.

Below: The old shopfront is no more and instead a somewhat more generic plastic replacement stands in its stead. Its modern equivalent, now home to a barber, also features tripartite fenestration, stallrisers and signage but this does not seem to offer the same quality or effective visual impression of its earlier occupier.

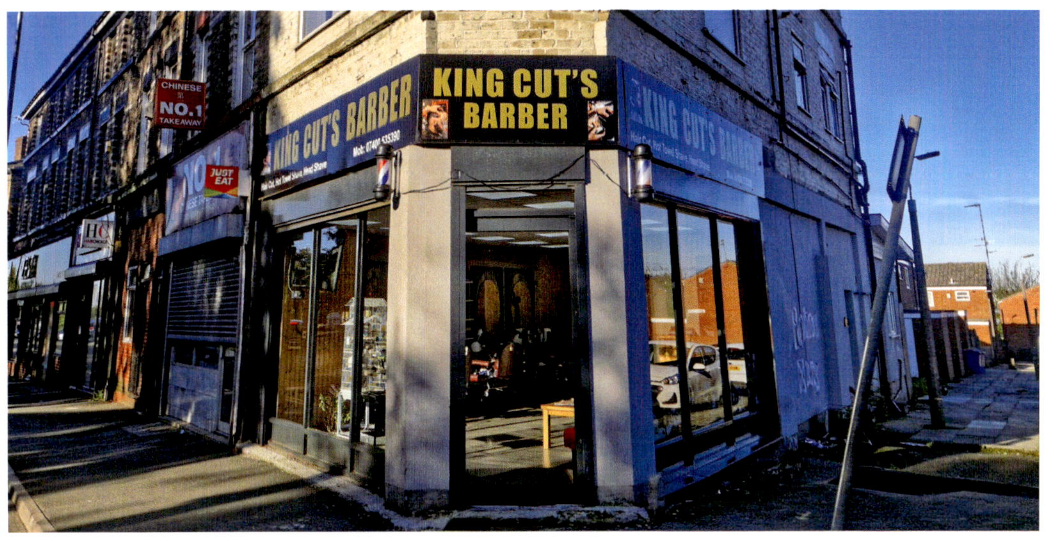

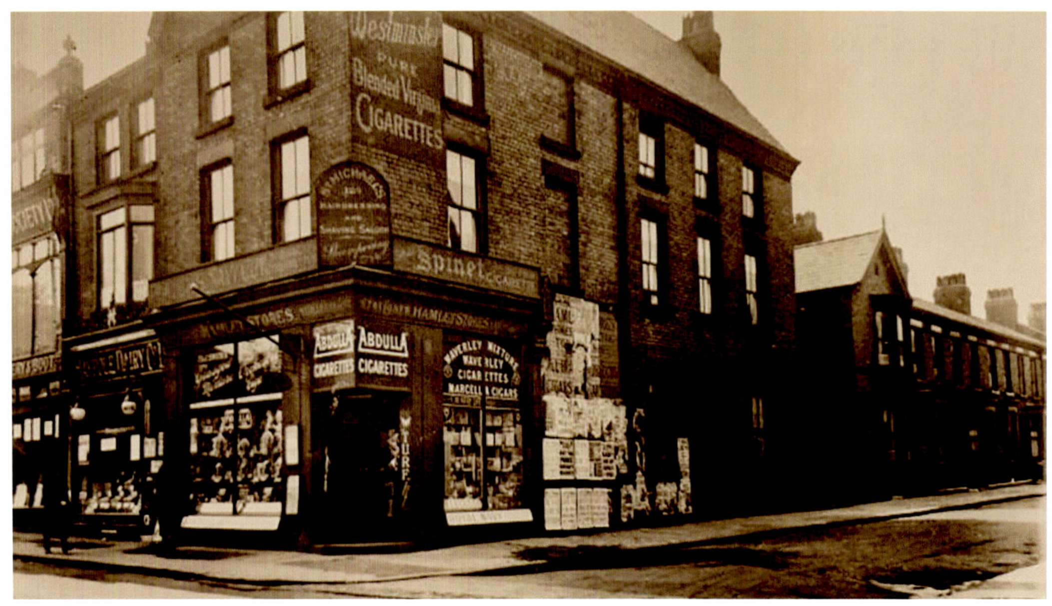

No. 124 Aigburth Road

Above: Hamlet Stores, a stationers and tobacconist which was kept by Mrs Elizabeth Beeson, is captured here in a view of 1930s Aigburth Road. Posters on the wall along Alwyn Street advertised newspapers such as the *Express*, *Weekly Post* and the *Herald*, whilst next door stood the Maypole Dairy Co. Ltd, butter merchants, and a shop belonging to the Liverpool Co-operative Society.

Below: This corner enjoys a less cluttered appearance, and the simplicity and form of the timber shopfront, despite an enlarged fascia, can now be better appreciated. Gone too are the adverts that had plastered the wall of Alwyn Street, but the current aspect of its Aigburth Road neighbours leaves much to be desired. The former stationer and tobacconist shop is now used as a patisserie.

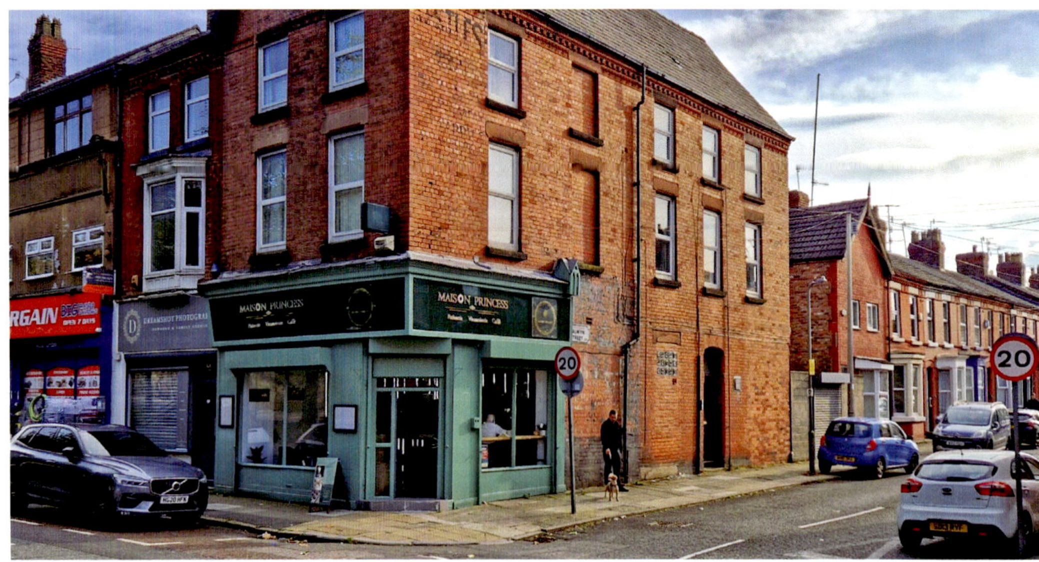

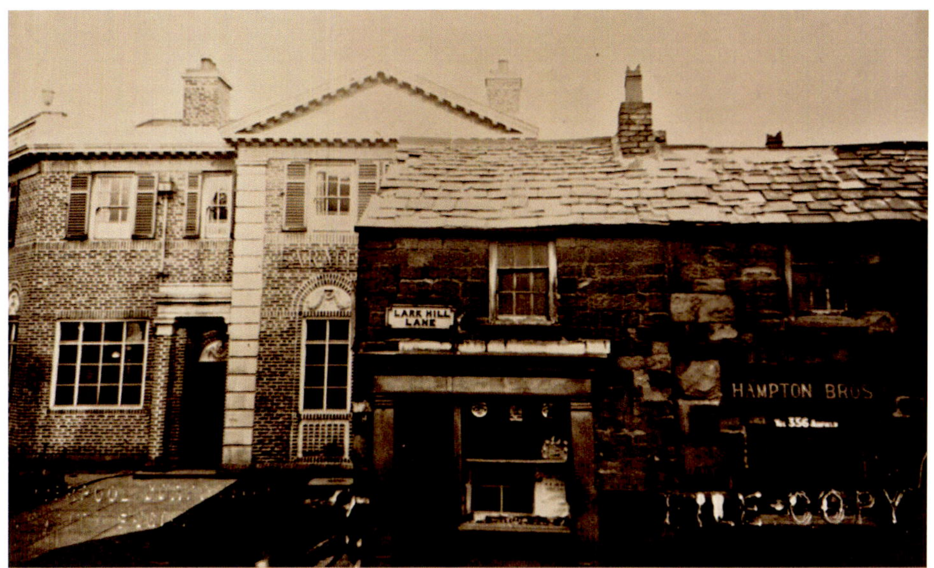

Lark Hill Lane

Above: Old sandstone cottages can be seen set against the relatively modern and extravagant Farmers Arms public house in this image from the 1920s. These quaint antiquated structures housed the business of Charles Brumfitt, a boot repairer at what was No. 45 Larkhill Lane, with bicycle makers Hampton Bros next door. A rudimentary shopfront greeted customers to the cobbler, whilst a modest moniker marked upon the stone lintel guided others to the neighbouring bike store.

Below: The aged cottages have since been demolished with few vestiges to be found to indicate the historic character of the street and the humble shops that previously stood there. The Farmers Arms however continues to serve the local community, and its impressive and detailed elevations can now be surveyed without interruption.

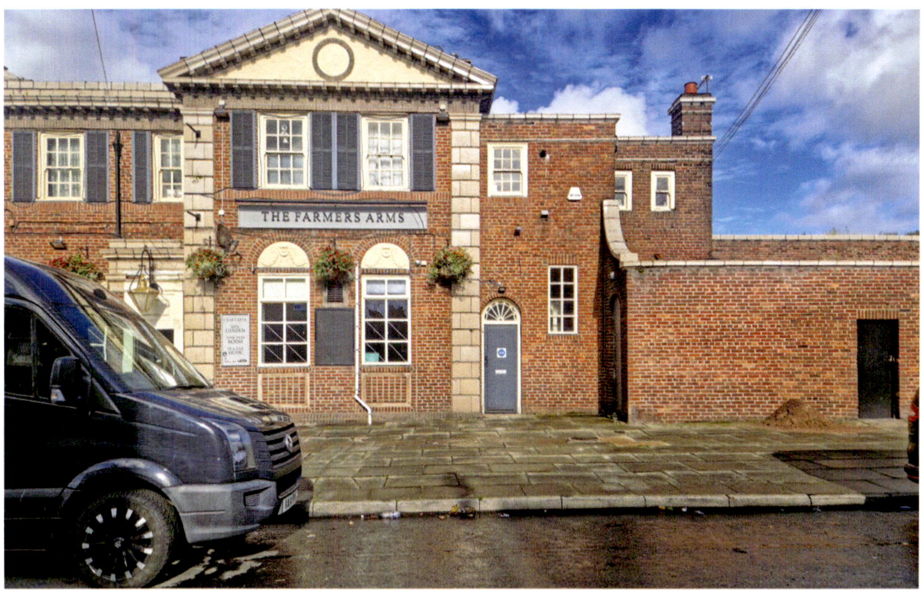

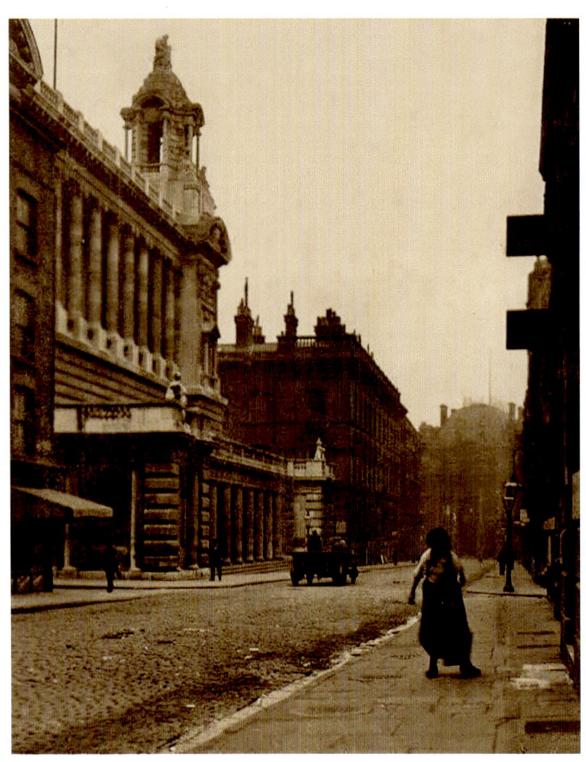

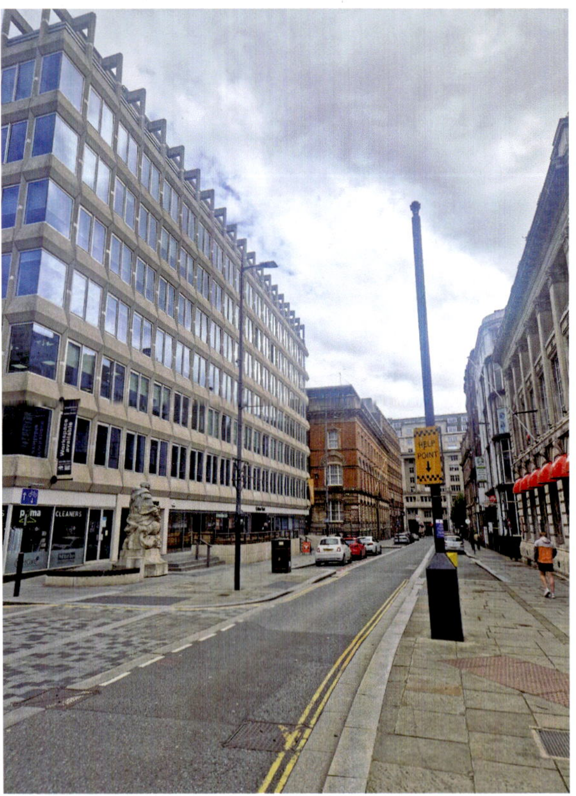

The Cotton Exchange, Old Hall Street

Left above: The impressive facade of the Cotton Exchange was seen here on Old Hall Street in approximately 1905. Its neoclassical appearance by Matear & Simon was bolstered by the addition of a pair of Baroque towers upon which sat colossal statues related to Liverpudlian commerce. At street level, an elegant loggia stretched across the front elevation with a colonnade of Doric columns, rusticated stonework and classical balustrading.

Left below: In an effort to modernise, the building was refaced in 1967, resulting in the loss of its original Edwardian character and the addition of a contemporary brutalist facade. Retail space was included in this new design by Newton-Dawson, Forbes and Tate, and nowadays a restaurant and coffee shop can be found behind the heavily glazed ground-floor units.

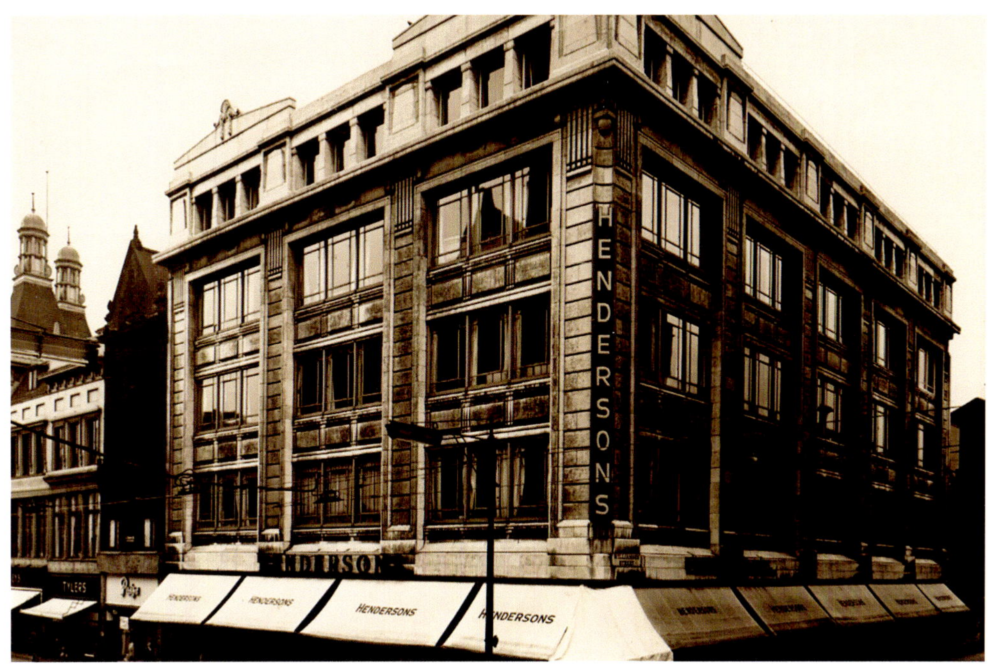

Hendersons, Church Street

Above: The large Church Street department store that was Hendersons is seen here in 1956. The steel-framed building itself was constructed thirty years earlier but the business dated to 1829. The architecture appeared thoroughly modern set against its more demure Victorian neighbours, with its multiple storeys offering shoppers an abundance of choice and selection.

Below: Tragedy emerged on the afternoon of 22 June 1960 when a blaze took hold of the upper floors following an electrical fire. Eleven people lost their lives and the store was rendered so unsafe that its demolition was ordered soon after. Today's building dates from 1962 and is divided into two separate premises with simple pale cladding across the ground floor, but an unusual, glazed curtain above.

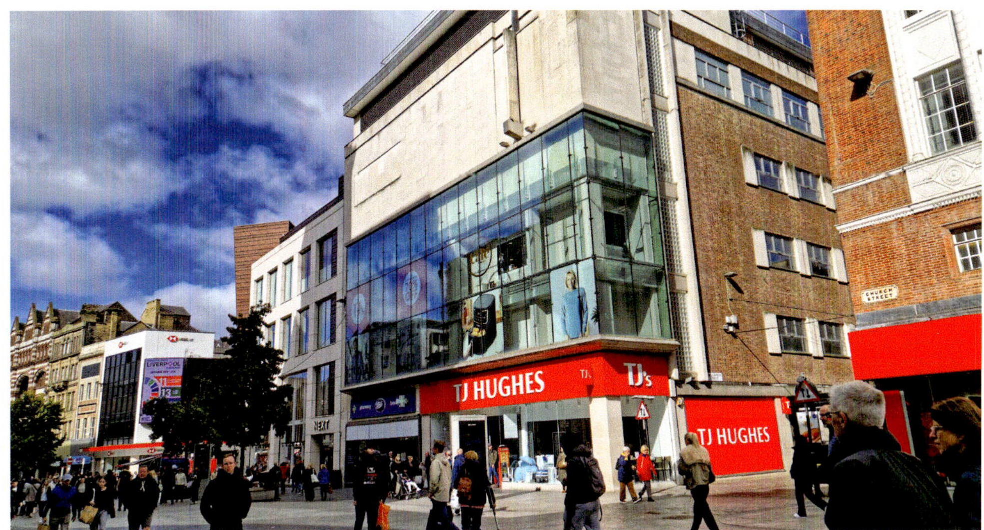

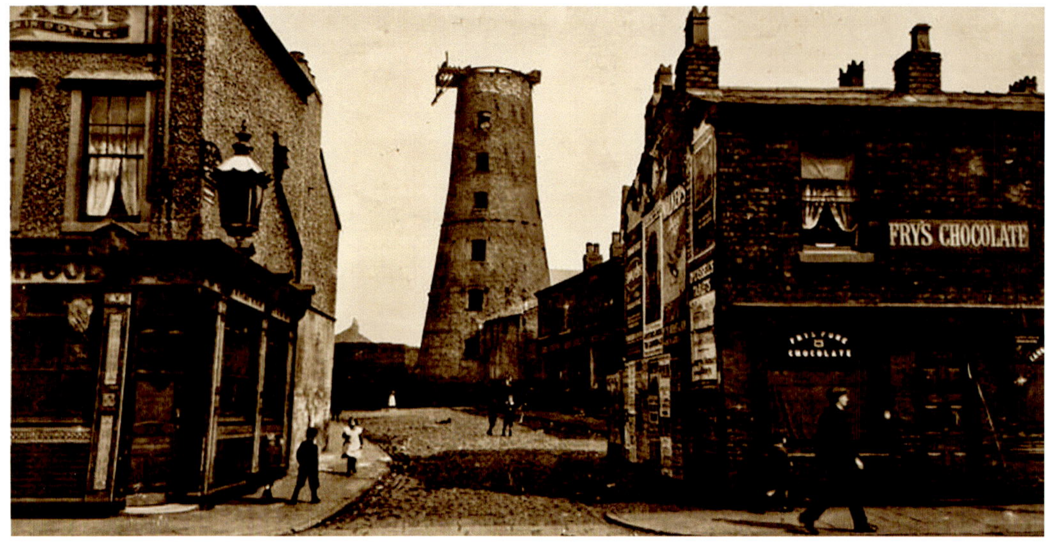

Springfield Square

Above: The Edwardian skyline of Walton Road featured an impressive windmill that soared above the populace. By 1927 its time as a mill had ceased and its foundations had been adapted as the stained-glass works of John Lewis who supplied many of the shopfronts across the city. Facing onto the highway a confectionary shop with probable domestic origins stood at the corner of Springfield Square, its gable covered in promotions.

Below: The twenty-first-century view tells a story of complete change with all remnants of the old windmill removed, and most of the architecture of the past destroyed. The former chocolate shop has been replaced by a box-like fireplace retailer, its stock displayed behind floor-to-ceiling glazing along with an illustrated fascia. This store too has utilised its exposed side wall to advertise goods to passing traffic.

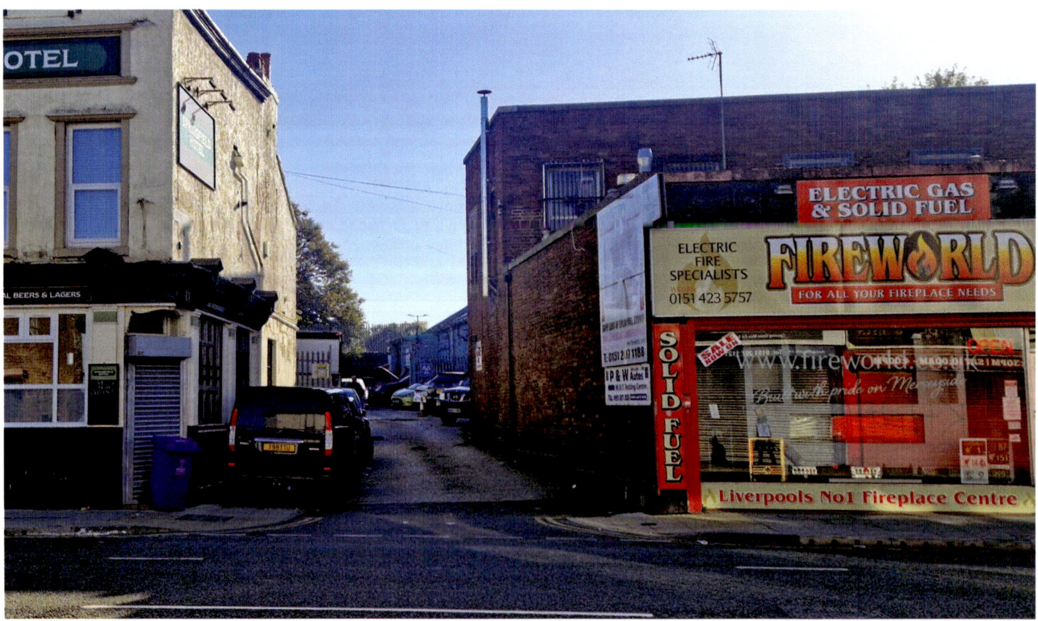

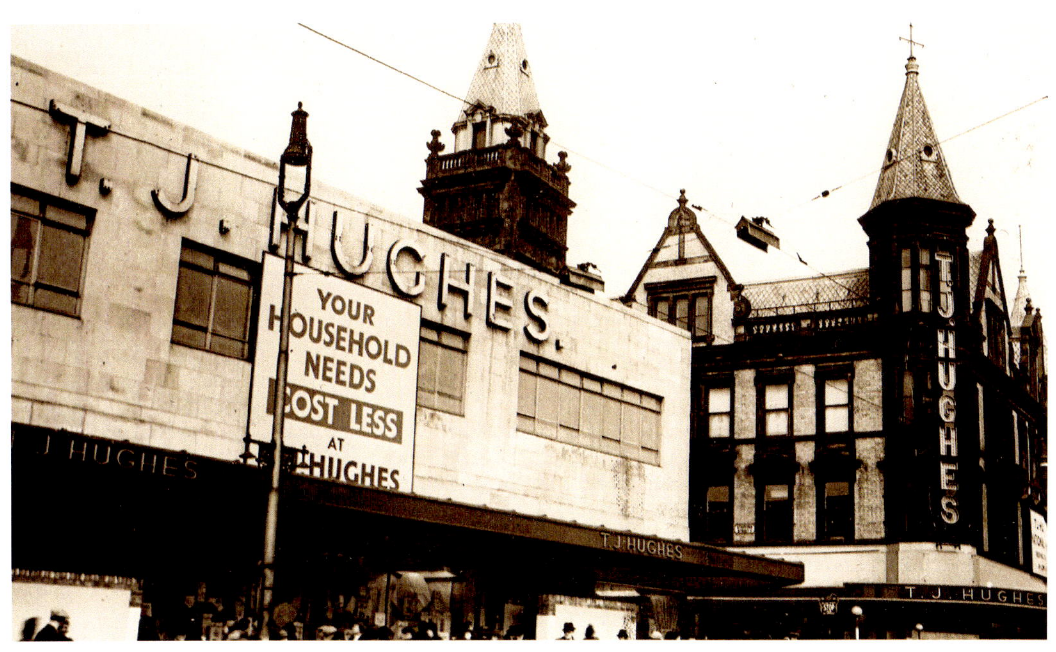

Audley House, London Road

Above: T J Hughes has been a familiar face on the high street since emerging in Liverpool in 1912. Their premises of Audley House was built in phases from 1880. Its large octagonal towers ascended over the shoppers of London Road, as did the mammoth signage and canopy positioned on the Stafford Street corner. In its shadow stood a distinctly subservient satellite store, Hughes House, designed with a contrasting 1920s approach.

Below: Audley House has been approved for residential conversion which will retain the impressive exterior, but its sister site next door has been demolished as part of a grand plan to bring about an additional 745 apartments to an area of the city well known for its student population. In 2023 T J Hughes moved to a premises in Church Street, bringing an end to its long, century-old presence in London Road.

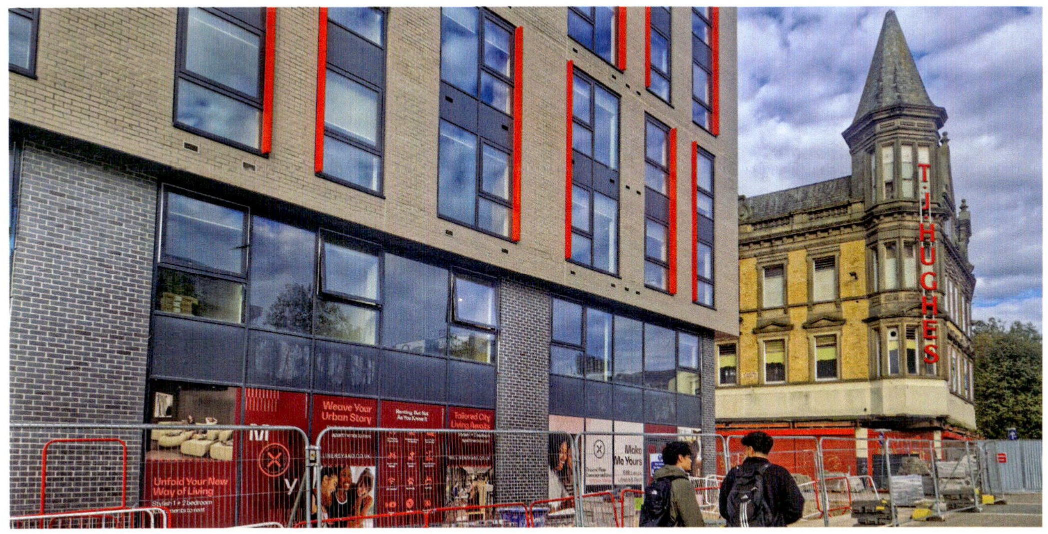

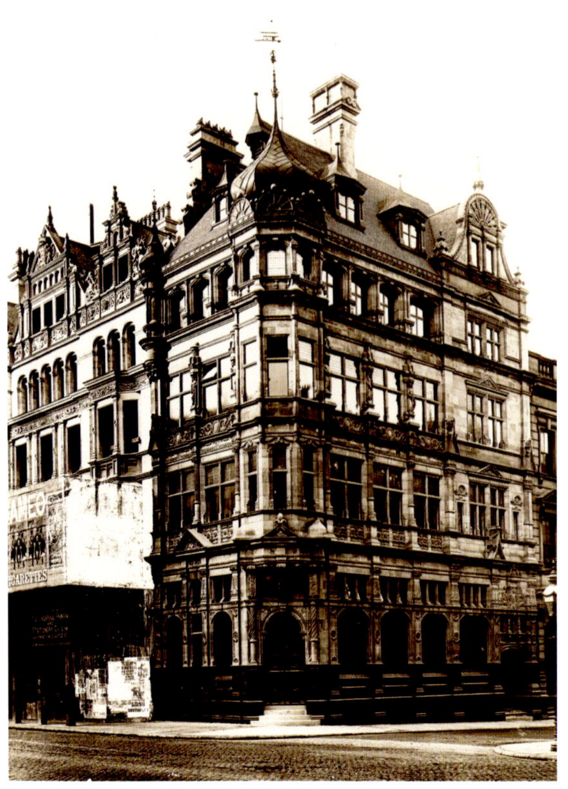

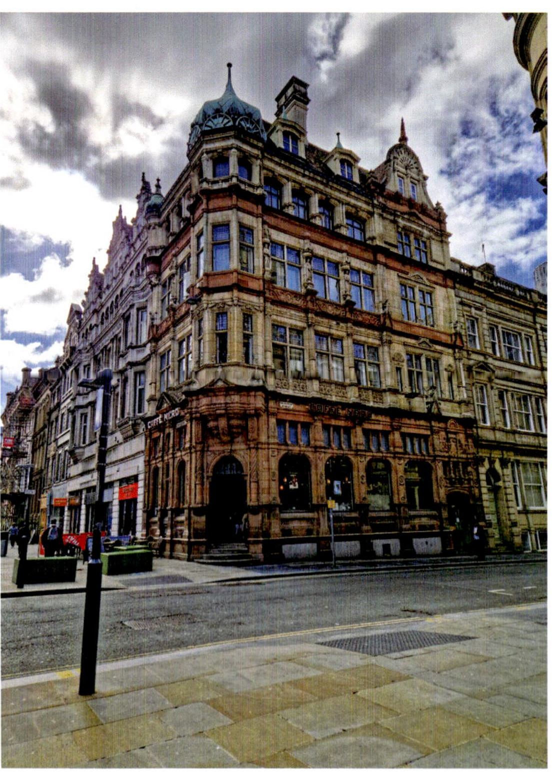

The Adelphi Bank, Castle Street

Left above: Originally constructed as the Adelphi Bank in 1892, this magnificent building was designed to impress. Architect William Douglas Caröe incorporated a wealth of architectural interest amongst alternative bands of sandstone and granite, with various carved columns, figures, reliefs and motifs wisely placed about the Castle Street and Brunswick Street elevations. The bronze entrance doors by Thomas Stirling Lee celebrated a theme of brotherly love, Adelphi being the Greek term for brothers.

Left below: The Grade II* building is now part of a chain of coffee shops with very little change to this nationally significant structure. Minor adjustments relate to some very subtle signage over the entrance and side elevations, with a mix of simple and reversible advertisements placed in the windows.

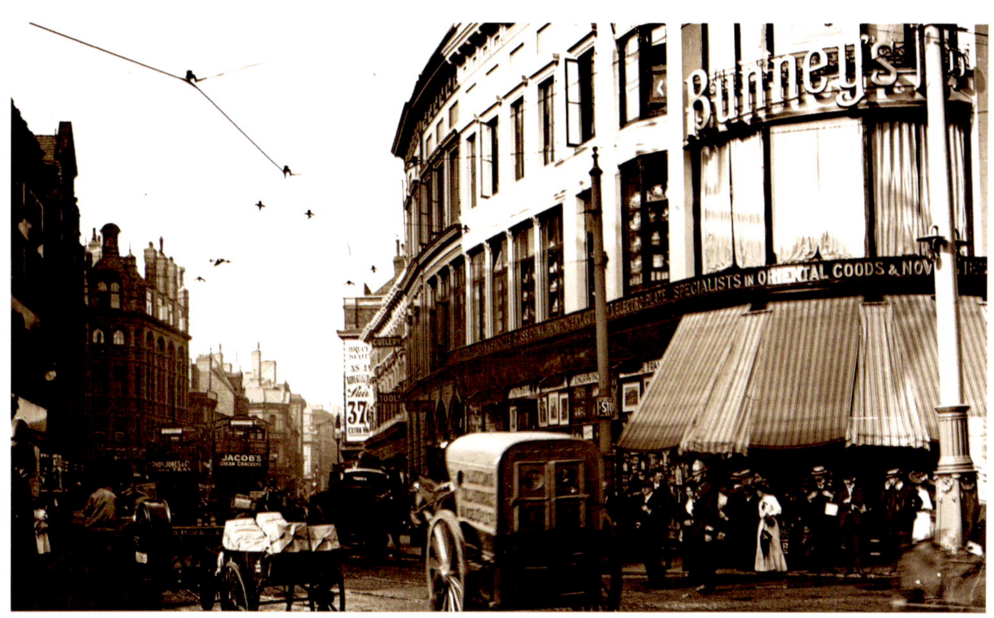

Bunney's, Church Street

Above: This early twentieth-century scene from outside Bunney's department store in Whitechapel shows Liverpool city centre bustling with shoppers and tradesmen as they go about their day. Established in the mid-Victorian era, Bunney's were specialists in oriental goods and novelties, all housed within an elegant Baroque Edwardian building. Nearby stood a branch of the outfitters Hope Bros Ltd, Chaloner and Co. tea merchants and Bagnall and Son merchant tailors, to name but a few.

Below: The order for the demolition of Bunney's was given in the 1950s with a view that the building should be replaced by a worthy, modern addition fit for a post-war era along with improvements to traffic easing at this congested city centre corner. Today's view shows a further retail development dating from 2014 with large masses of glazing, stone render, copper cladding and a huge digital screen.

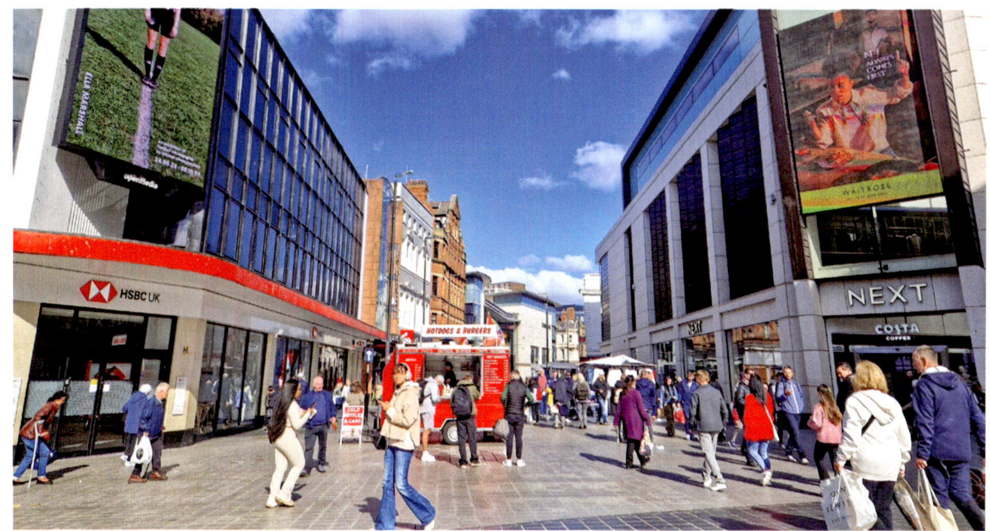

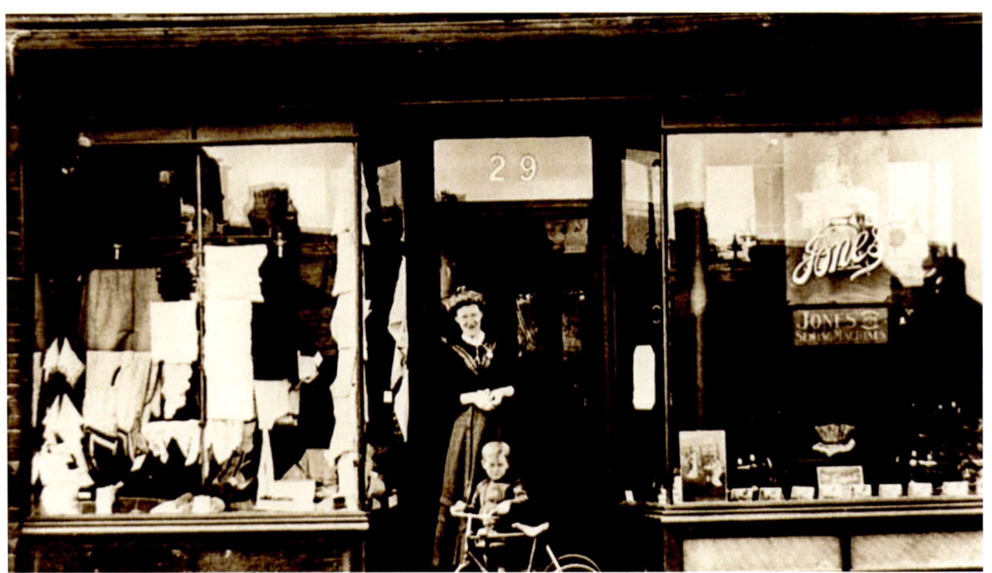

No. 29 Warbreck Moor

Above: In this maternal scene, a double-fronted shopfront faces onto Warbreck Moor with its spotless windows positioned neatly within timber frames. Inside hung various white wares upon hangers whilst advertisements for Jones Sewing Machines sat behind its counterpart. In between stood a recessed doorway with a simple numbered panel fixed overhead.

Below: The road outside has been altered with the installation of metal safety railings, and the shopfront itself looks very different too. The business is now a hairdressers with twin panes of partly obscured glass providing privacy for staff and visiting customers. Across the fascia a small and proportionate italic name sign has been set over the doorway, along with the business phone number.

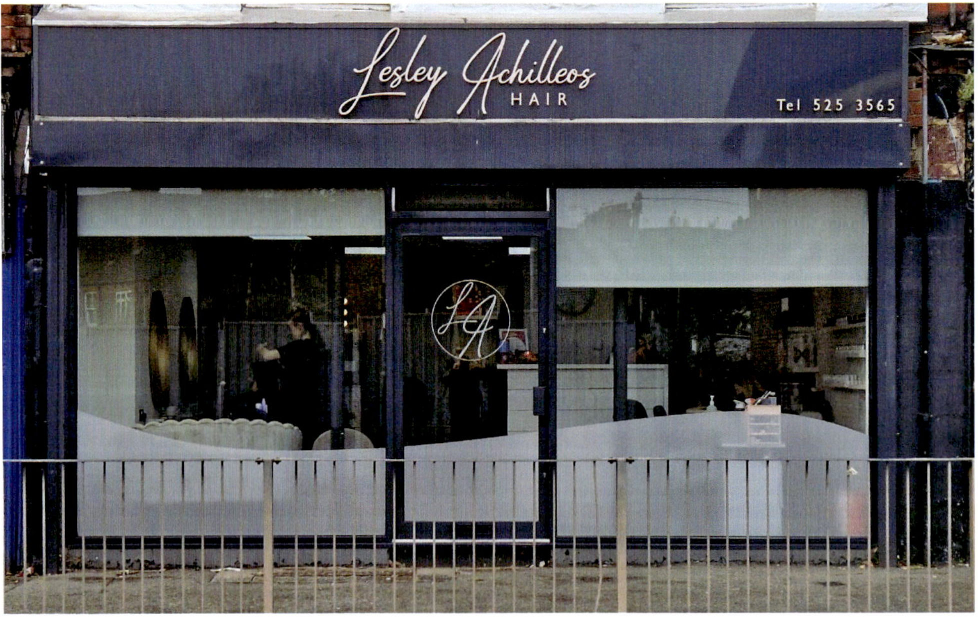

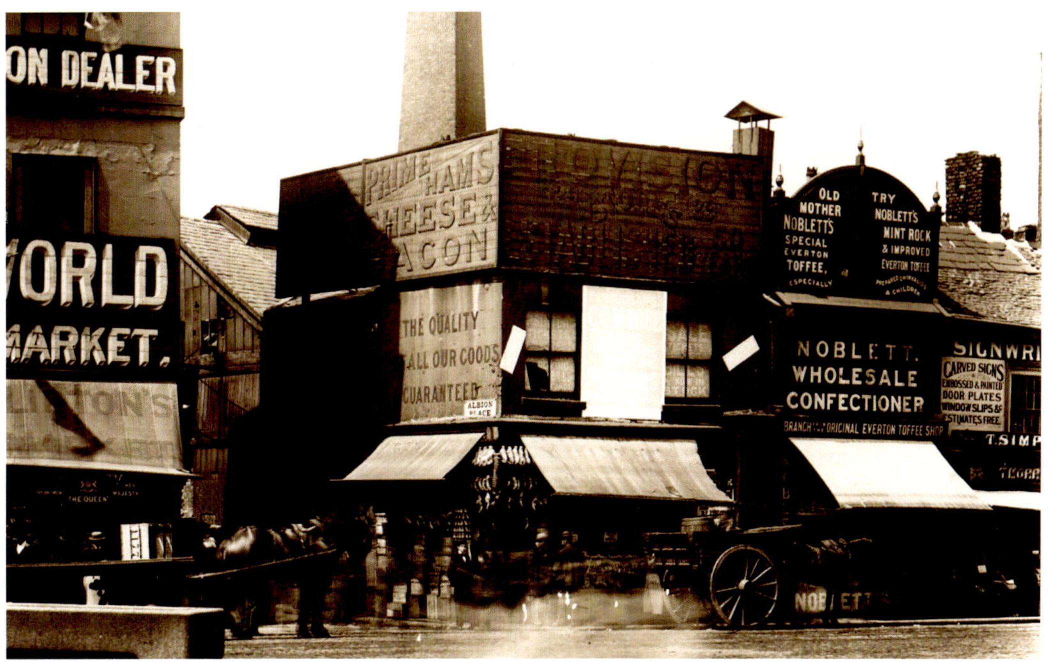

Albion Place

Above: The shops here in Albion Place were rather simple and appear to have evolved piecemeal with little architectural cohesion. Baskets were piled high outside the provisions store with more stock hung from above, alongside an almighty timber advertising board affixed to the roofline. A whimsical depiction of Old Mother Noblett adorned the signage of a neighbouring confectioner, complete with finials, whilst a signwriter and decorator plied their trade next door.

Below: Works to construct the Mersey Tunnel in 1925 prompted the razing of the old properties of Albion Place and the surrounding area to facilitate an approach road into the new engineering marvel. Nothing remains of the dense commercial cityscape that once lined the streets here.

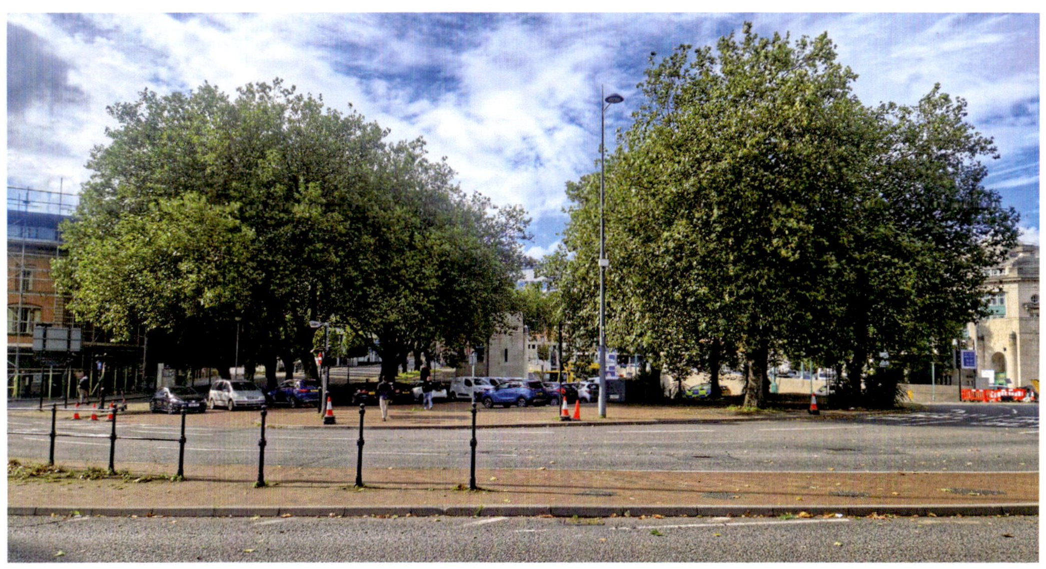

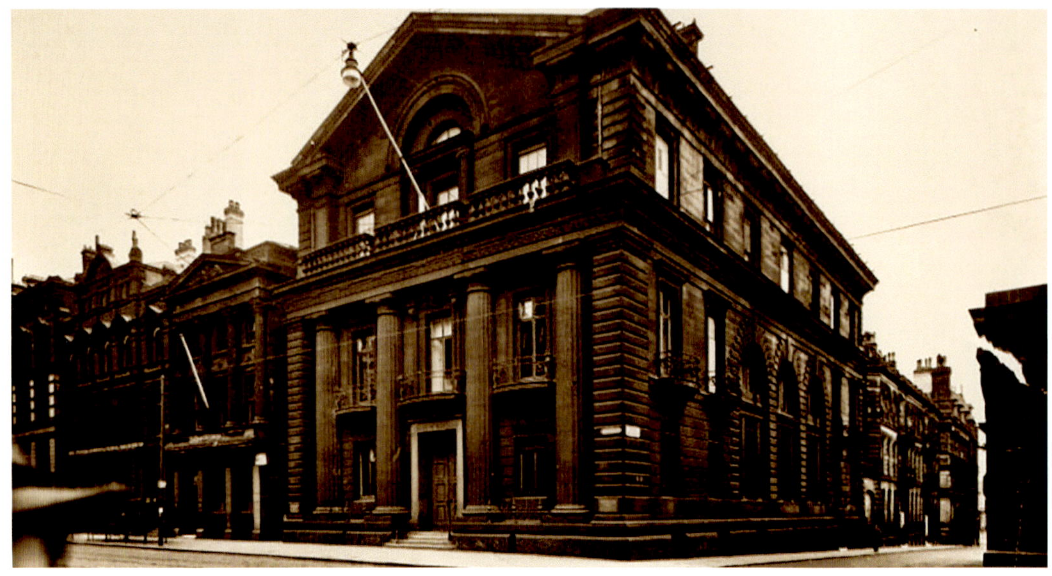

The Bank of England, Castle Street

Above: One of the most impressive buildings in Liverpool was the Bank of England which stood at the corner of Castle Street and Cook Street. This Victorian masterpiece, not unlike a Roman temple, exemplified the power and ambition of the city when built in 1845. Next door stood the Norwich Union Building alongside the Dominion, Colonial and Overseas Branch of Barclays Bank. Despite their remarkable appearance, these neighbours did not quite match the monumental splendour of the old bank.

Below: The Grade I listed building has stood empty for many years and its potential back into the banking industry is limited. However, plans have recently been completed to transform the splendid property into a restaurant offering a unique dining experience for patrons to enjoy. Many of its neighbours have already switched to the lucrative business of hospitality.

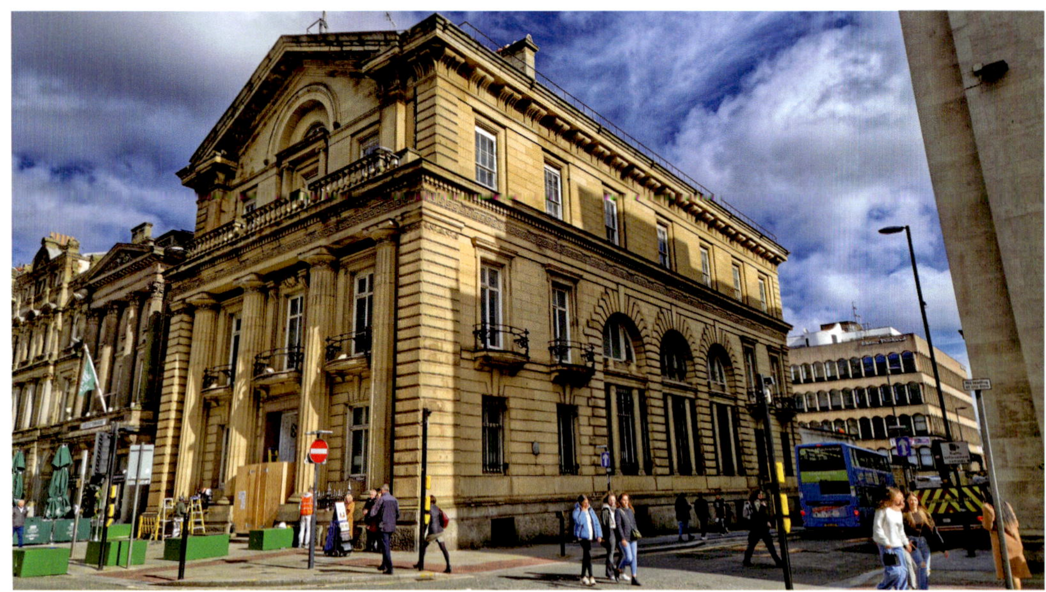

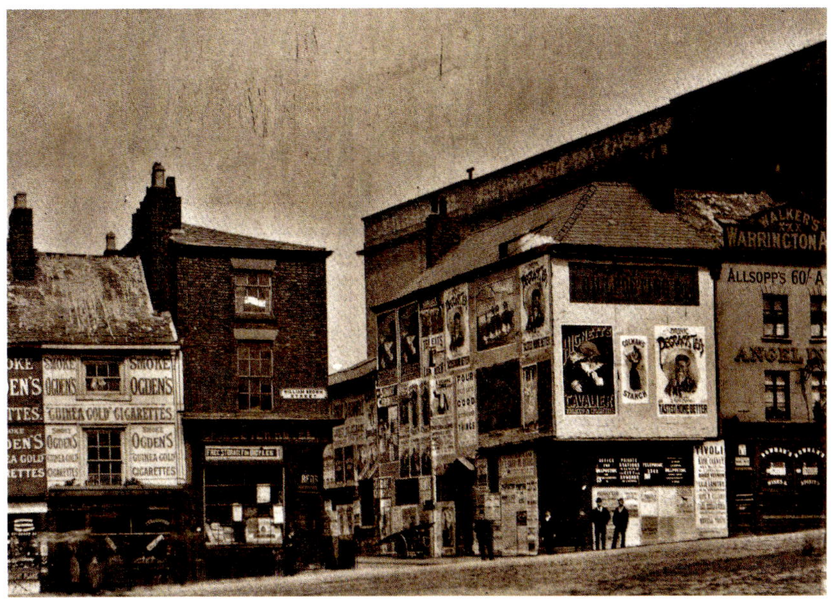

William Brown Street

Above: The historic remnants of what was Shaw's Brow stood over the cobbles as the efforts of a bill-posting company engulfed their elevations at the junction of Livesley Place. Nearby the Leicester Hotel, which offered free storage for bicycles, headed a diffident terrace of shops selling items such as cooking sauces and tobacco, with advertisements for Ogden's Cigarettes applied directly to the face of the buildings.

Below: In 1860 wealthy benefactor William Brown MP donated funds to build a new museum and library, and the street was renamed in his honour. In 1906 the museum was extended with a new building shared with the Liverpool Central Technical School. The historic shops which had withstood the first wave of gentrification could no longer resist the march of redevelopment and today the street consists of Grade II* buildings dedicated to education, arts and culture.

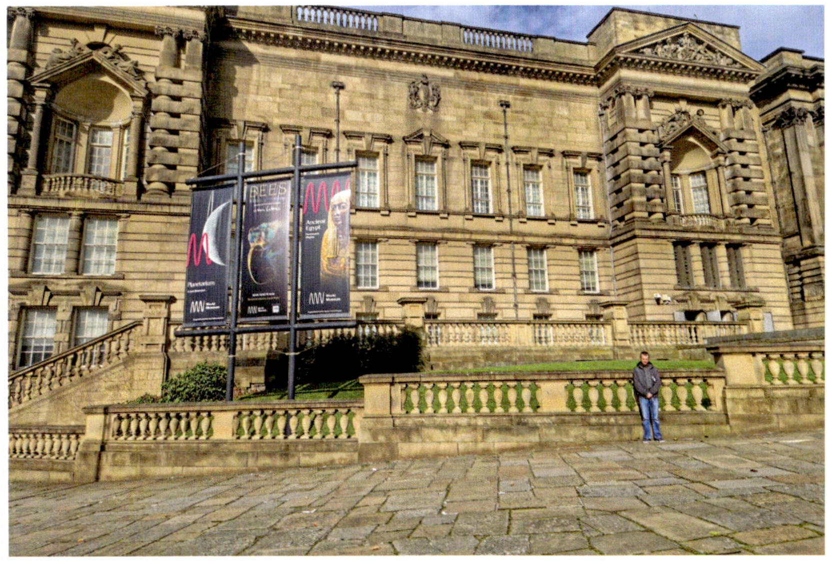

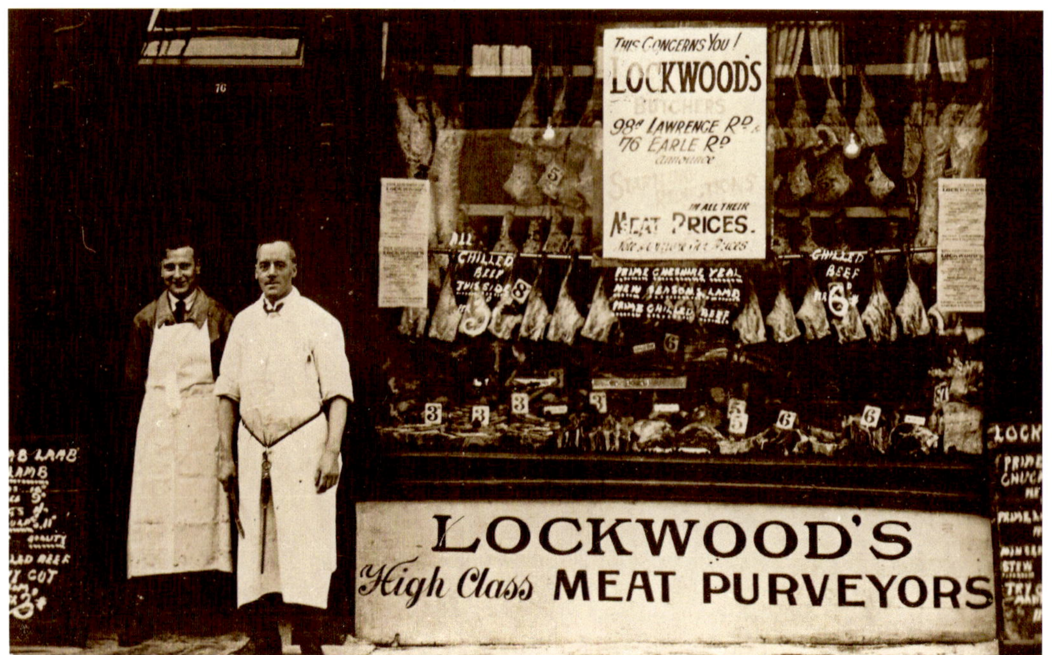

No. 76 Earle Road

Above: Lockwood's meat purveyors are seen at No. 76 Earle Road with their simple but effective shopfront. A large printed sign attracted attention to the window display which housed the firm's latest cuts. Handwritten prices were added to the glass to suit the market, whilst more permanent signage was placed upon the stallriser below. Further promotions could be found on blackboards positioned on the pavement.

Below: Many of the earlier buildings along Earle Road have been dismantled after an extensive compulsory purchase scheme was instigated in the 1980s. The scene today is far more residential with many semi-detached family homes now facing out onto the road. The construction of such dwellings has improved living conditions; however, their arrival indelibly changed the motley character of the street.

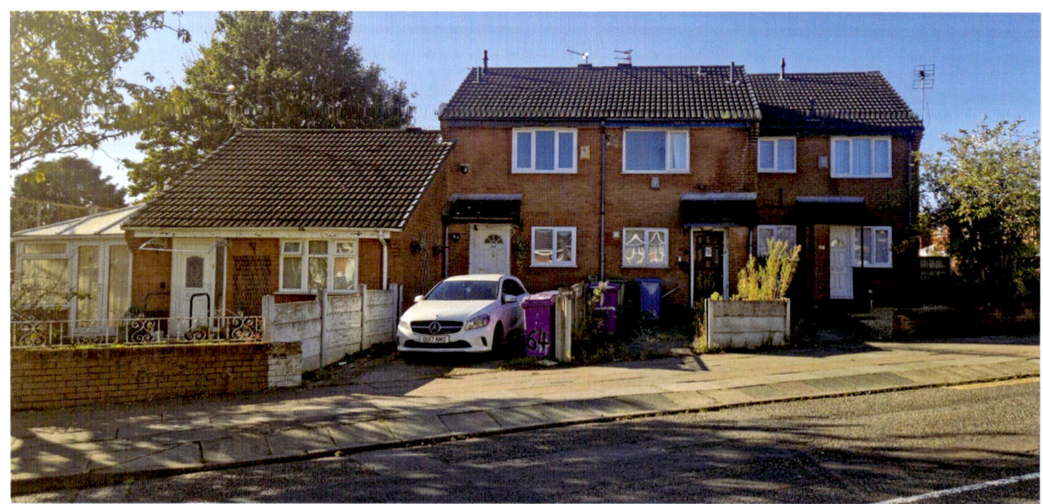

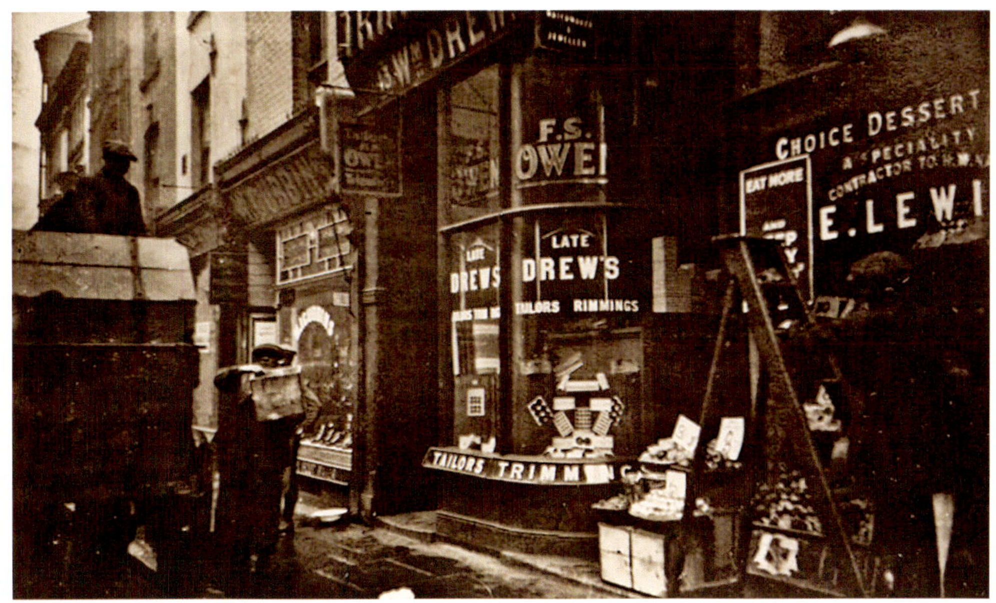

Richmond Street

Above: As men unload merchandise outside the large, curved-glass windows of F. S Owen's tailors at No. 13 Richmond Street, the scene depicts a mix of hanging signage, window graphics and even the groceries of E. Lewis advertised outside on the pavement. Alongside stood the premises of Cubbins Bootmakers with their collection of highly polished footwear seen in the window display.

Below: There has been considerable change to this part of Richmond Street with the loss of the traditional shopfronts and changes of use. The view now depicts more simplistic construction with oversized pilasters and plastic signage of a chain of betting shops which has consumed the adjacent store. Further down, a similar series of losses have continued.

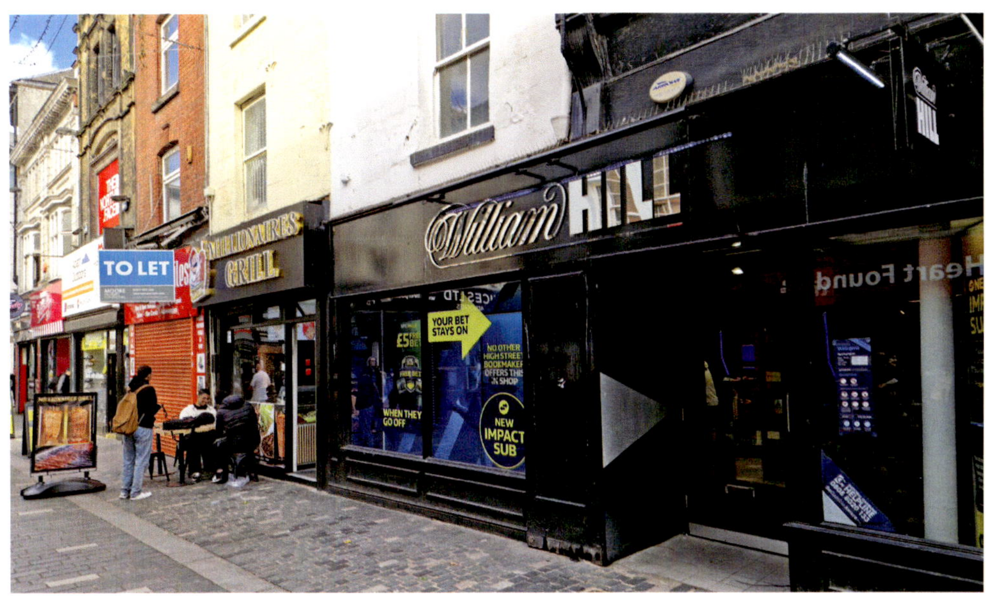

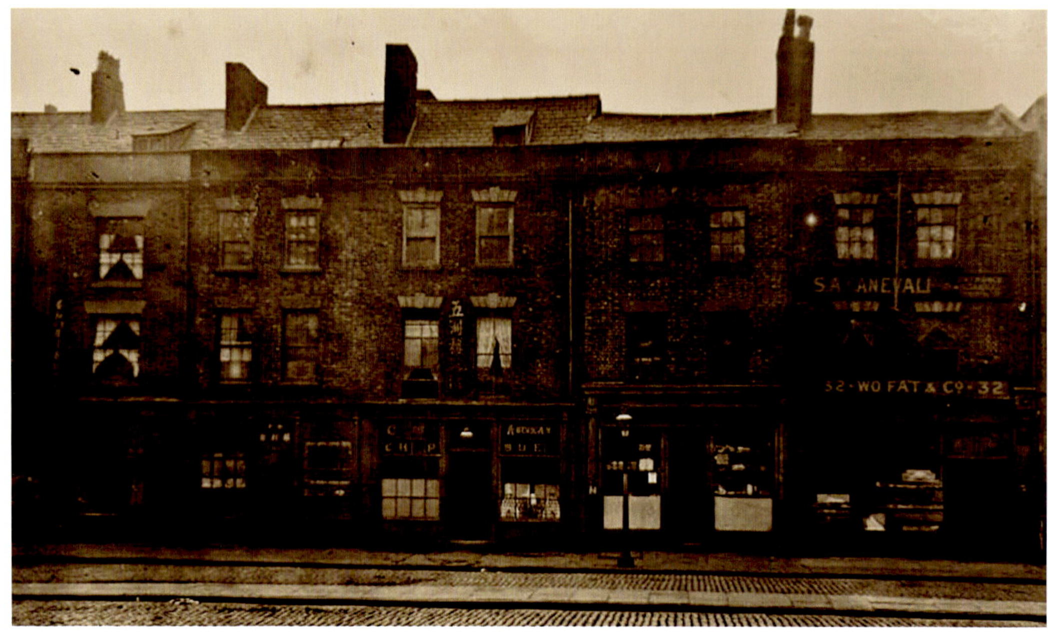

Cleveland Square

Above: A tired row of shops stood in what was the original Chinatown of the city, Cleveland Square. This photograph taken in 1919 shows Eng Chow Low's restaurant, the Lai Kee lodging house, the premises of shopkeeper Way Hin Kwong and the tobacconist Wo Fat. Despite their slightly dejected appearance the old brick buildings still possessed the fundamental and appealing architectural features of their prime.

Below: Cleveland Square was one of the many locations across Merseyside to feel the might of the German Luftwaffe and it was largely destroyed during the Second World War. The square today is now home to a mix of low-density housing and small businesses, with no clues as to the heartbreak and carnage that occurred here all those years ago.

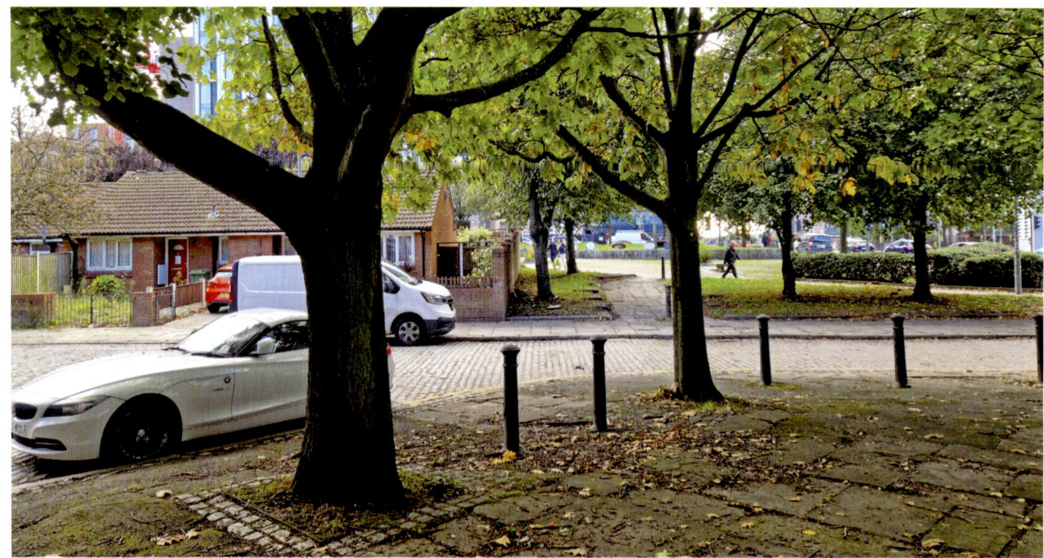

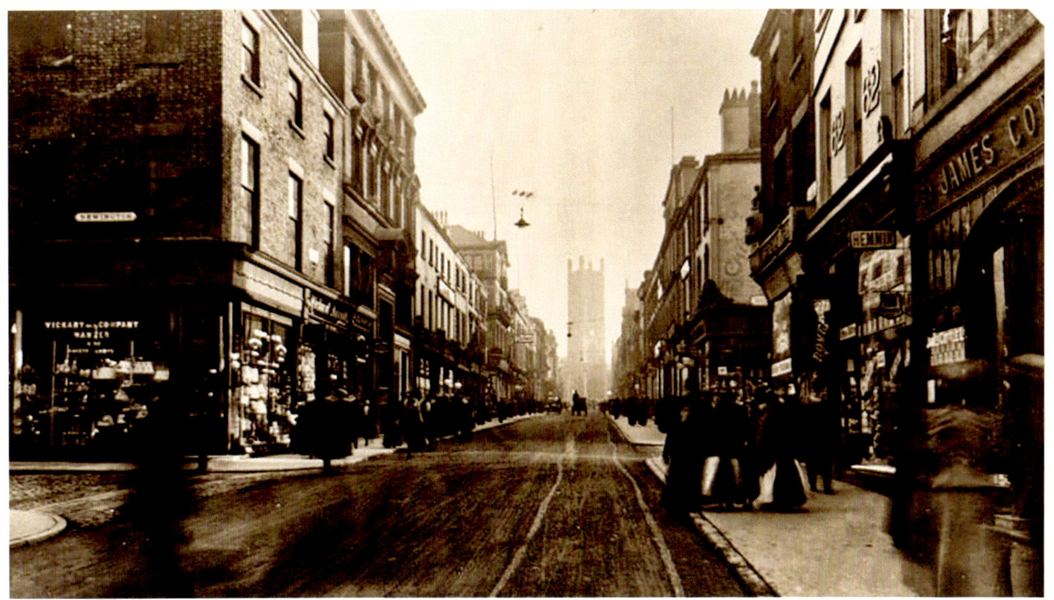

Bold Street

Above: Taken from the middle of Bold Street with Newington nearby, a mirage of blurred suits and dresses meandered through Liverpool's key shopping route in 1910. The arched entrance of confectioner James Cottle could be seen to the right, alongside James Hemming's stationers and Sutton's mantle warehouse. Across the street stood the corner premises of A. J. Vickary and Co. lamp manufacturers, whose various shades filled the shop windows.

Below: Much of Bold Street's remaining architectural interest can be found on the upper elevations with the majority of its older shopfronts removed in the name of progress. The corner premises have been adapted into a branch of the sandwich chain Subway, with a new frame, glazing and large signage. Similar interventions can be found across the pedestrianised street with the insertion of more contemporary shopfronts.

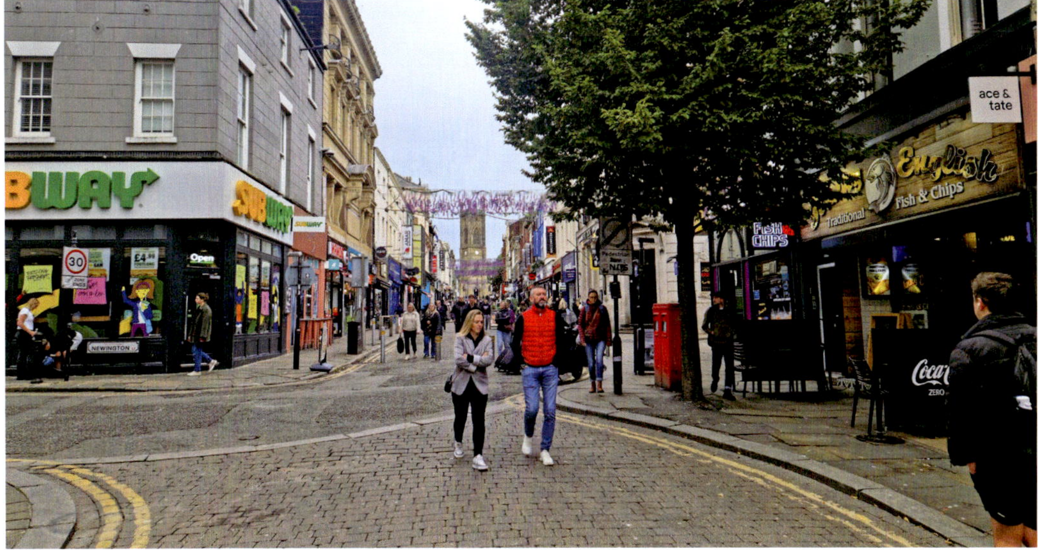

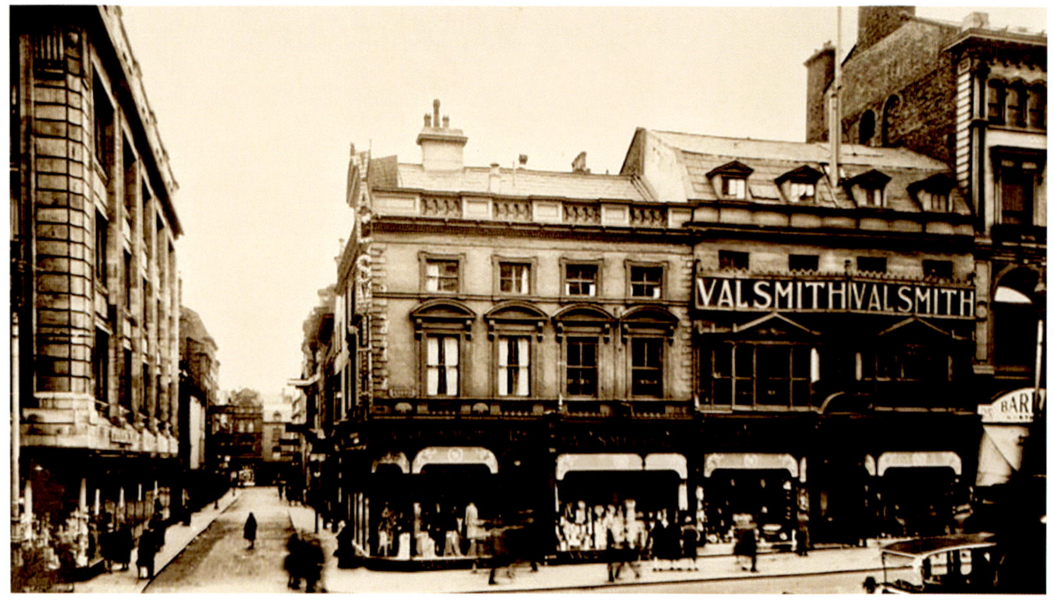

Church Street

Above: The unmistakable premises of Madame Val Smith millinery, drapers and haberdashery once stood at the junction of Church Street and Williamson Street. The company was established in the 1880s and this 1920s view shows the building with a very exuberant exterior, with an array of smart window displays packed with the latest styles and fashions of the time.

Below: This Church Street corner appears very different thanks to famed architect Herbert Rowse who designed this building in 1931. Finished in a Romanesque Revival style, the building was originally a bank with no shopfront at all, but a series of beautiful stone arches set across the ground floor. Alas, the move to retail saw the permanent removal of these exquisite features.

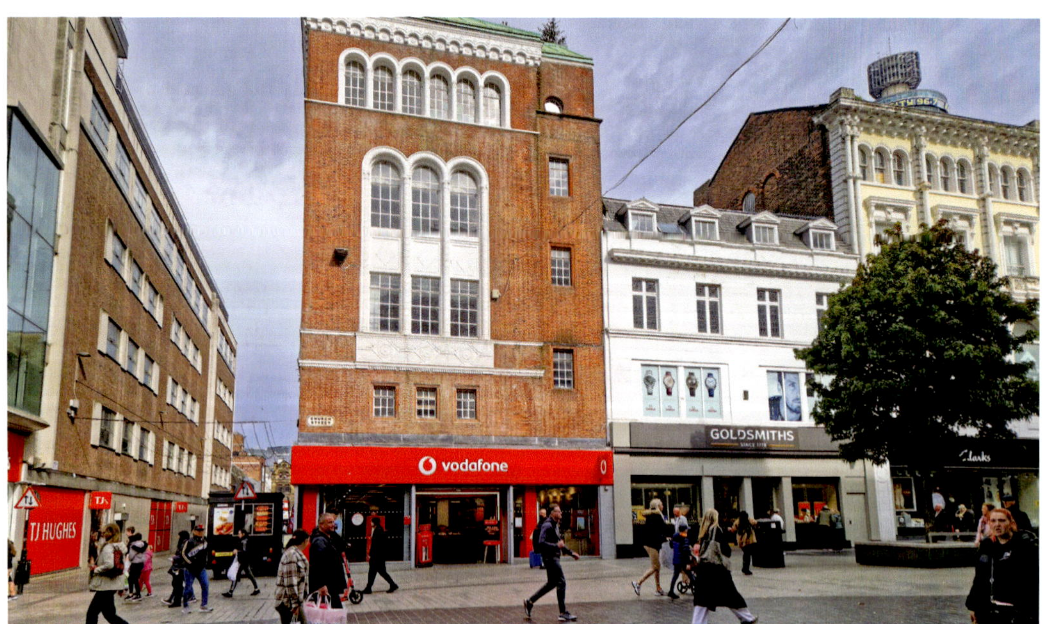

No. 1 Castle Street

Right above: No. 1 Castle Street was the premises of Mansfield & Son's boot and shoe purveyor whose large plate-glass displays could be seen between Tuscan granite pilasters. Its large awnings advertised the brand accompanied by a sophisticated font across the fascia. A dentilled cornice added detail along with a classical motif around a recessed corner doorway.

Right below: A restaurant now occupies the ground floor of No. 1 and the 1970s building next door. Both structures are listed at Grade II for their respective significance; however, there have been some alterations over time, such as the creation of a new entrance and the insertion of new windows. The pavement has also been considerably widened which allows for alfresco dining in the shadow of the Town Hall.

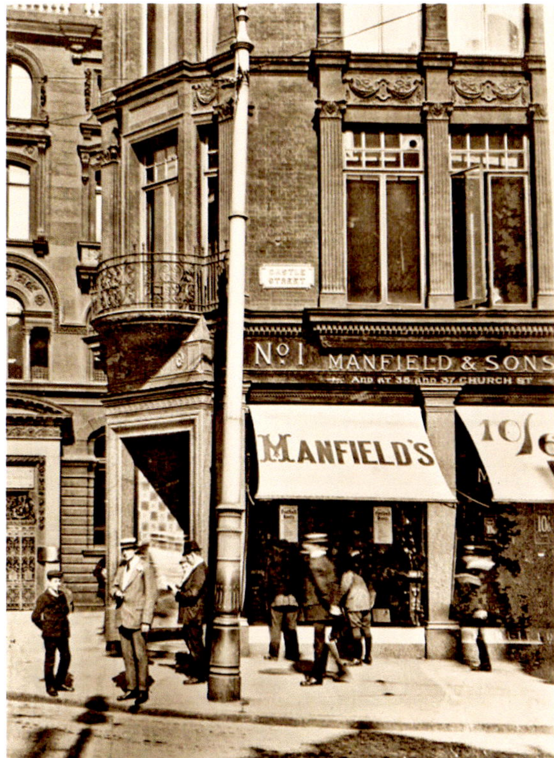

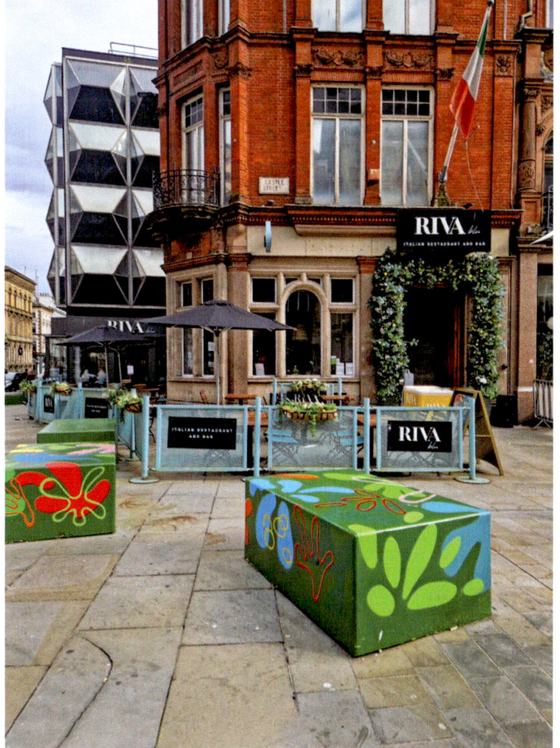

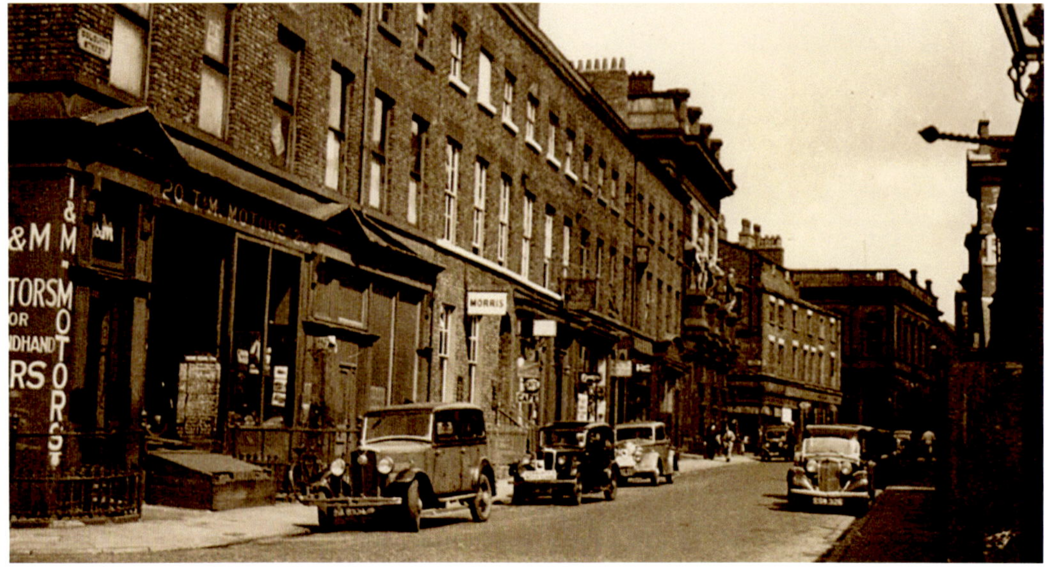

Colquitt Street

Above: This corner premises in Colquitt Street featured a distinctly classical influence with its pair of huge doorway pediments at the second-hand car shop of T. M. Motors. Nearby along this Georgian terrace could be found the heating engineers William Morris & Bros, whilst at the junction of Wood Street towered a series of imposing figures watching down from the Egyptian Museum.

Below: The former vehicle vendor has become a bar, and structural alterations have seen the addition of bi-folding doors and a small balcony decorated with some dramatic signage. A convenience store with its own conspicuous signage stands next door; however, many of the older buildings, including the museum, have been replaced by apartments whose seven storeys rise over the street.

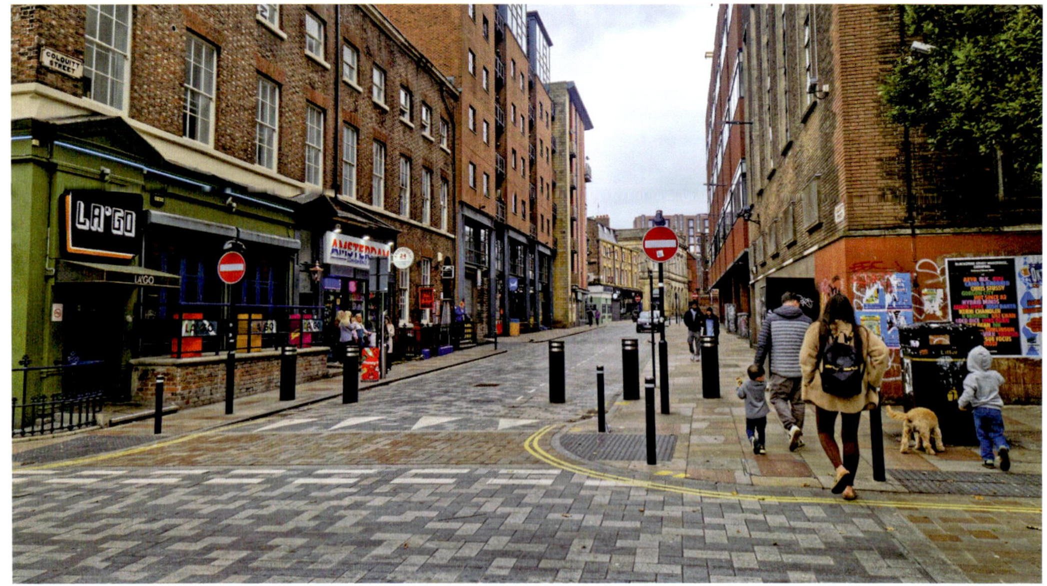

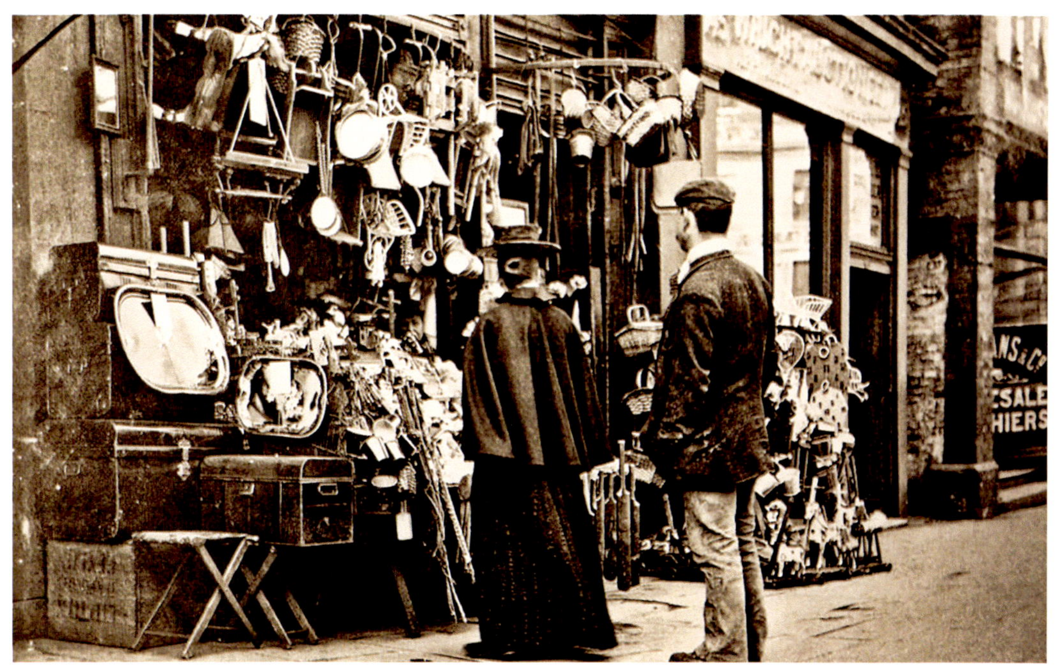

Dale Street

Above: This humble but well-stocked unit in Dale Street, not too far from the historic Chorley Court, represented the livelihood of John Parry. It appears that a large proportion of his wares obscured his shopfront, with various toys and bric-a-brac stacked high on display. Next door the auction house of Mr Wright appeared somewhat less cluttered with a simple but orderly style.

Below: The site is now occupied by No. 151 Dale Street which was constructed for the Blackburn Assurance Company and completed in 1937. Chorley Court, the birthplace of American founding father Robert Morris, was razed to the ground along with the other antiquated properties in the vicinity to allow for the creation of this Art Deco endeavour by architect William P. Horsburgh, clad in Portland stone with classical decoration.

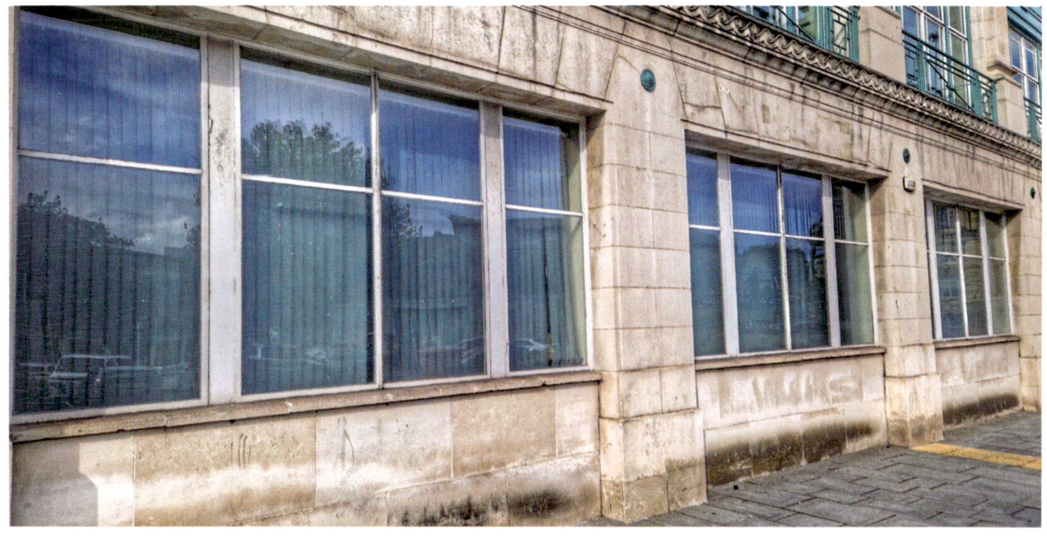

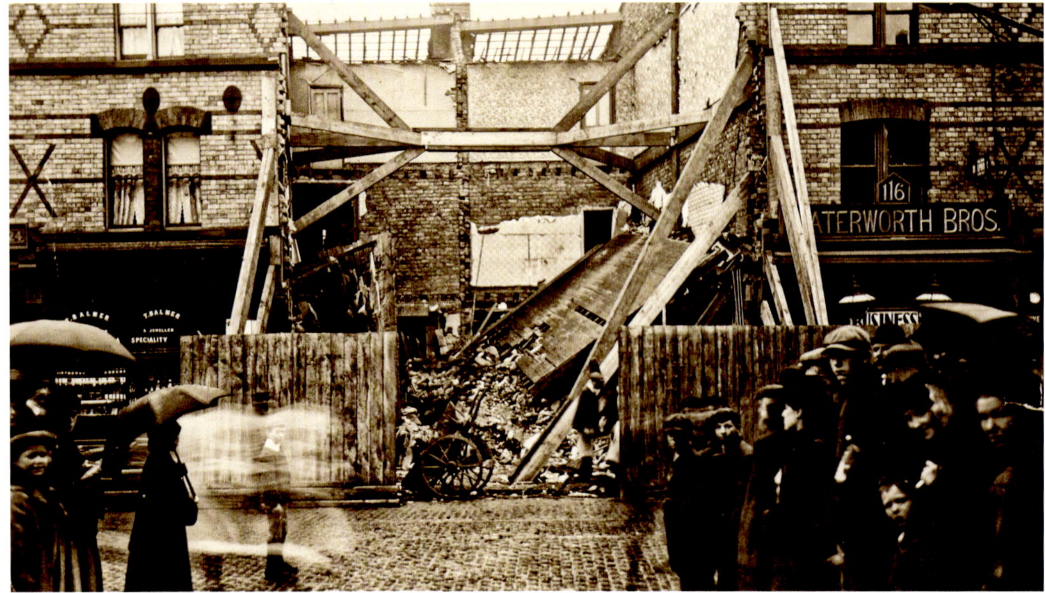

Lodge Lane

Above: Disaster befell these Lodge Lane shops in the summer of 1907 when Davies and Pritchard's haberdashery and millinery business collapsed out onto the street. Luckily the early morning event caused no casualties, but the building and all elements of its shopfront and stock were unceremoniously destroyed. The neighbouring grocery store of Mr Waterworth and that of Mr Balmer's watchmakers and jewellers were left at serious risk.

Below: This part of the street was cleared of debris and appears to have been left largely undeveloped. In more recent times the land has been used as an event space known as Tiber Square after receiving a public grant to transform the area for the local population. The investment has seen the introduction of new paving, planting and seating areas to help create a dedicated place for community events and celebrations.

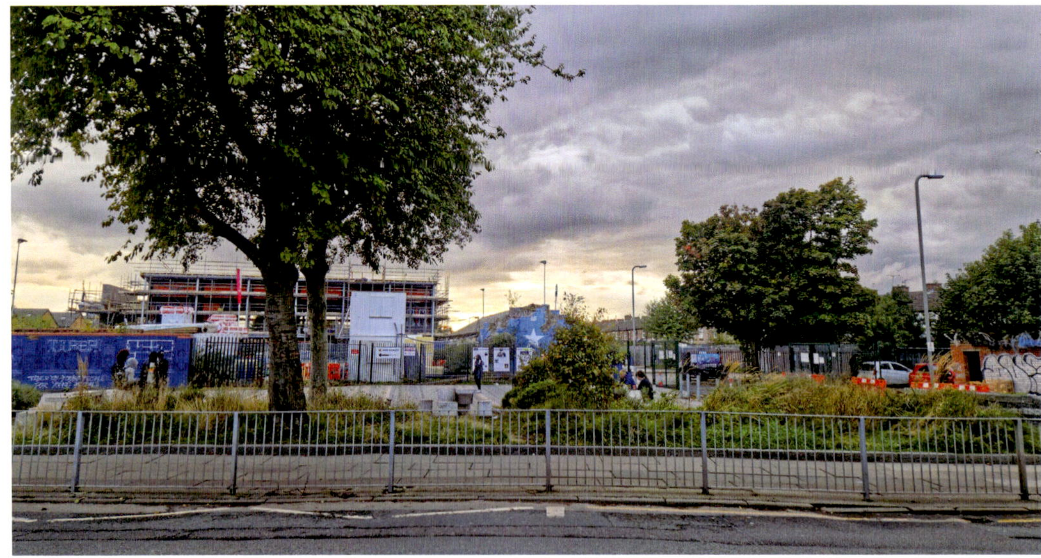

Highfield Street

Right above: This corner of the city dates from the mid-eighteenth century with Highfield Street once leading to the market of Pownall Square. By the early twentieth century, the route was awash with businesses such as public houses, greengrocers, cocoa rooms, provision merchants and various other trades and professions. As a result, shopfronts here had somewhat eclectic designs reflecting the diversity of the neighbourhood.

Right below: Little is left of the history of Highfield Street with various buildings destroyed in the Blitz or demolished through later development. A rare survivor is a former pub on the corner of the square last known as The Wedding House, however, its use as a hostelry has long disappeared. New apartment buildings have since appeared around the square with suggestions that the space itself may become a pocket park.

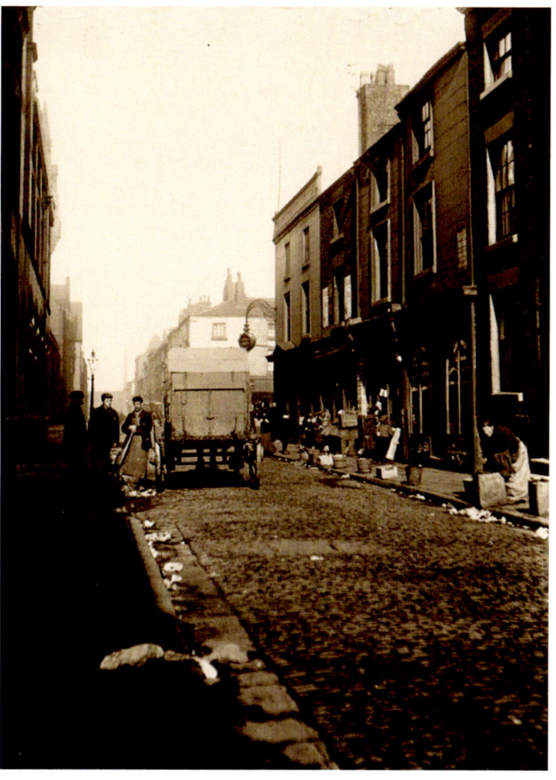

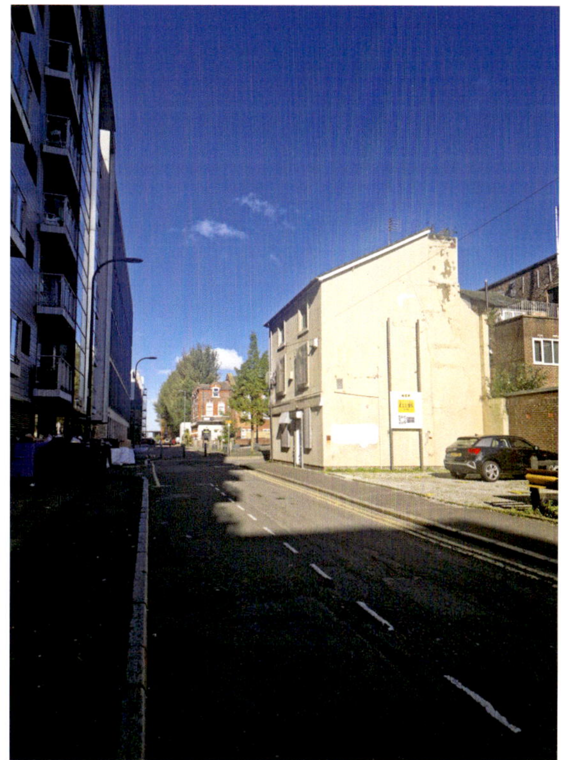

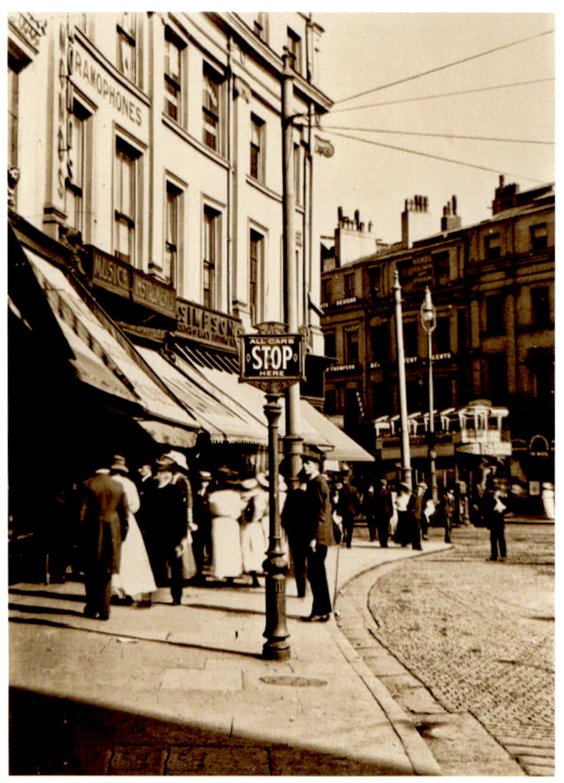

St George's Crescent

Left above: A close-up look at St George's Crescent reveals a multitude of shoppers peering beneath the awnings of shops including Archer & Sons musical instrument makers and Simpson & Harvey hatters & umbrella merchants. From this Castle Street perspective, the sequence of timber sash windows across the upper floors and the examples of carefully crafted bespoke signage can be appreciated.

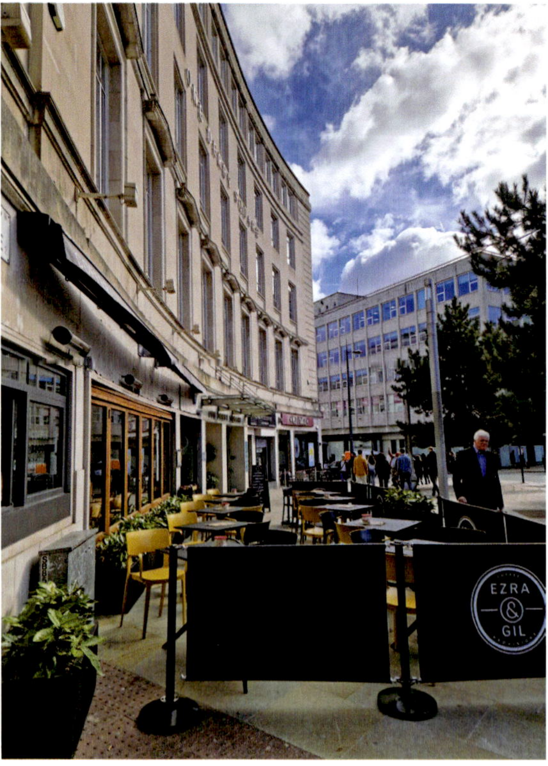

Left below: It is evident that the design for this replacement building, One Derby Square, took inspiration from its predecessor, with a gentle curve guiding pedestrians through this part of the city centre. Retail uses have been replaced by restaurants and coffee shops, with an increase in paving and the planting of trees to bring a touch of nature to this built-up urban environment.

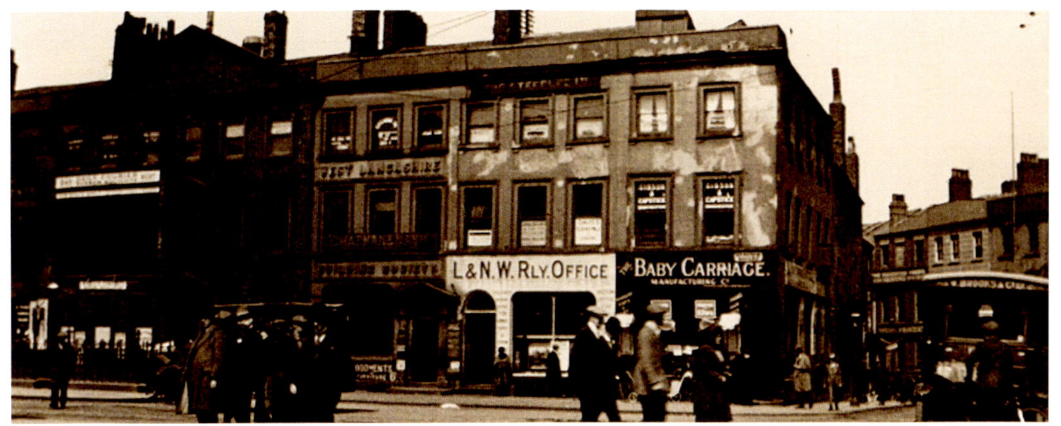

Clayton Square and Houghton Street

Above: A 1920s view of Clayton Square at the corner of Houghton Street with its substantial Georgian terrace. The shopfronts were moderately simple and consistent, with the London and North Western Railway Parcel Office, the West Lancashire Building Society and the Baby Carriage Manufacturing Company occupying the principal ground-floor units. A novel illuminated stage by 'Adlights' was commissioned by the *Daily Courier* to promote their newspaper and advertisements to shoppers below; however, this undoubtedly harmed the appearance of the otherwise magnificent building.

Below: The building we see today dates from 1924 and was designed by Walter Aubrey Thomas not as a department store, but as a hotel that never was. Plans were altered and the premises were taken on by Owen Owen who relocated from London Road. The high-end clothing store Flannels now trades from here and has reinstated a number of lost architectural details such as stone surrounds and marble stallrisers, as well as carrying out a series of essential repairs.

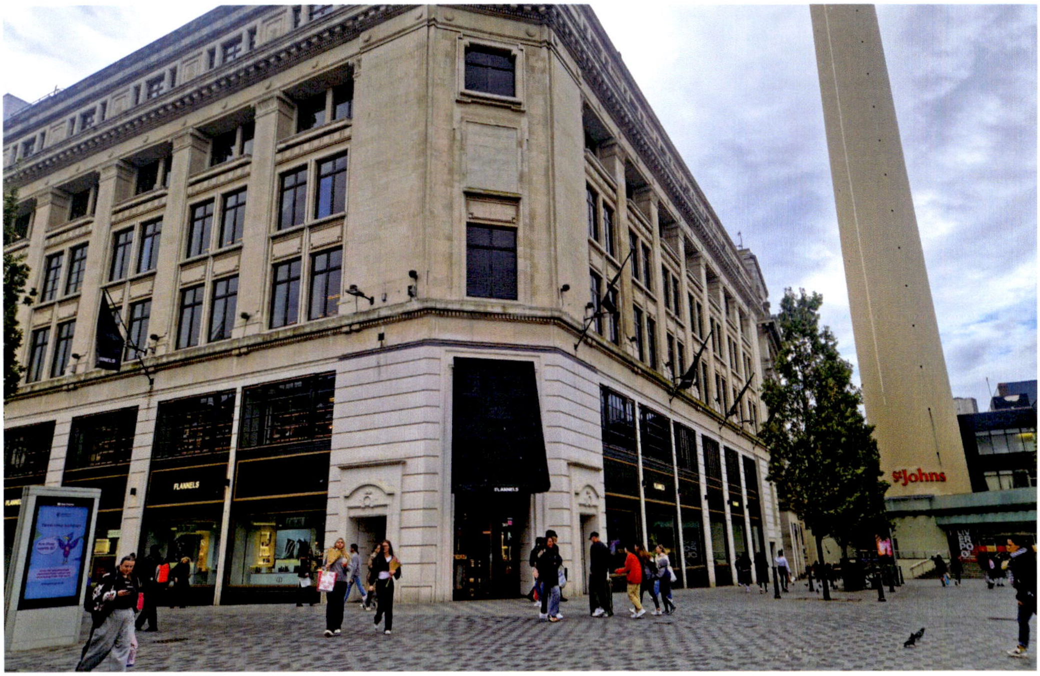

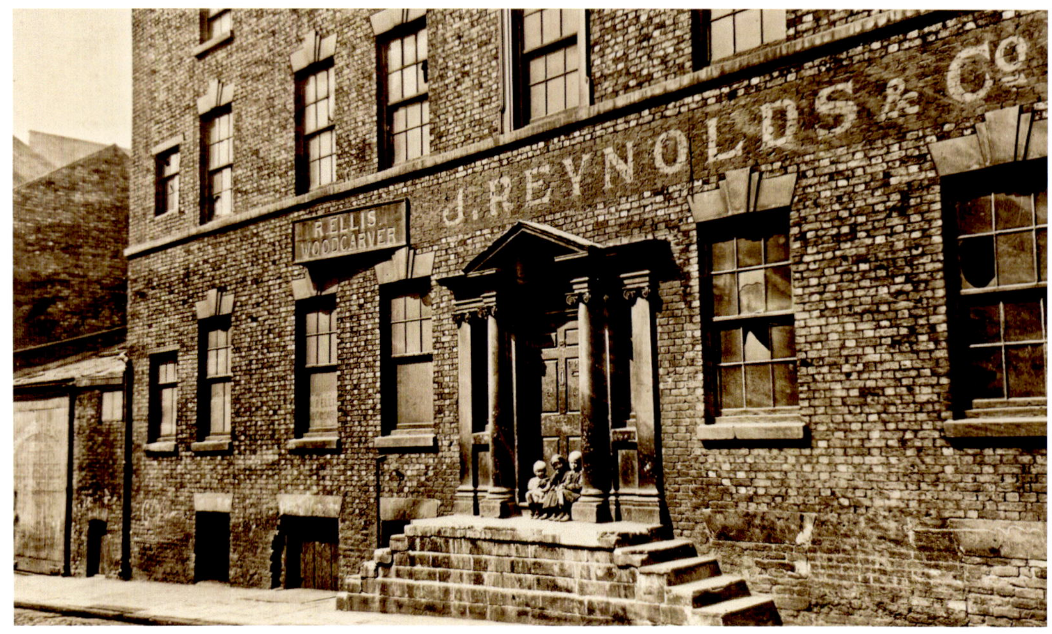

No. 2 York Street

Above: An early twentieth-century photograph of York Street and the premises of J. Reynolds and Co. basket manufacturers and R. Ellis woodcarver, whose advertisements could be seen across the main elevation. Originally built in the late eighteenth century, the building was once a merchant's dwelling with associated warehousing, later adapted for commercial use but retaining its domestic Georgian aesthetic.

Below: The Grade II listed premises is now home to several small businesses including a cosmetics company and a tattooist. The exterior of the building features an arrangement of signage relating to these professionals and there has been some alteration to the building fenestration. Safety railings have also been added to the precarious stone stairs up to the entrance.

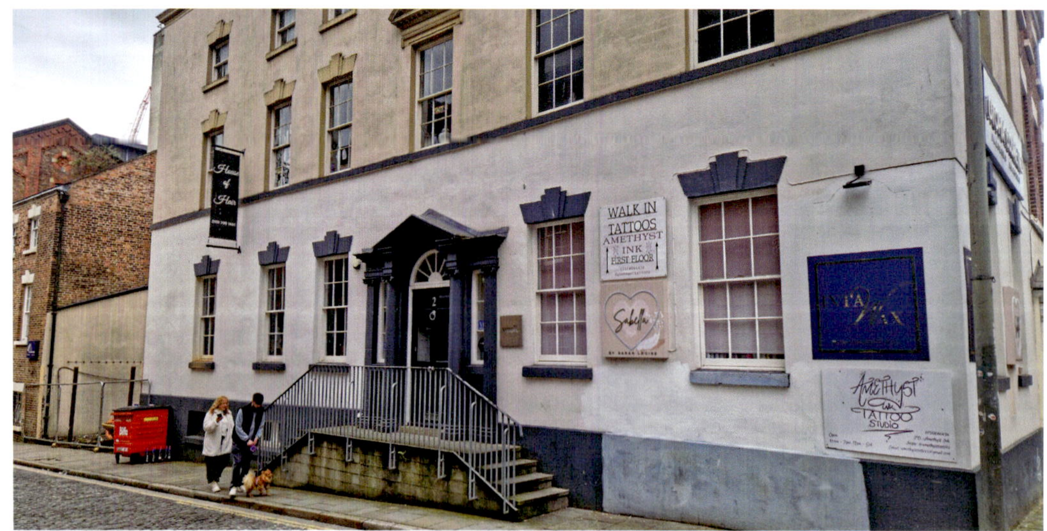

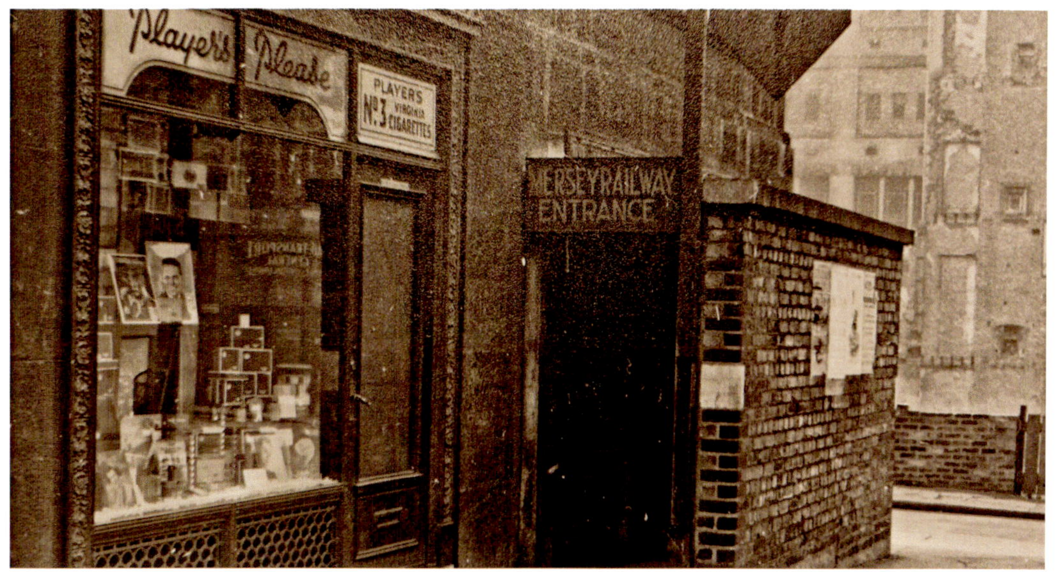

James Street Station, Water Street

Above: Directions for the air raid shelter project over the Water Street entrance to James Street Station in the mid-war image from 1944. The adjacent shop incorporated into India Buildings has fortunately survived the surrounding carnage and boasted a decorative pierced stallriser and an integral fascia, with ornamental mouldings to the surround. A simple timber door gave access to the shop under a trio of segmented windows.

Below: The shopfront remains one of the more inspired versions to be found across the city and is one of four such installations to be observed across this elevation. Unfortunately, the Grade II* India Buildings suffered substantial damage during the Second World War but was later repaired under the guidance and supervision of its original architect Herbert Rowse.

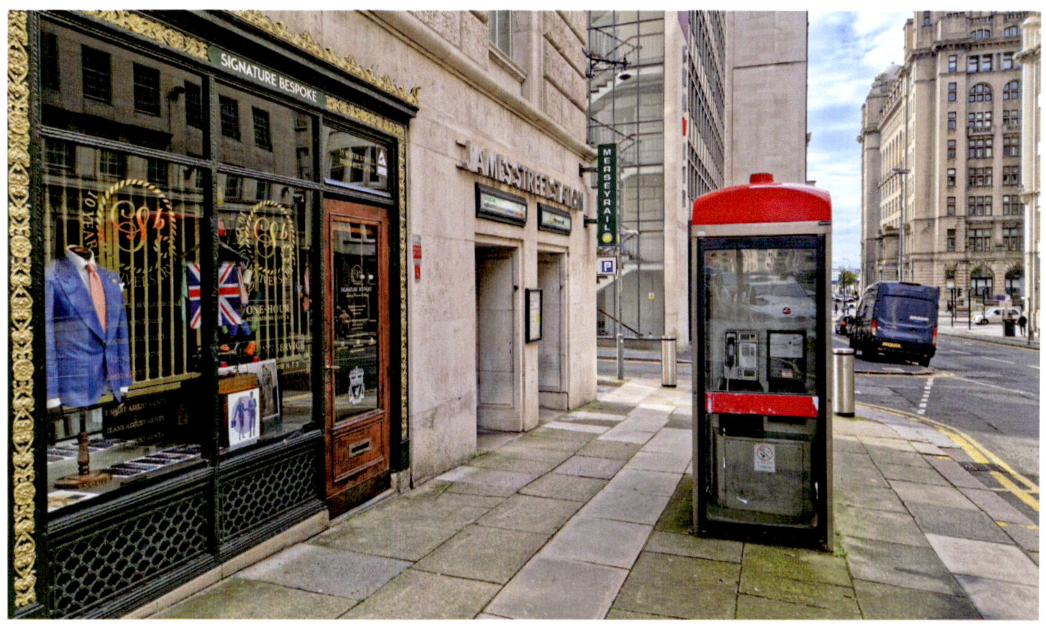

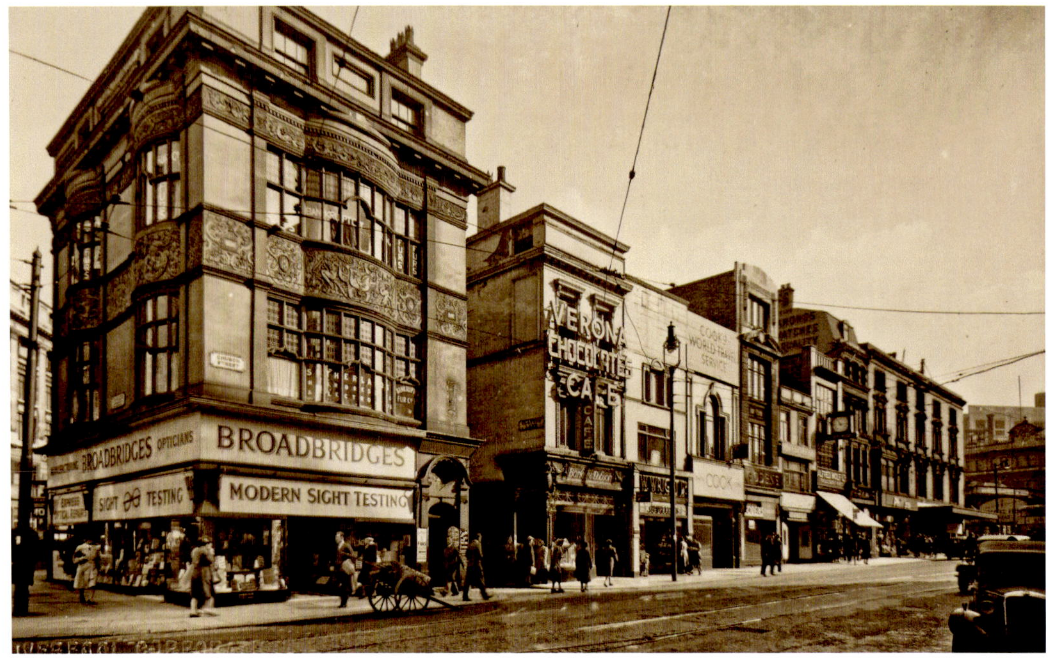

Church Street and Parker Street

Above: Enormous signs advertised the services of Broadbridges opticians at the corner of Parker Street and Church Street and somewhat detracted from the lavish exterior of the late nineteenth-century decoration above. At ground level, more modern twentieth-century windows drew in customers as further along the road a diverse assortment of shopfronts and architecture added interest to the street scene.

Below: Now pedestrianised with added street trees, the key visual interest in these properties can be found across the upper floors, although the removal of such extreme mid-twentieth-century signage is arguably an improvement. As one of Liverpool's principal shopping avenues, the shopfronts of Church Street will undoubtedly continue to be adapted and upgraded as fashion dictates.

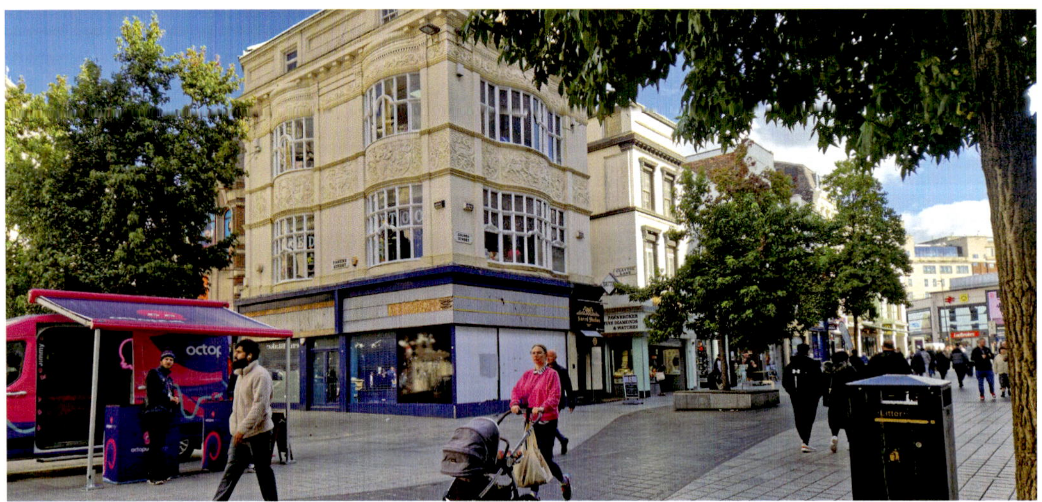

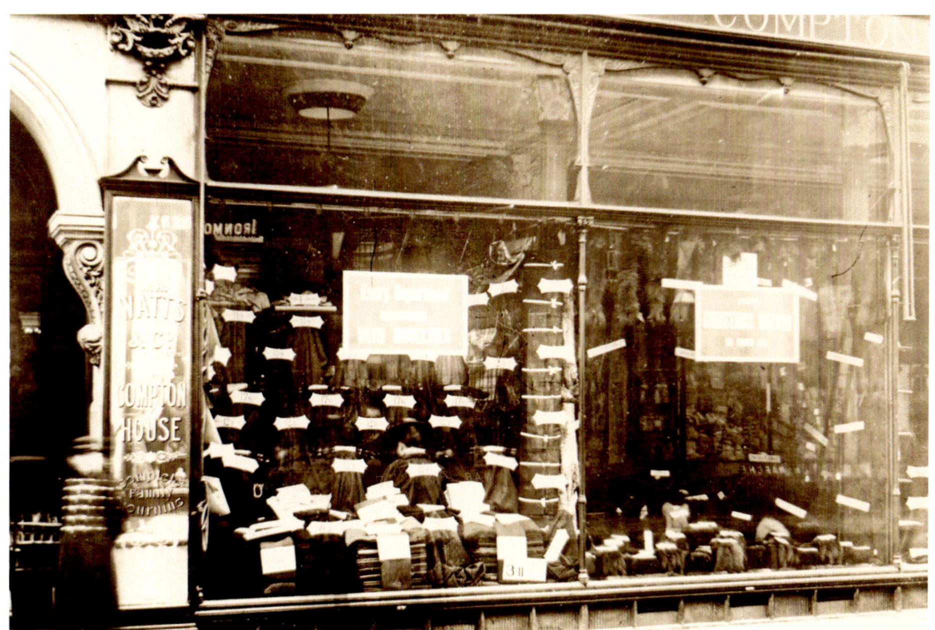

Compton House, Church Street

Above: Compton House began life in 1867 as a department store, but financial difficulties saw the building subdivided into a hotel and its retail department allocated below. This image depicts Watts & Co. who sold all manner of goods from this high-class address, with decorative window exhibits, tasteful mirrored signage, carved scroll brackets and even a uniformed doorman.

Below: Compton House stands as one of the city's most recognisable buildings and was home to Marks and Spencer for almost a century. In 2023 the company vacated the Grade II listed building for a new site in Liverpool One, bringing an end to this historic tenure. At the time of this more recent photograph the building was being prepared for use by a national sports retailer.

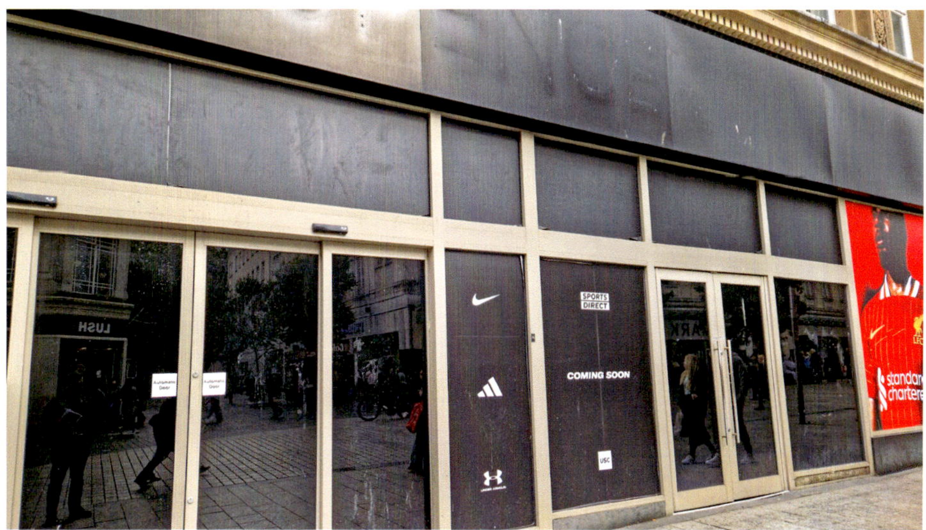

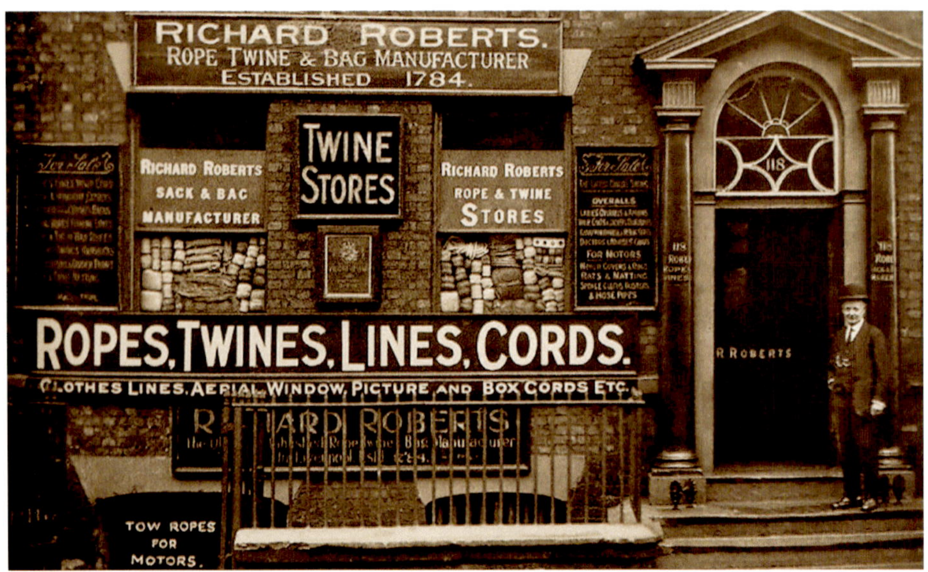

No. 118 Duke Street

Above: The shop at No. 118 Duke Street could not be missed with its arrangement of signs across the main elevation. This was the business of Richard Roberts who manufactured rope and twine, continuing a line of work first established in 1784. The remarkable doorway is seen complete with a pair of Tuscan columns and an intricate glazed fanlight topped by a stone pediment.

Below: A sorry sight with pseudo windows, metal netting and worthless graffiti on what is now a vacant building, having been so for thirty years. The Grade II listed property is noted as the birthplace of the leading eighteenth-century poet Felicia Hemans, but its condition has certainly deteriorated since those early days. It is hoped a new and appropriate use can be found for this former dwelling which respects its historic and cultural significance and aesthetic appeal.

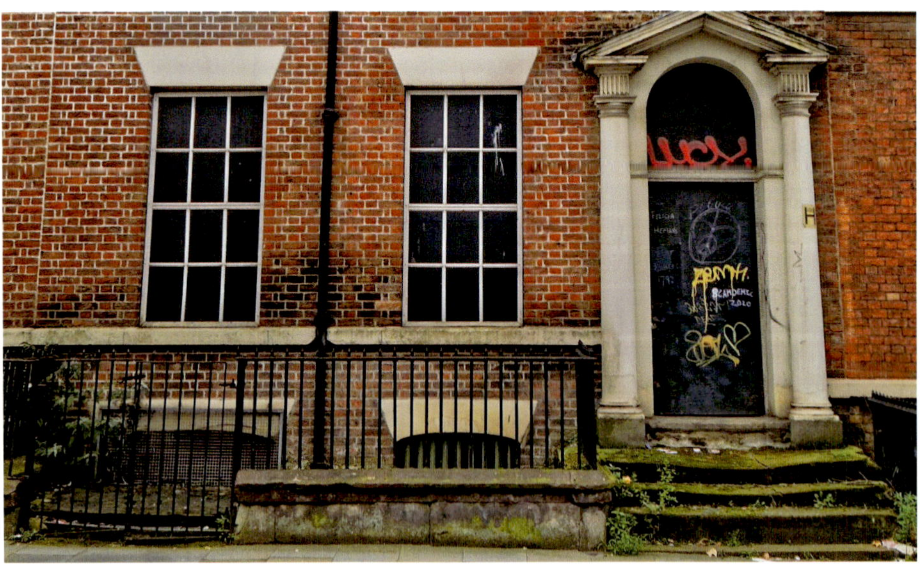

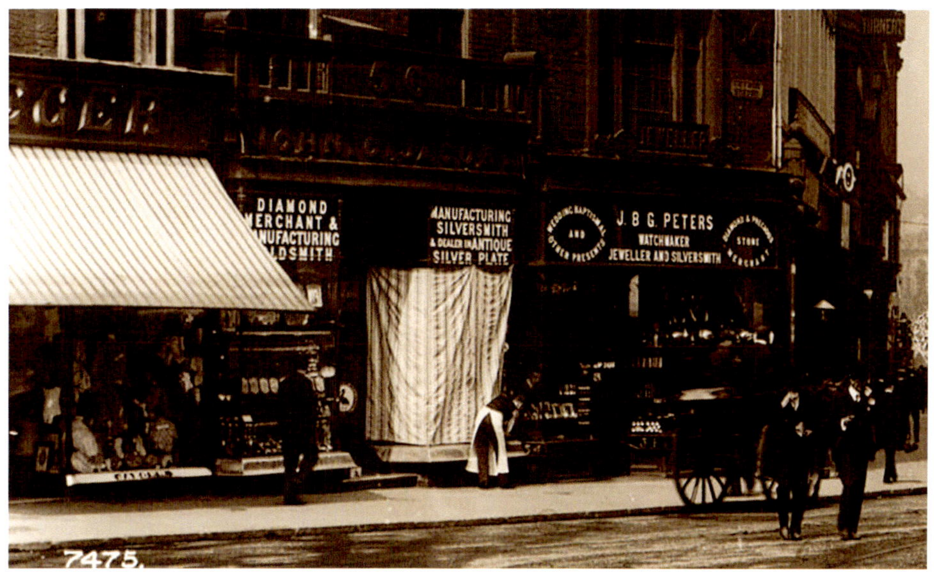

Church Street and Hanover Street

Above: An interesting mix of shopfronts once graced the corner of Church Street and Hanover Street, as seen in this early twentieth-century image. A large fabric awning overshadowed the plate glass of No. 54, which neighboured the store of John Jacob. His name could be seen embossed above the recessed entrance doorway and beneath a simple balcony. Decorative consoles supported the signage of the adjacent jewellers which also featured a very elaborate first-storey window.

Below: The eight-storey Premier Buildings arose at this spot in 1914 to the designs of Gerald de Courcy Fraser. This giant flat-iron-style block was home to Boots the Chemists and the area became known as Boots Corner shortly after opening. A branch of Lloyds Bank now operates from the ground floor with wrap-around glazing across both Church Street and Hanover Street.

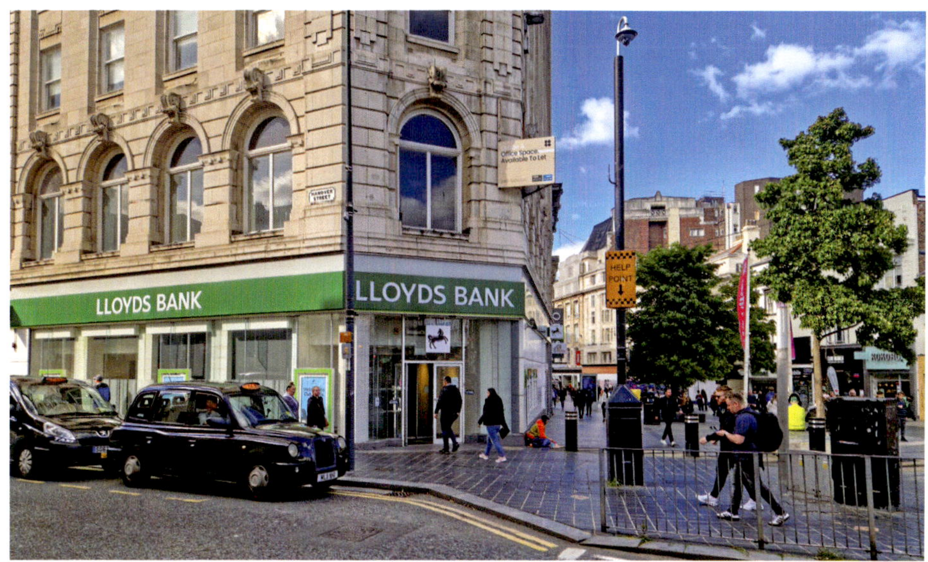

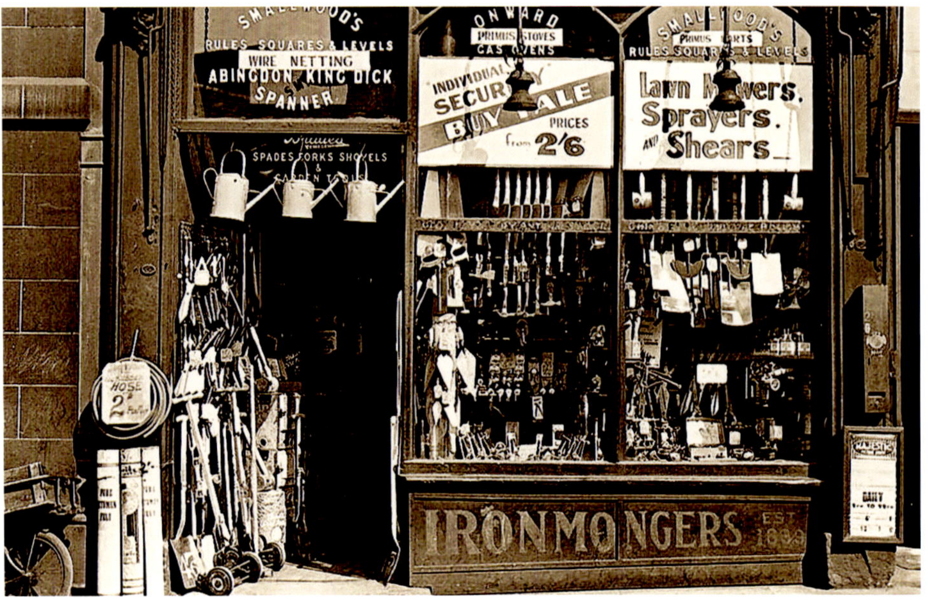

No. 5 Prescot Street

Above: This small but well-stocked shop at No. 5 Prescot Street was home to Smallwood's ironmongers. No space had been spared at this premises with various tools and equipment positioned in almost every available position. The shop featured a faded advertisement for its stallriser whilst more modern additions could be seen across the fascia, between a pair of subtlety decorative pilasters.

Below: The attraction to this shopfront has been somewhat diminished with the use of uninspiring materials such as a plain brick stallriser and lacklustre singular glazing, with none of the decorative details which had previously existed here. The shop is now in use as a restaurant with multiple paper adverts and menus stuck onto the inner window and door.

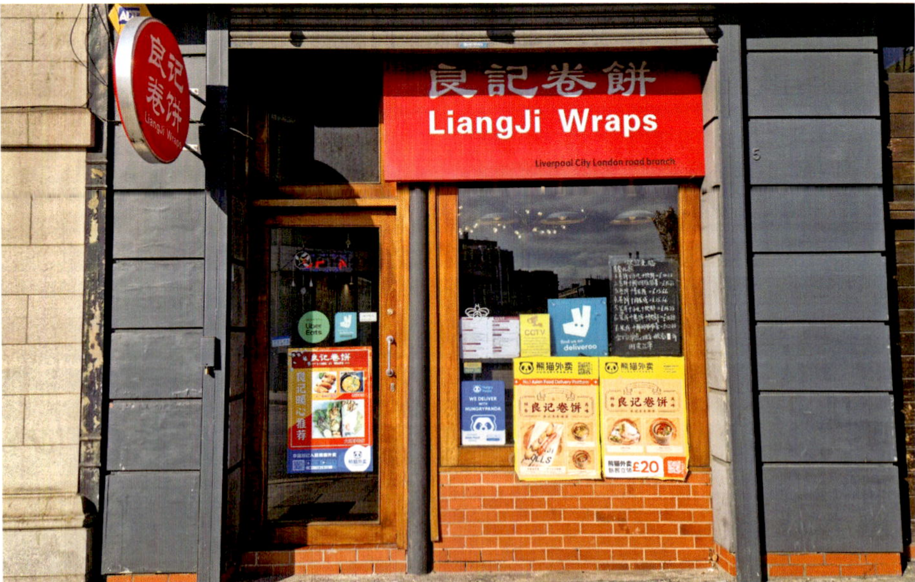

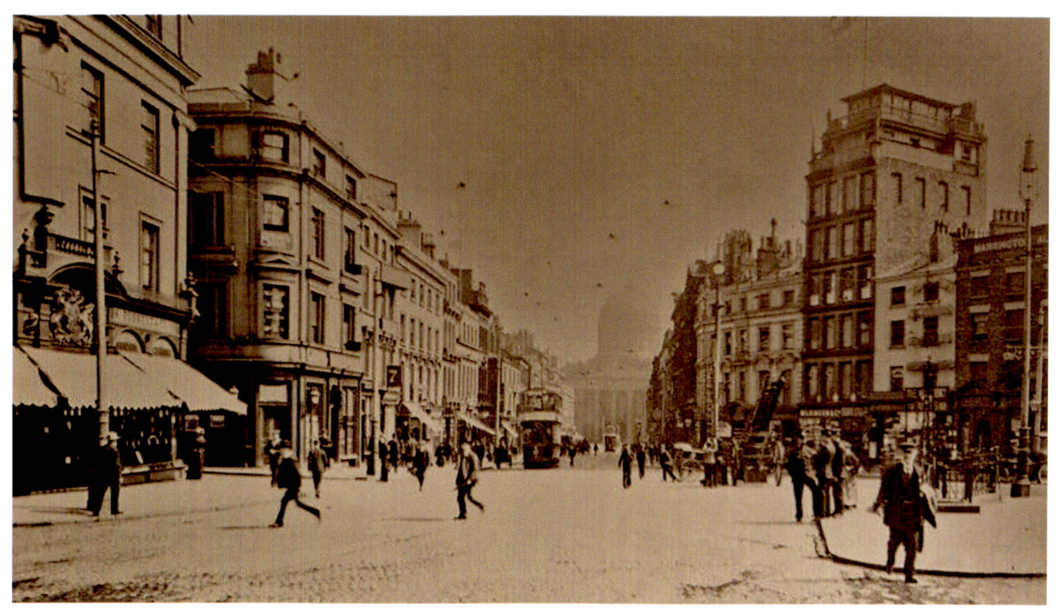

South Castle Street

Above: South Castle Street is shown with the awe-inspiring Custom House seen on the horizon. The Corinthian Buildings with their princely coat of arms, urns and finials housed a gentleman's outfitters, whilst the shopfront nearby with its large illuminating lanterns was home to a tailor. Similar high-end shopfronts adorned the landscape, each meticulously designed and constructed in this architecturally eclectic part of the city.

Below: The street and those in the surrounding area were heavily bombed during the Second World War, leaving much of the area as a sea of rubble and wiping South Castle Street off the map. Twentieth-century office structures such as Merchants Court and Graeme House now border Derby Square, with the Queen Elizabeth II Law Courts now standing in the distance.

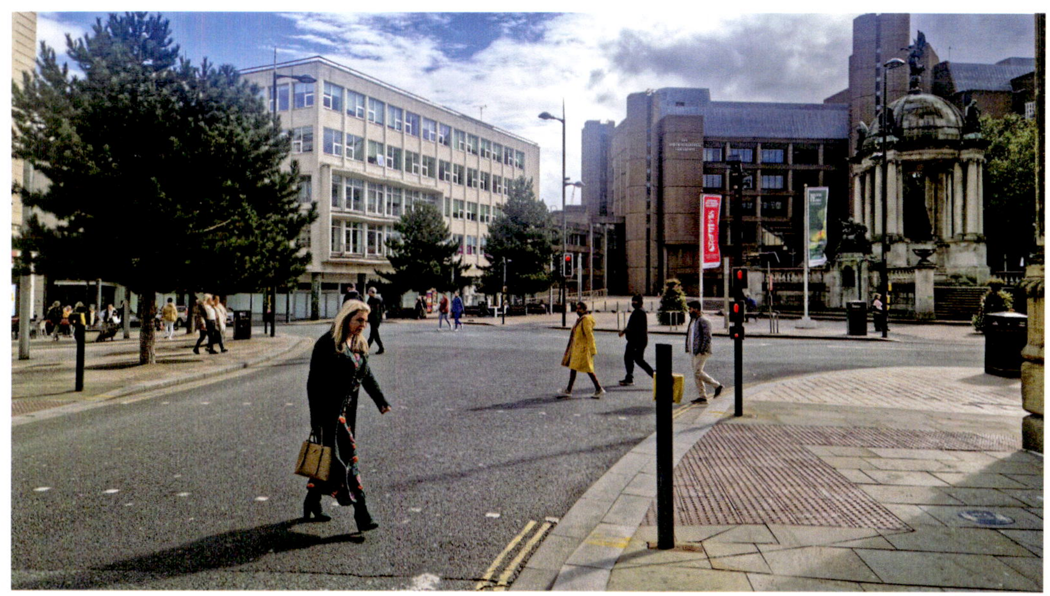

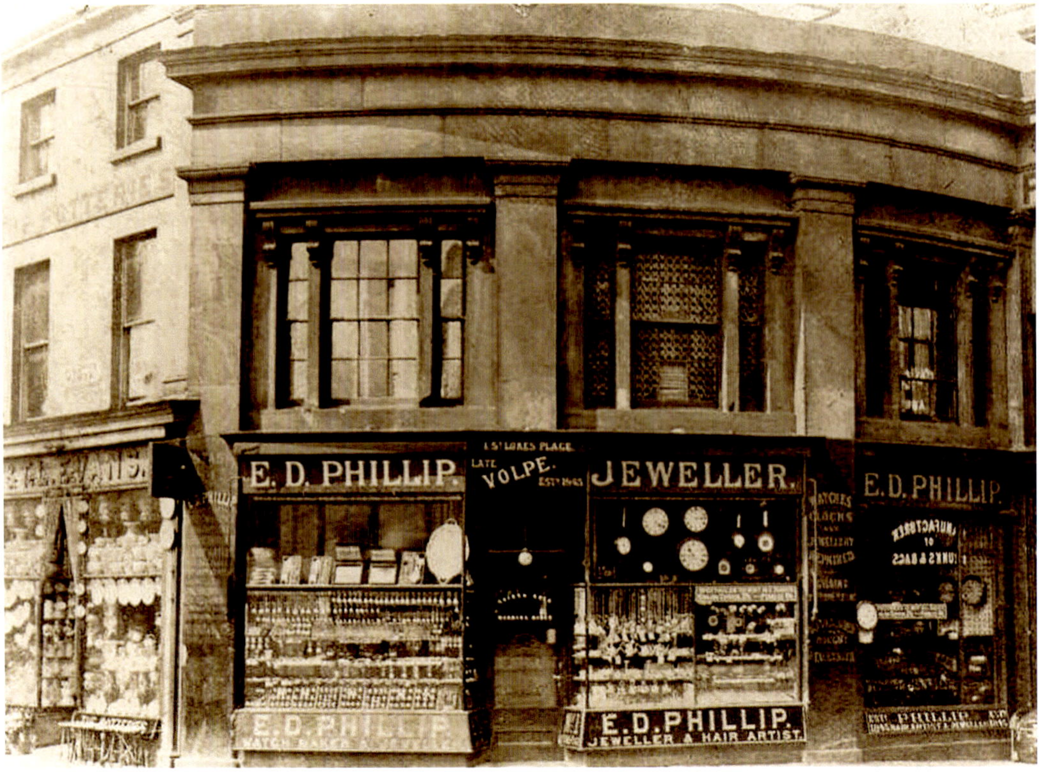

St Luke's Place

Above: A classic Victorian-style shopfront graced the business of Edmund Dixon Phillip, a watchmaker and jeweller whose mix of stock filled window displays here at St Luke's Place. He had taken over the premises from Raffaele Volpe, a hairworker and jeweller. The curved building's robust stone facade had also been utilised for advertisements across a shopfront which sat firmly beneath a trinity of windows and substantial classical columns.

Left: The present building dates from around the turn of the last century and was built to accommodate a range of different retailers stretching almost the entire length of the street. However, this particular unit has become part of a pizza parlour which has undergone extensive installations of glazing with very little in the way of outward decoration or finesse.

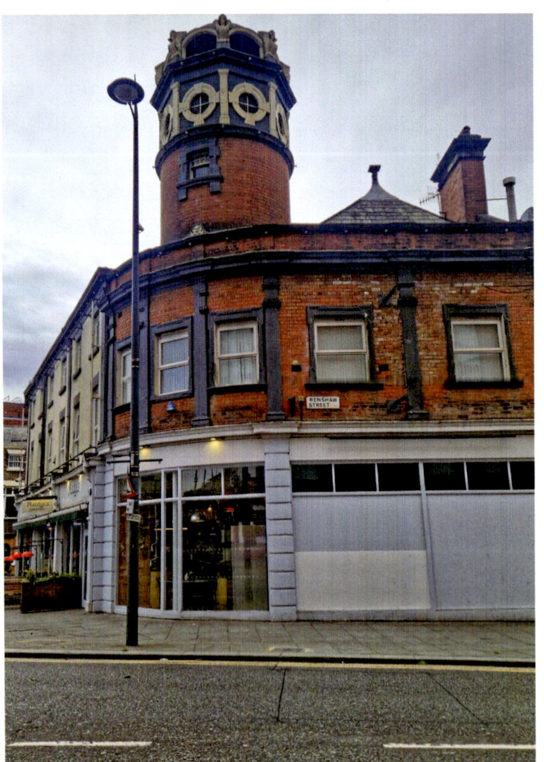

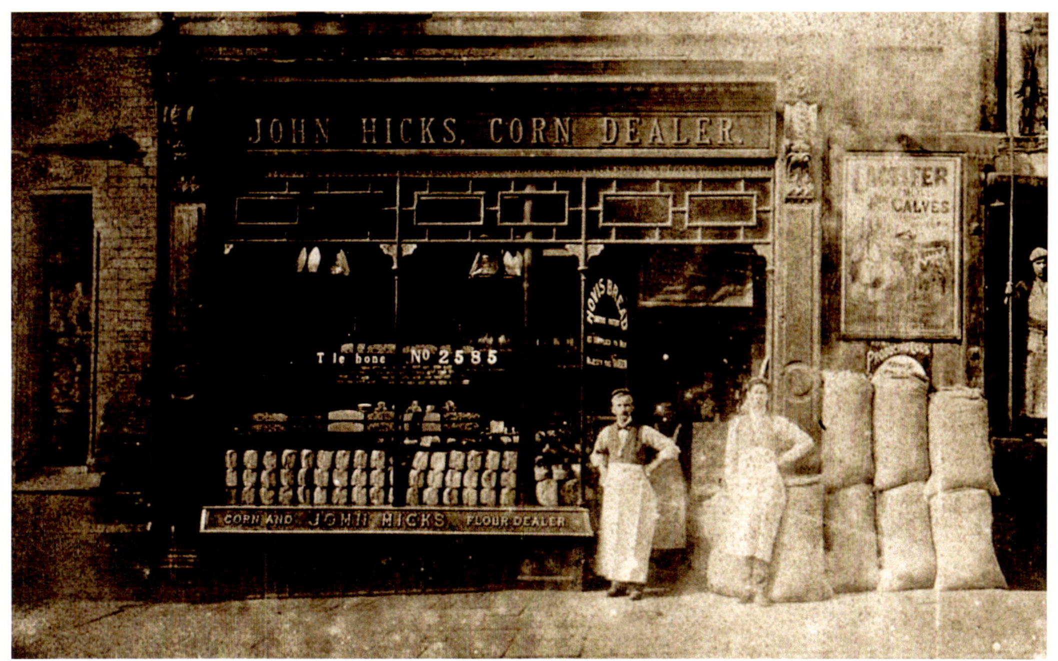

No. 83 High Street

Above: A combination of the commercial and industrial is depicted at the multipurpose premises of corn and flour dealer John Hicks. His store at No. 83 High Street in Wavertree doubled as a warehouse complete with a vigorous pulley system for lowering and raising produce. His shopfront took on a more genteel approach with perfectly proportioned signage sitting within a tripartite frame adorned with dentil detail, decorative corbels and pilasters.

Below: The fundamental structure of these buildings has mercifully survived the years with the former shop and adjoining warehouse structure still standing. The shopfront has been extensively altered to meet its more recent requirements which has resulted in the placement of numerous plastic windows and domestic doors across the front elevation, along with a substantial oversized fascia.

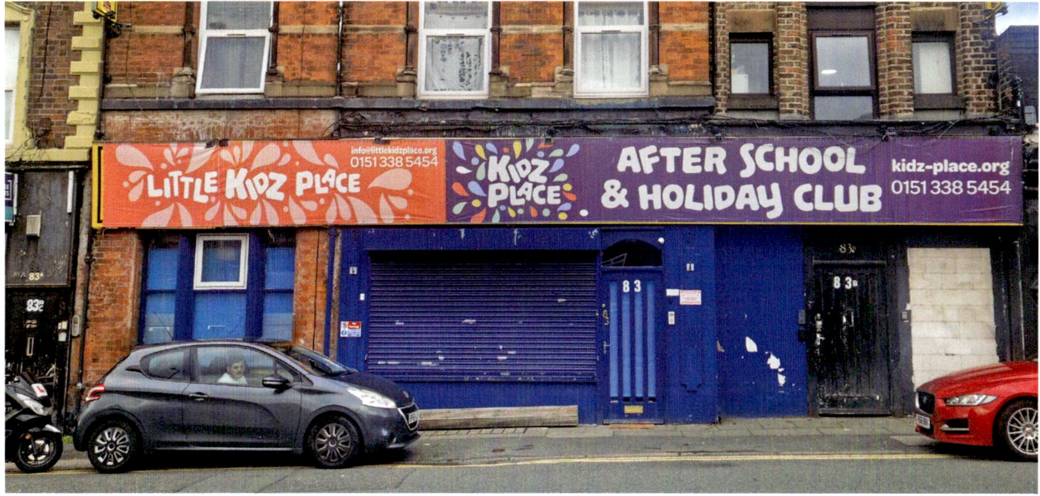

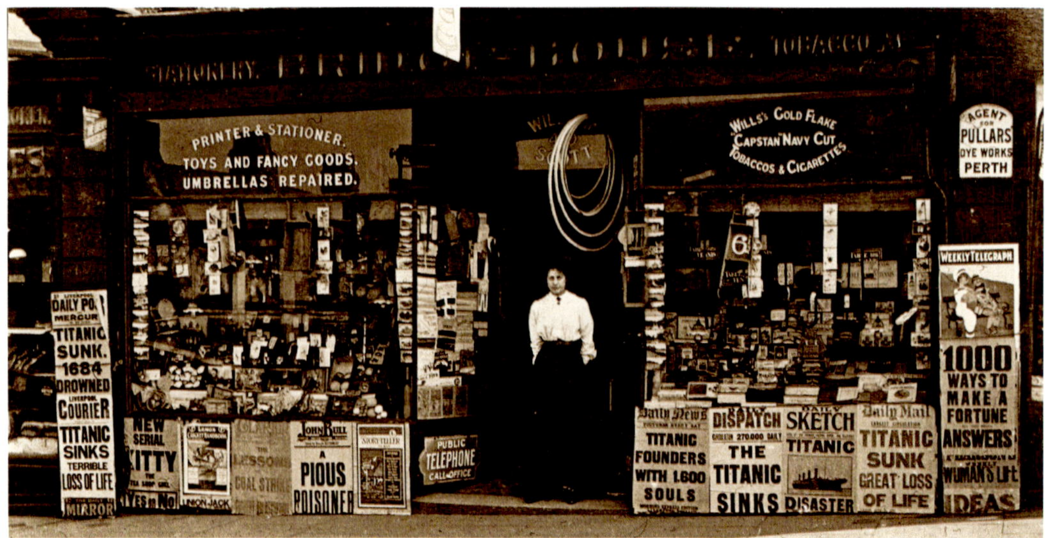

No. 40 Penny Lane

Above: The latest shocking headlines drew the eye to this shopfront at No. 40 Penny Lane, no less so than the terrible news of the sinking of the *Titanic*. Elsewhere the well-stocked projecting display spaces were flanked by a pair of powerful corbels whilst the name of the shop was painted boldly across the fascia. Presumably the shopkeeper herself posed in the recessed doorway at this important moment in human history.

Below: The building bears a remarkable resemblance to its original appearance with only modest modifications apparent to the shopfront. These include an adjustment to the recessed doorway which now opens straight onto the pavement, and a change to the glass panels which now feature central glazing bars. The interior however is undoubtedly much different from the old newsagents which has since become a glazing company.

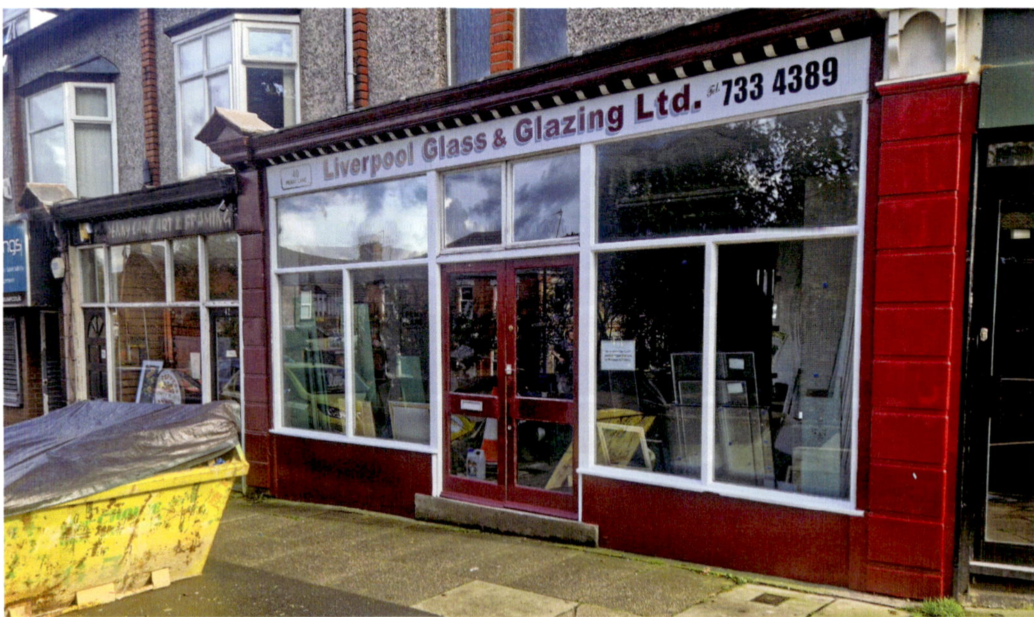

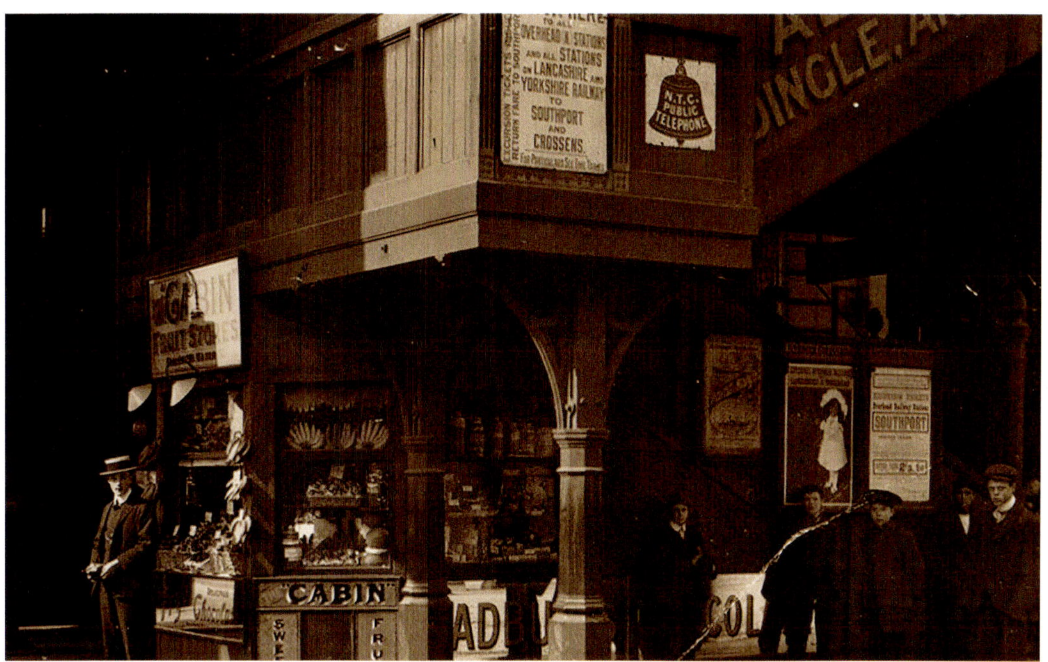

The Strand

Above: A small shop known as the Cabin once stood beneath the overhead railway not far from the pier head. This was a simple timber unit built into the railway infrastructure from where both sweets and fruits could be purchased by passing commuters via a serving hatch. Its windows were stocked full of produce with a distinctive mirrored advertisement for chocolate placed across the boards.

Below: The overheard railway was severely damaged during the Second World War and its repair was deemed too great a financial commitment in a post-war Britain. The structure was totally dismantled by 1959 along with the small shop here at Pier Head Station. Traffic on the Strand now runs through this site with Liverpool's famous Three Graces standing nearby.

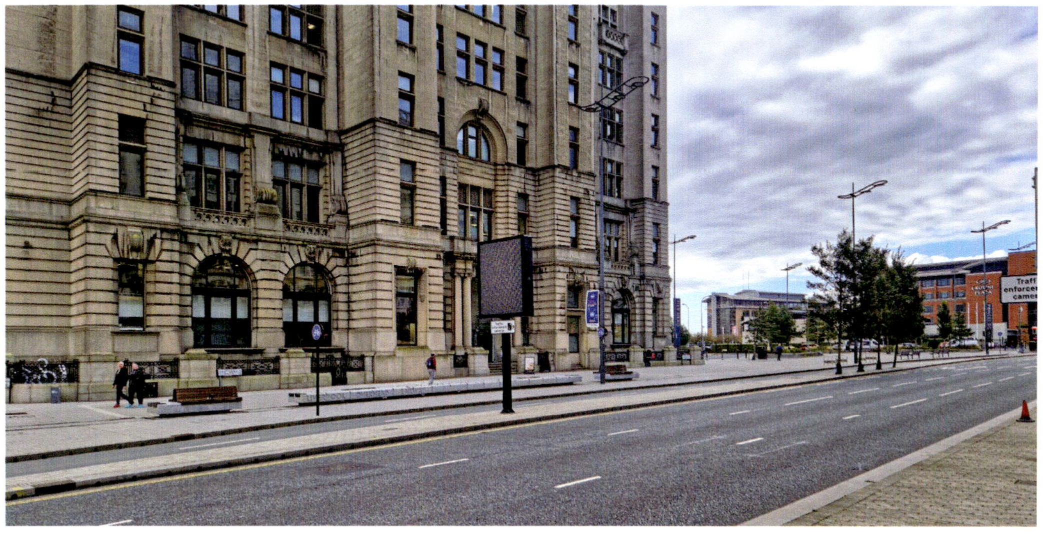

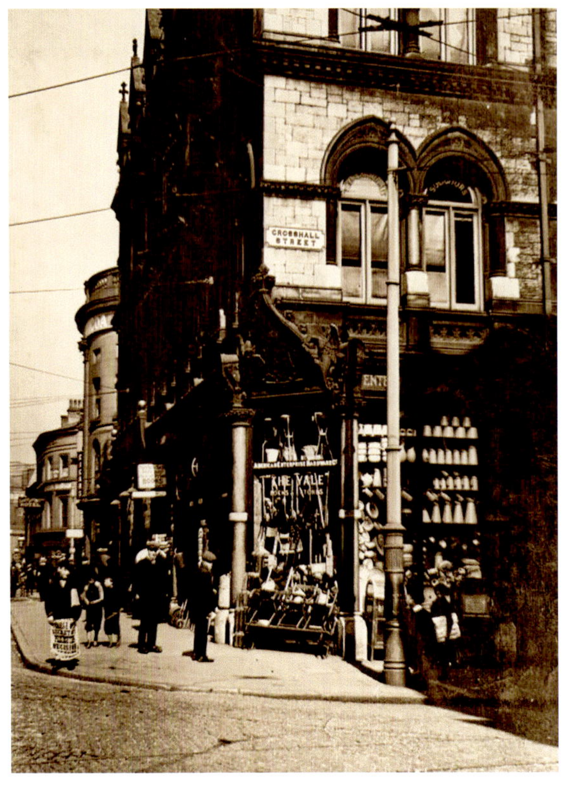

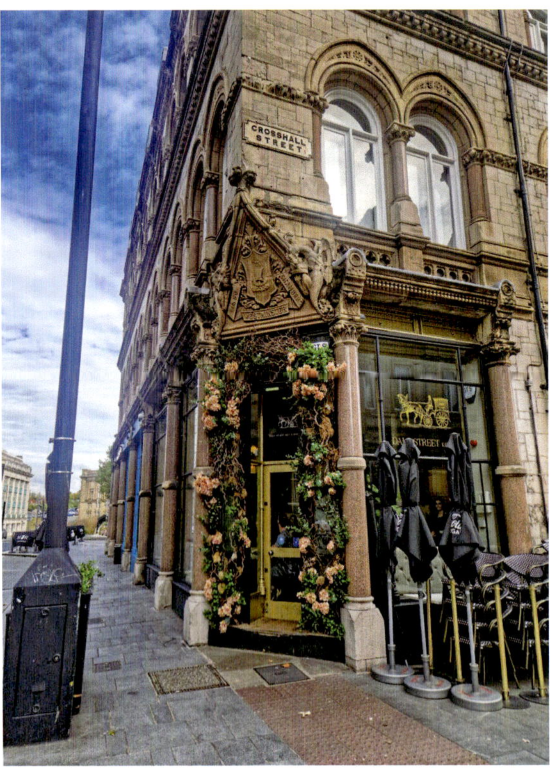

Crosshall Street

Left above: The shop of the Enterprise American Hardware Company once occupied the corner of Crosshall Street and Dale Street which boasted an incredible stone cartouche flanked by dragons with a fabulous array of granite pilasters positioned across the main elevations. This premises was part of a larger building known as Westminster Chambers which was completed in 1880 in a lively Gothic style.

Left below: The quality of the building has seen it placed at Grade II on the National Heritage List for England. Although no longer a shop, the premises still boast an incredible appearance in its latest incarnation as a restaurant known as the Dale Street Kitchen and Bar. The original entrance has also been reinstated on the corner of the building.

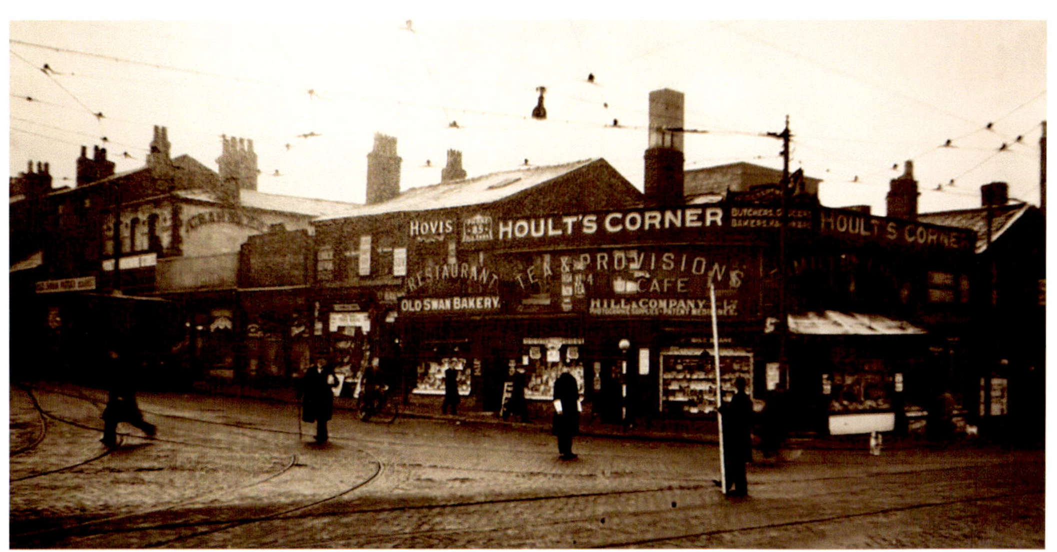

Hoult's Corner

Above: This area of Old Swan was known to many as Hoult's Corner thanks to James Hoult and his grocery, butchers, bakers, and hardware emporium which occupied the curve of St Oswald Street and Prescot Road. Hefty lettering advertised the goods and services on offer, with small individual shops set into the frontage. Large panes allowed for the showcasing of necessities, but with internal awnings fitted when required. The structure also housed other businesses including a chemist, restaurant, cafe and a sweet shop.

Below: The old shops here were demolished in 1939 in readiness for the Art Deco construction that was St Oswald House, a new crescent of municipal flats with retail below. This too felt the wrecking ball in 2022. The global supermarket giant Tesco now occupies the site, with Hoult's Corner now nothing but a barren and characterless car park.

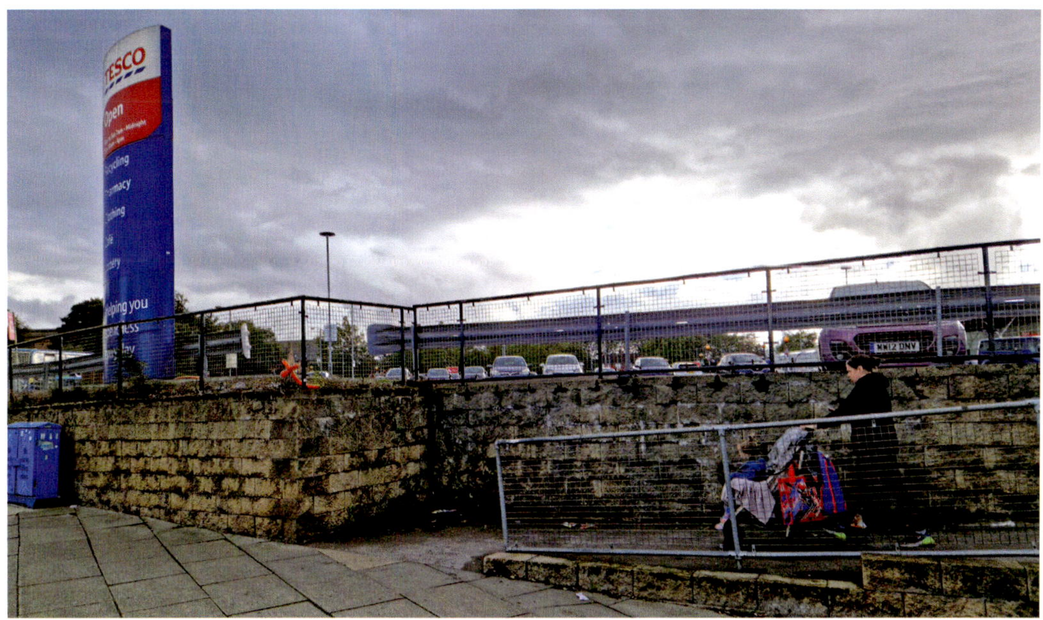

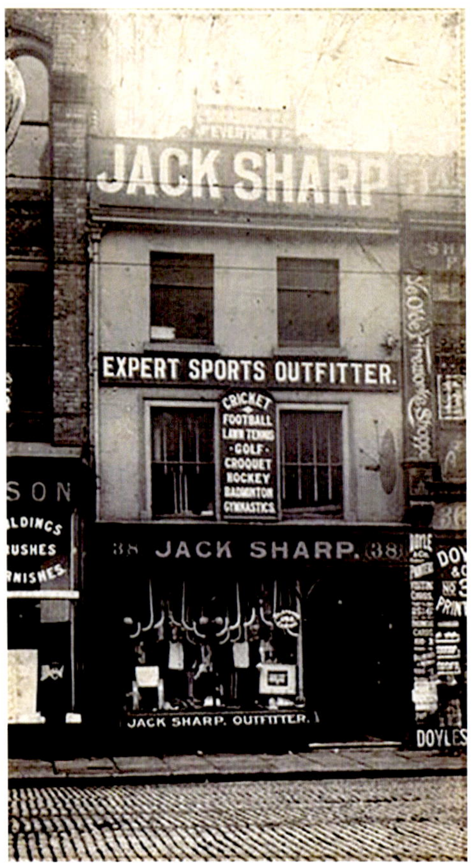

No. 38 Whitechapel

Left above: Before opening his sportswear business in 1903, Jack Sharp enjoyed a career as both a professional cricketer and professional footballer for England in both sports. His eponymous store traded from No. 38 Whitechapel selling a range of sports equipment, clothing and even Everton tickets on match days. With his name unmistakably painted across the facade, eager football fans could often be found queuing outside along the pavement before fixtures.

Left below: The business was a great success, so much so that the shop was enlarged to meet demand. In 1988 the company was purchased by retailer JJB Sports who promised to keep the famous name above the door. However, Jack Sharp was eventually dropped and JJB itself later fell into administration in 2012. Much of this part of Whitechapel has been regenerated in twenty-first-century development and the site is now part of a branch of the travel agents Trailfinders.

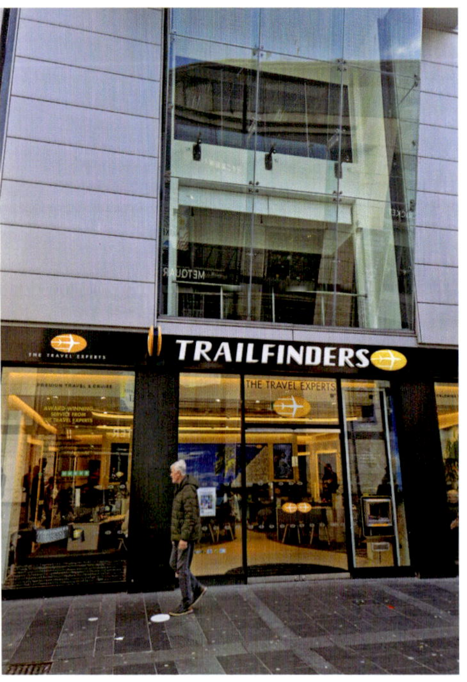

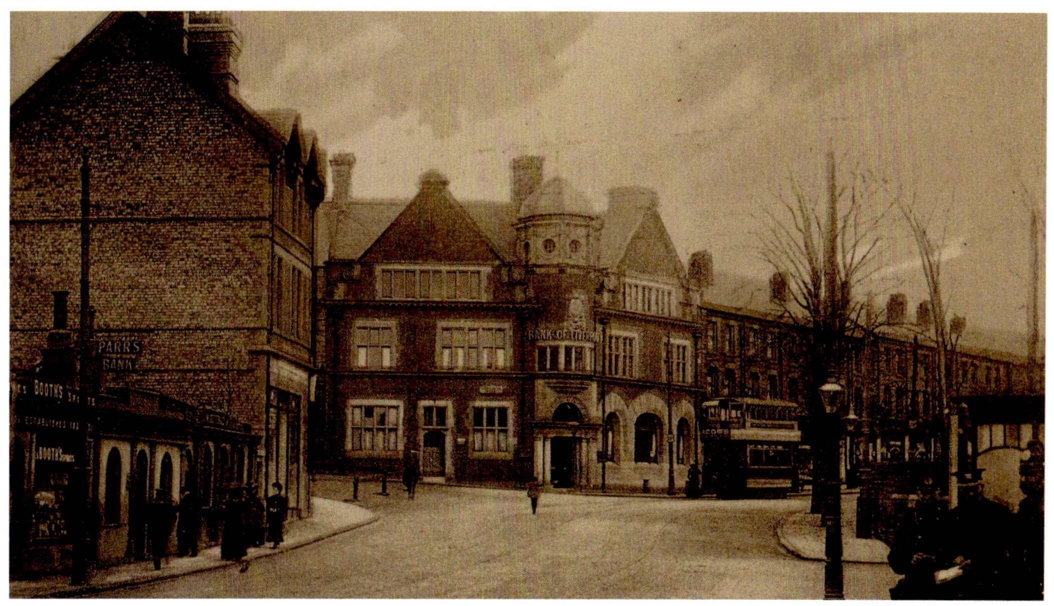

Aigburth Road

Above: The corner of Aigburth Road and Ashfield Road was once dominated by an exquisite branch of the Bank of Liverpool. This landmark building, finished with an octagonal cupola, was built in 1900 and complemented a busy through road in the south of the city lined with multiple shops and businesses. To the left, a somewhat more reserved branch of Parr's Bank could be seen occupying the curve, adjacent to Booths Wine and Spirits merchants.

Below: The Grade II listed bank remains a key feature on the streetscape but is now in use as a bar known as the Old Bank Ale House. The view itself is highly comparable to that of a century ago; however, the single-storey buildings have been demolished and the land repurposed for apartments. The former Parr's Bank has too ceased to be, instead operating as a branch of Boots the Chemist.

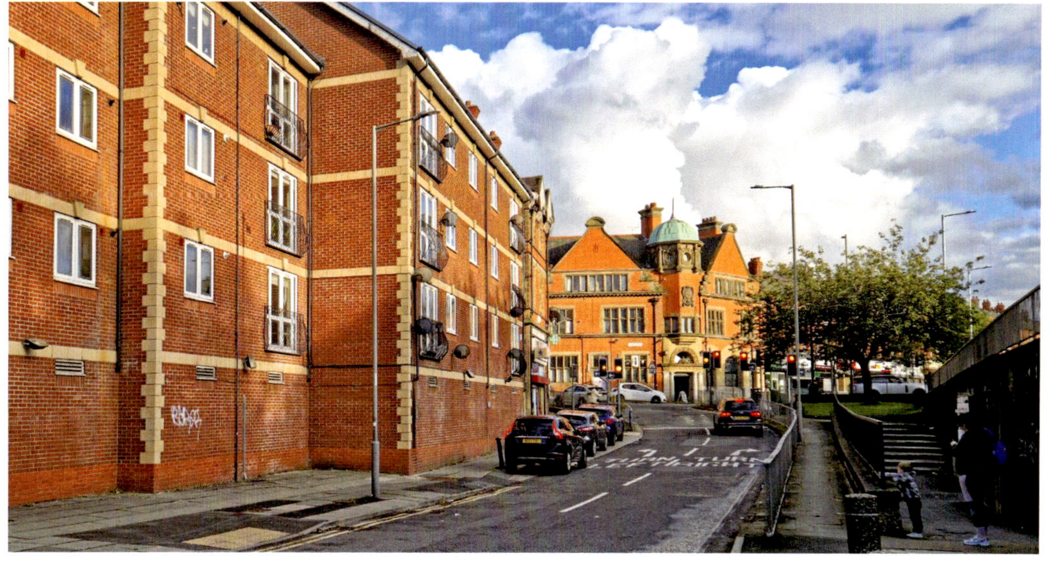

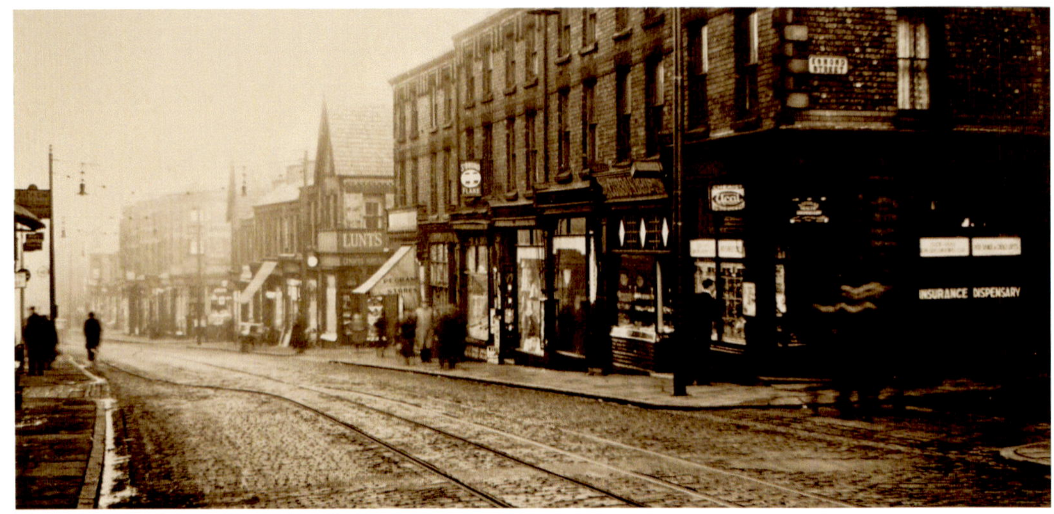

Breck Road

Above: The tramlines of Breck Road passed by the multitude of businesses, which contributed to the active commercial character of the street for generations. The premises of Melling's chemist with its corner shopfront and projecting signage served as a finale to an interesting terrace. Further down, the patterned windows and glazed bricks of Cubbin's Bakers enticed those who passed by to consider a savoury snack, whilst a succession of elegant and varied shopfronts looked out across the busy townscape further into Anfield.

Below: Some of the earlier and well-designed individual units of Breck Road have been amalgamated into wider shopfronts which do not offer quite the same visual interest. Breck Road, like many other once bustling areas across the UK, has suffered a downturn in tenancy with many shops closed and boarded up. The road is yet another victim of wider societal changes in our buying habits and consumer expectations.

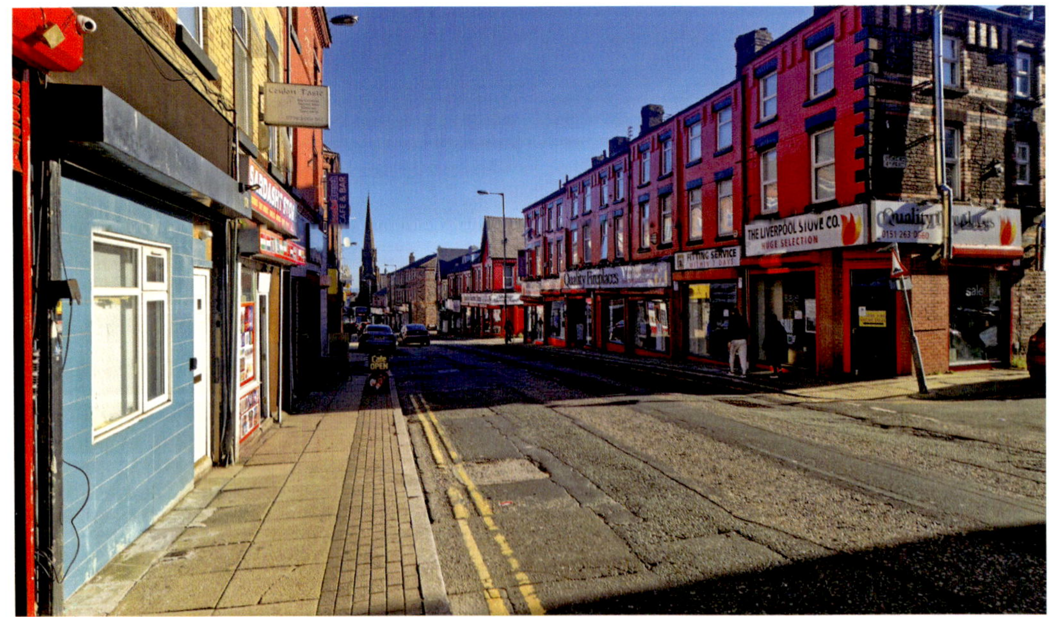

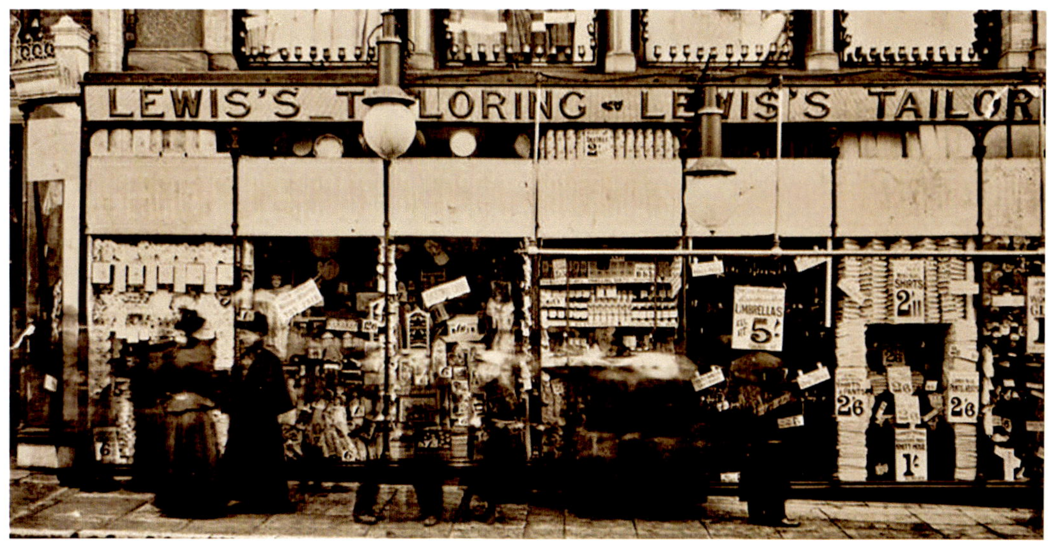

Lewis's, Ranelagh Street

Above: The view of the city's famous department store Lewis's as seen from the pavement of Ranelagh Street, with its large plate-glass windows used to maximum effect. Toys occupied one of the windows with others packed with umbrellas, shirts and even toilet rolls. Large lamps were fixed to the fascia to light up the stock in darker hours, whilst a series of smaller lights illuminated the windows of the upper floors.

Below: Lewis's was badly bombed during the Blitz and in 1947 it was redesigned by Gerald de Courcy Fraser, operating until its eventual closure in 2010. Large windows again line the Ranelagh Street elevation of this Grade II listed building, betwixt columns of Portland stone in a classical yet modern style. Despite an uncertain future, the eight-storey structure stands as one of Liverpool's most treasured buildings.

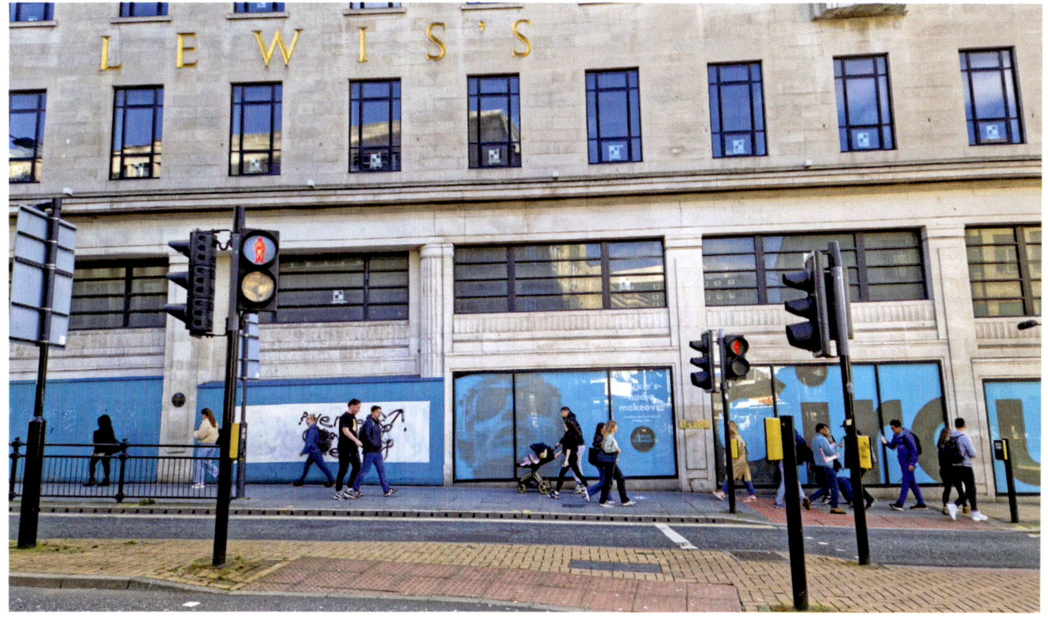

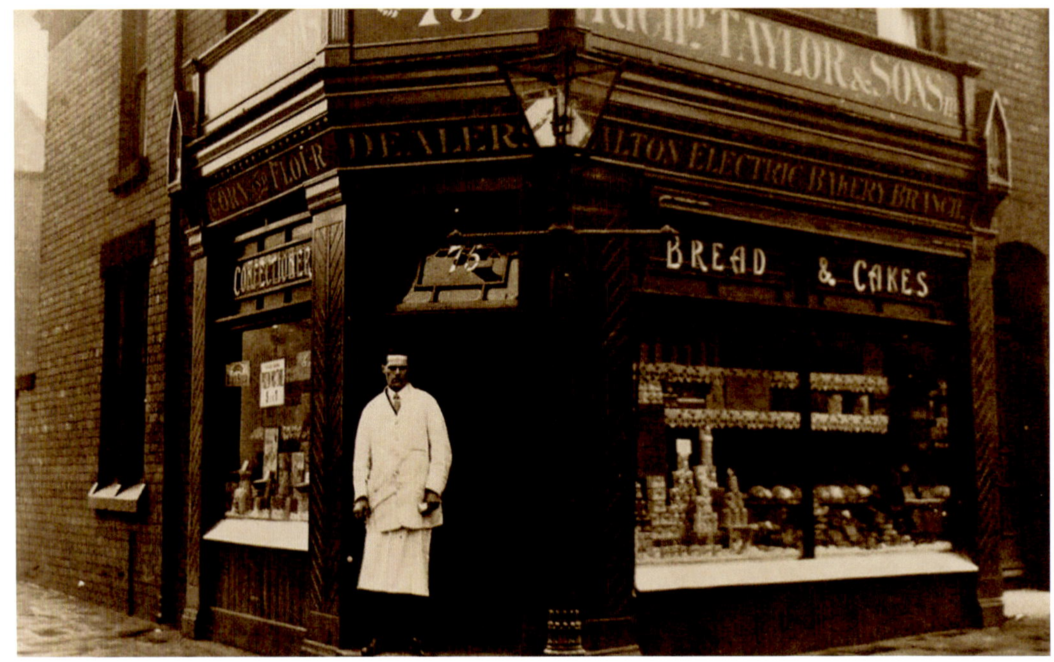

No. 75 Hall Lane

Above: A delightful bakery under the auspices of Richard Taylor & Sons stood at No. 75 Hall Lane in the 1920s. The corner premises had an understated yet pleasing appearance with balanced signage across the windows and fascia, along with well-dressed product displays. The doorway also featured a beautiful bespoke transom window which could be opened for added ventilation.

Below: The building can still be found but its appearance has been exceptionally weakened by the loss of its original corner entrance, large panes of glazing and the introduction of plastic signage and roller shutters. A newsagent now operates from the address, but the business certainly lacks the draw and appeal of its early twentieth-century occupants.

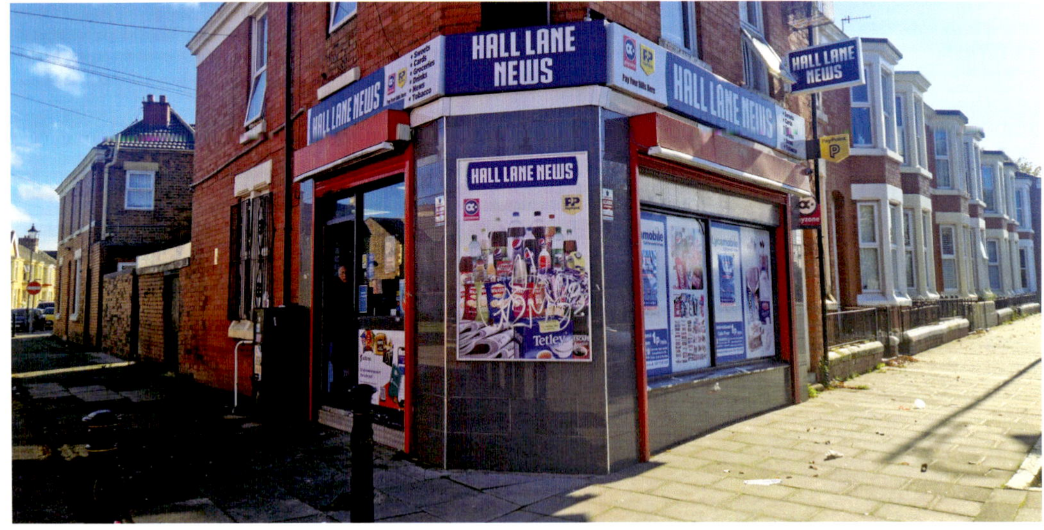

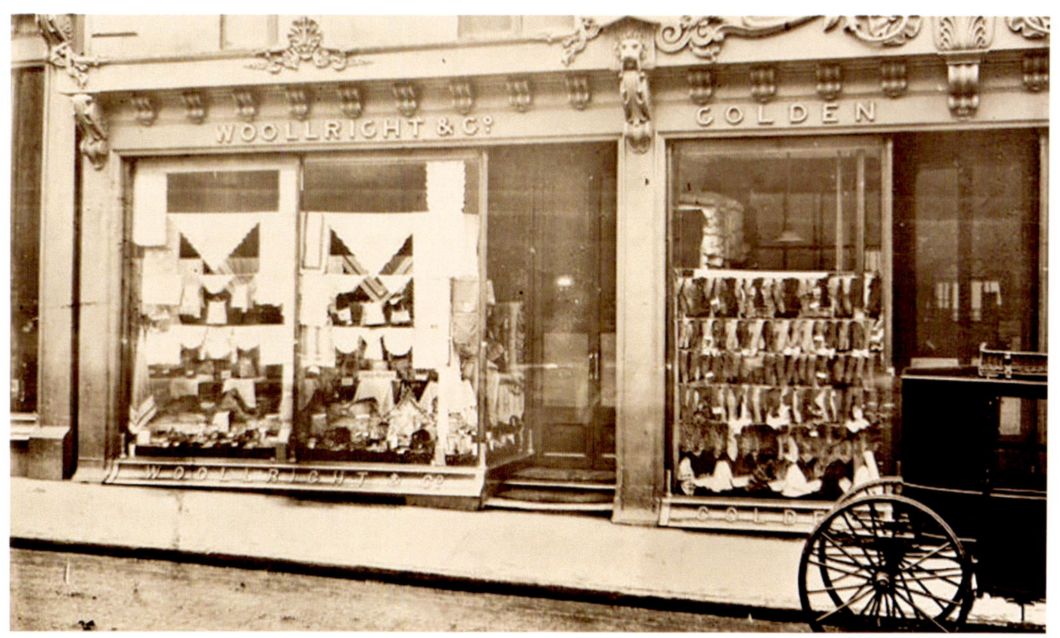

Nos 18–26 Bold Street

Above: This exceptional shopfront of Woollright & Co. silk mercers and haberdashers once stood at Nos 18–26 Bold Street in the heart of the city centre. Also known as The Golden Eagle, the property boasted an eponymous statue above its door as part of an illustrious shopfront which featured ornate lion cornices, decorative cartouches and a mixture of fancy ornamental elements.

Below: The eighteenth-century building was eventually levelled, and the land made good to host Radiant House. Christened the 'Queen of Bold Street' on opening in 1938, the unmissable building designed by Ernest Gee featured the avant-garde showroom and offices of the Liverpool Gas Company. It is faced in quartzite with fluted columns of Swedish marble which had braced a classical portico. Today it is occupied by the Albert's Schloss bar.

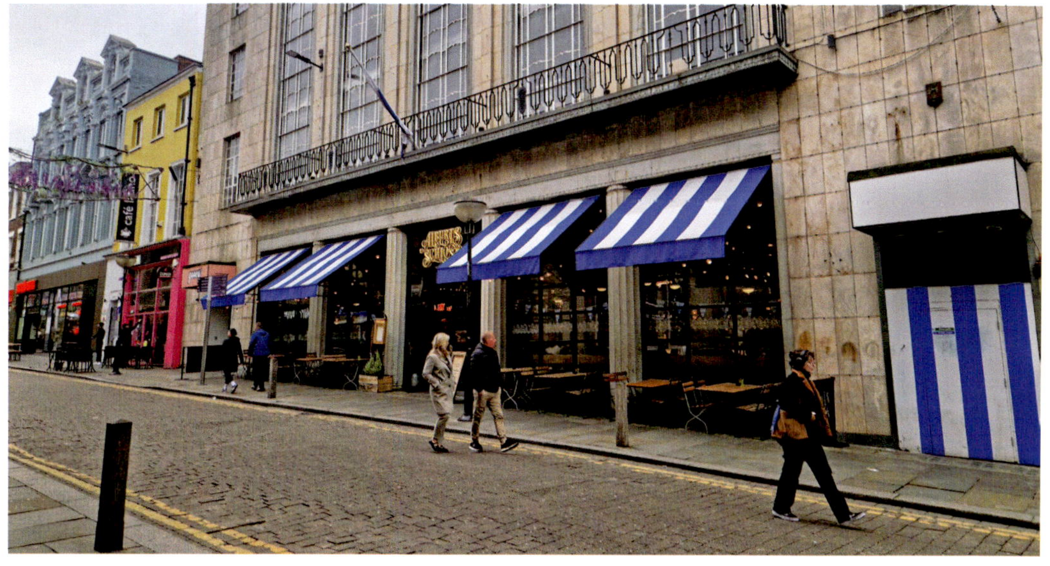

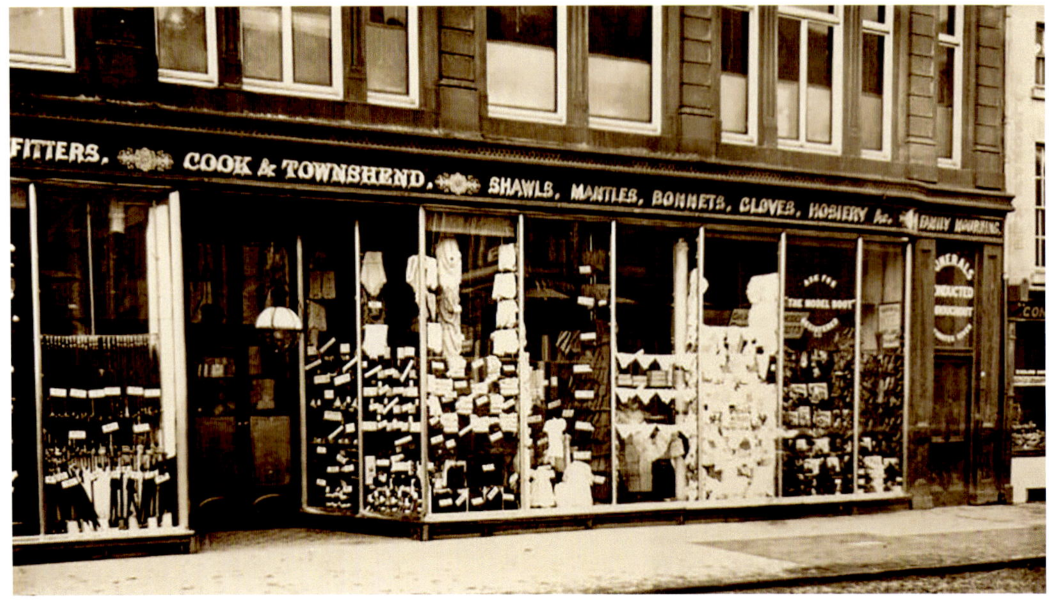

Cook & Townshend, Byrom Street

Above: Cook & Townshend once traded from a substantial store at Nos 5–29 Byrom Street. Their main elevation featured near complete floor-to-ceiling windows, interrupted by only symmetrical doorways and lighting. Shawls, pinafores, aprons and umbrellas were just some of the merchandise on show in an effort to compete in what was once a very commercialised part of the city.

Below: The firm announced its closure in 1920 and the following decade saw widespread infrastructure works commence around the vicinity. Today's commuters heading to and from the north of the city pass over the sites of these old shops, overlooked by the Blackburn Assurance Company and newly constructed blocks of student accommodation.

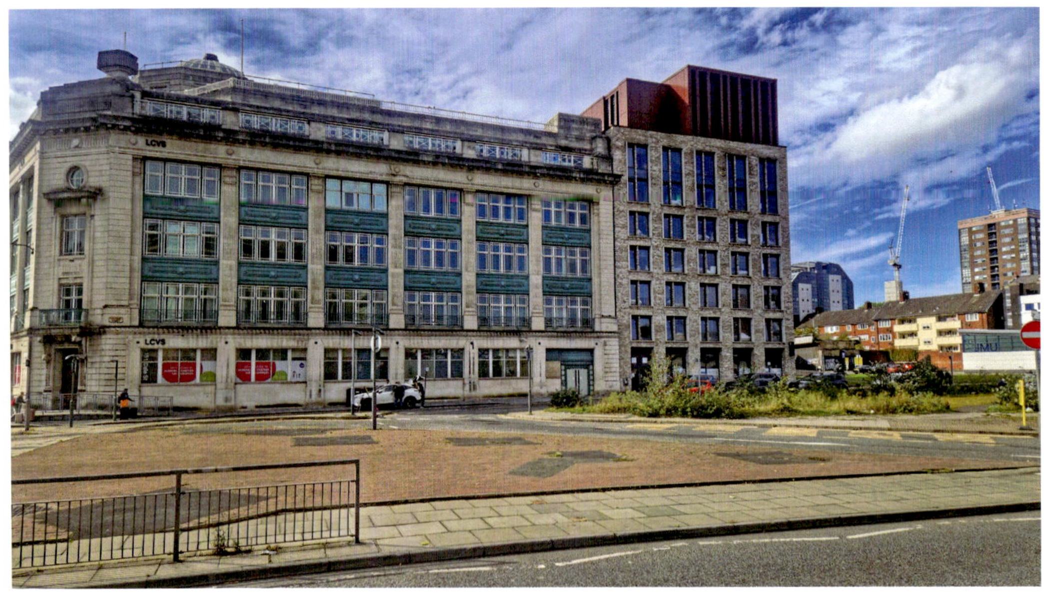

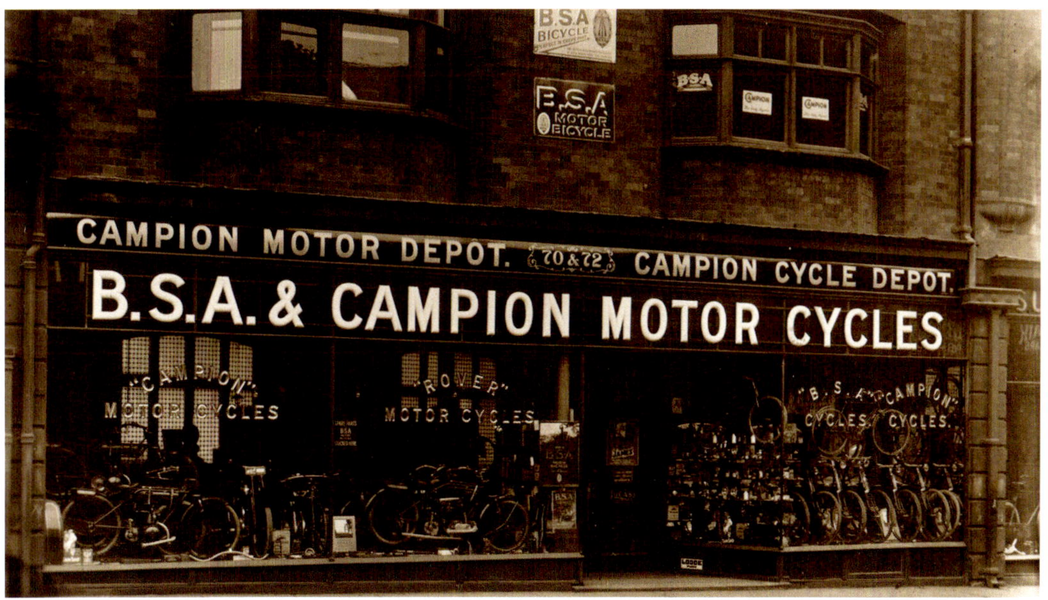

No. 70 Renshaw Street

Above: Motorbikes and bicycles were out for all to see at the Campion Depot at No. 70 Renshaw Street. By purposeful design, this rather simple shopfront featured the thinnest of glazing bars and the most minimal of stallrisers to take advantage of the display space facing out onto the pavement. The company's giant lettering panels sat neatly upon a metal frame positioned across the entire elevation.

Below: There have been various changes to this old shopfront, with movement to the doorway, the surrounding framing and fascia, and of course branding as the necessities and fancies of respective businesses have evolved over time. The current use is one of an unsightly convenience store which has taken on a number of these former shops, the whole row having previously been occupied by the Rapid Hardware store.

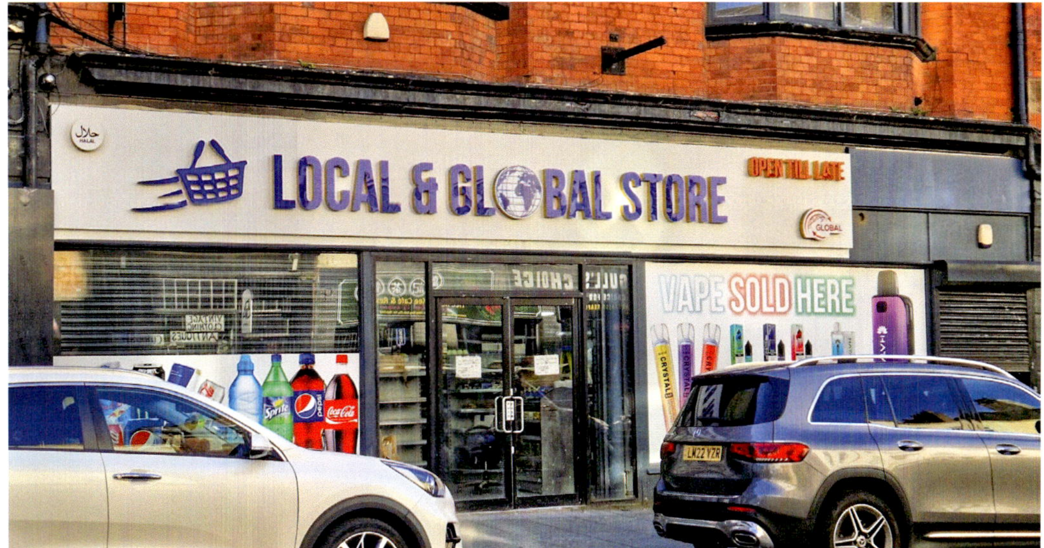

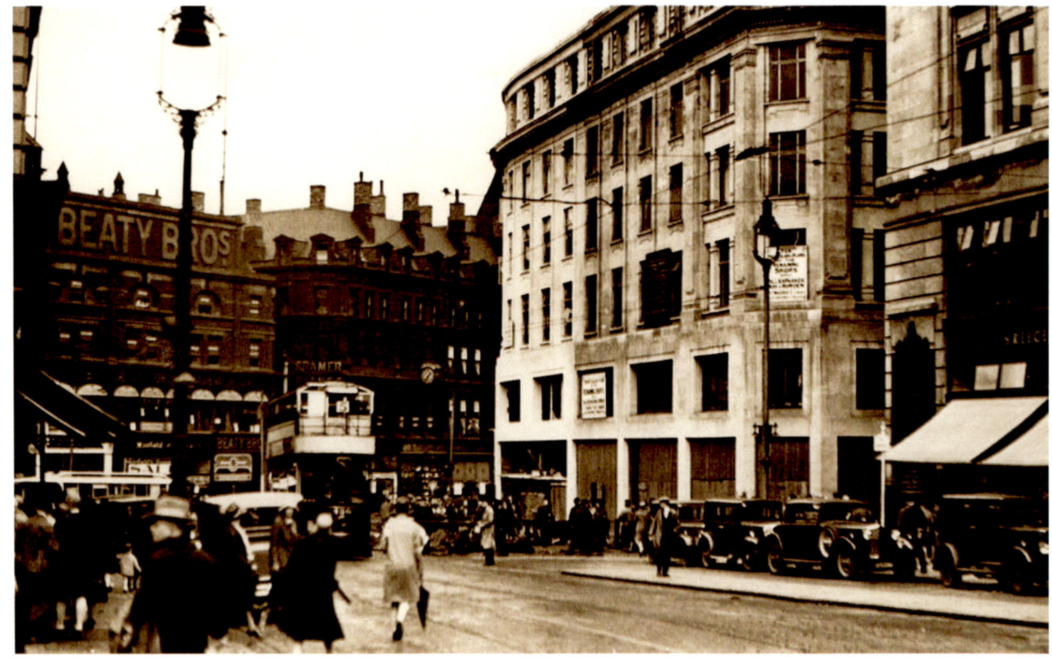

Parker Street

Above: The scene as witnessed down 1920s Parker Street and the gigantic signage of Beaty Bros loomed high over the public below. The construction of a new commercial block at the junction of Church Street neared completion with large apertures in its Portland stone facade left for the insertion of ground-floor shopfronts. The design signalled a move towards a new wave of architecture as shoppers embraced modern, twentieth-century developments.

Below: Parker Street continues as one of Liverpool's designated retail zones; however, the appearance of some of the buildings in this area have been altered in their form and detail, particularly across ground floors. The substantial property of Spinney House, a 1955 creation by Sir Alfred Shennan built for Littlewoods, now dominates the view across to Church Street which is now a branch of the clothing retailer Primark.

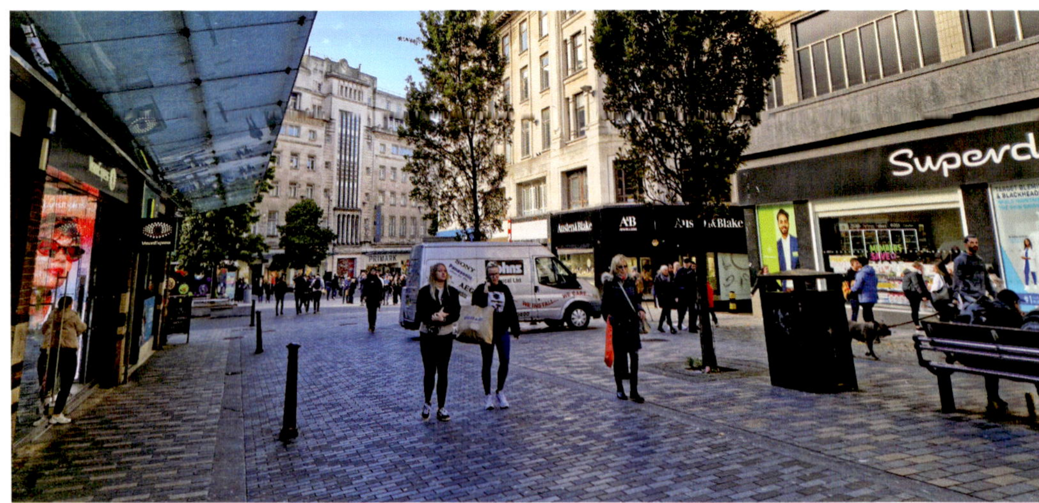

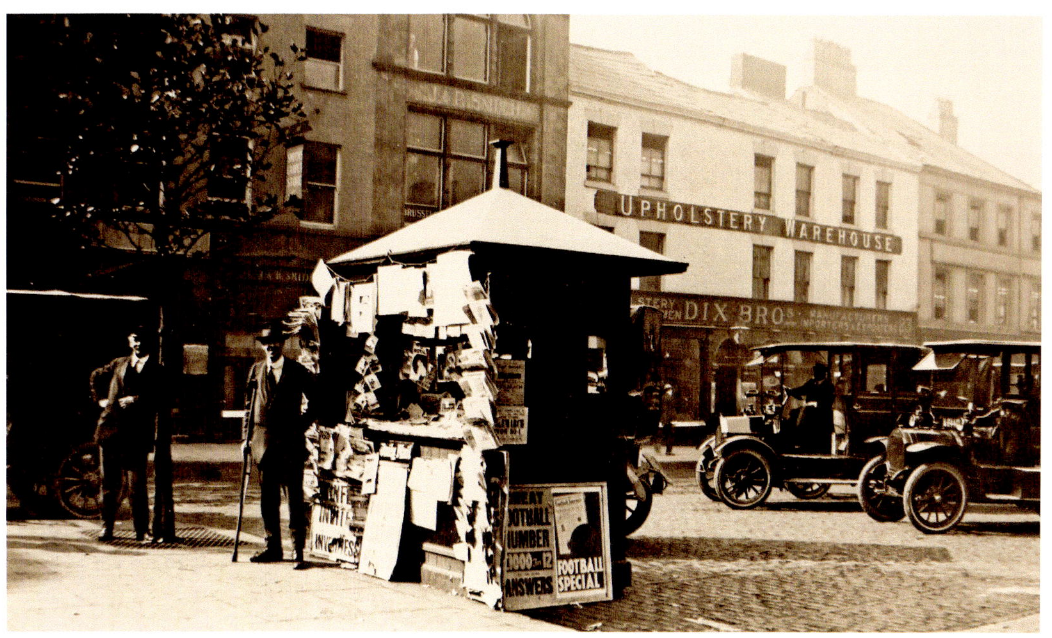

Williamson Square

Above: A popular parking spot for early automobiles, Williamson Square was first formed as a residential conclave in 1745. The character of the area changed significantly with the construction of the Theatre Royal in 1772. This dash of drama contributed to the introduction of hotels, shops and businesses all eager to offer their good and services to paying audiences. By the 1920s these buildings on the southern part of the square were occupied by Smiths Carpet Store and the Dix Brothers Upholstery Warehouse, respectively.

Below: The Williamson Square of 2025 is entirely pedestrianised and hosts several bars and shops around its periphery. Its architecture has continued to alter over time, with the older shops and warehouses now lost to more recent construction housing a barbers and a souvenir store. The Georgian Theatre Royal no longer exists but the Grade II* listed Playhouse has stood on the square's eastern element since 1866.

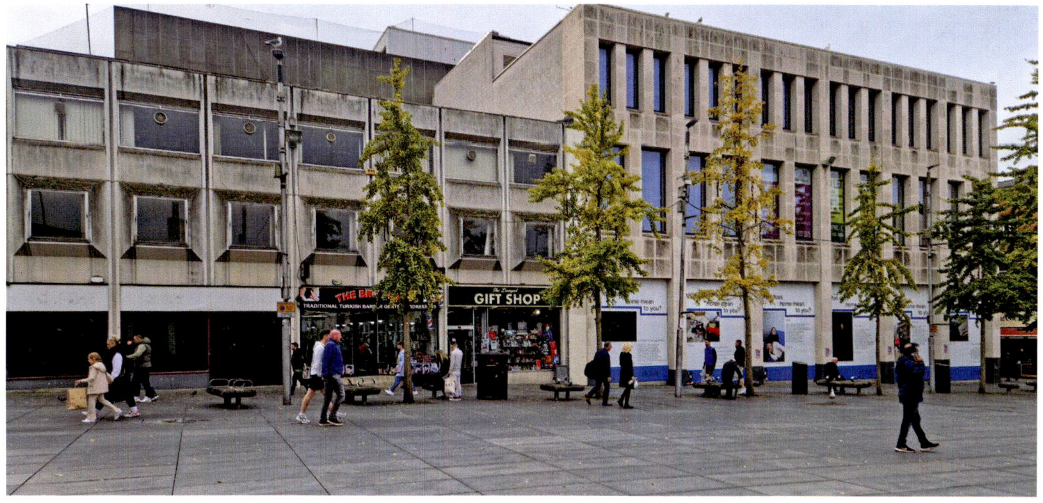

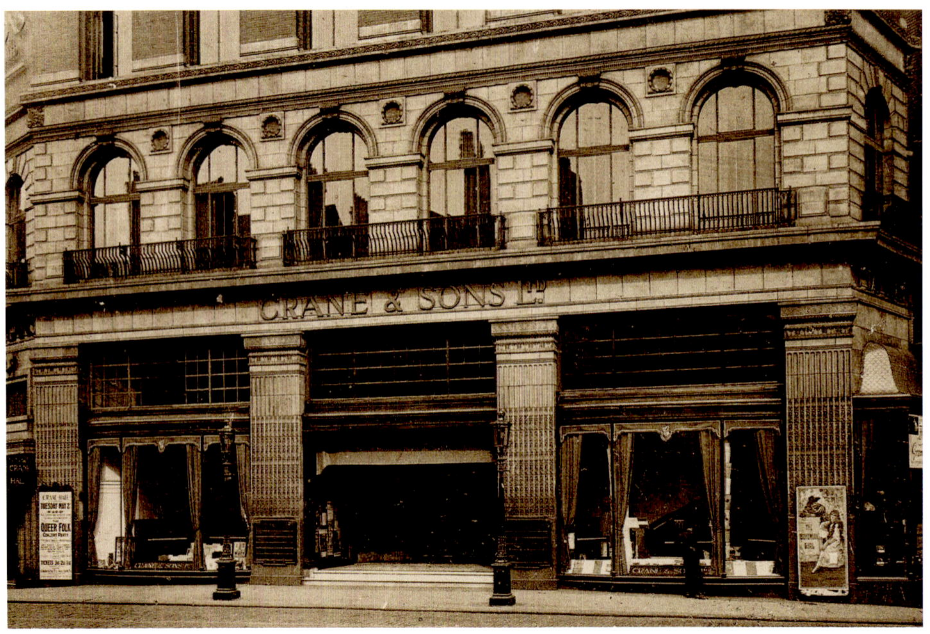

Crane & Sons, Hanover Street

Above: This scene in Hanover Street shows the premises of instrument manufacturers Crane & Sons, who described themselves as the largest piano and organ firm in the world. The building was constructed in approximately 1915 and featured five storeys with a theatre within. The principal facade included well-proportioned round-headed windows set between ornamental wreaths and balconies, as well as imposing pilasters adorned with intricate decoration bracing a pair of stylish window displays.

Below: The Grade II listed building is now home to a combination of bars which has seen extensive alterations to the ground floor. This has unfortunately resulted in the removal of its outstanding glazing and the division of the former retail space with the introduction of modern shopfronts and associated lighting, signage and security items. Upstairs the 380-seat theatre remains in situ.

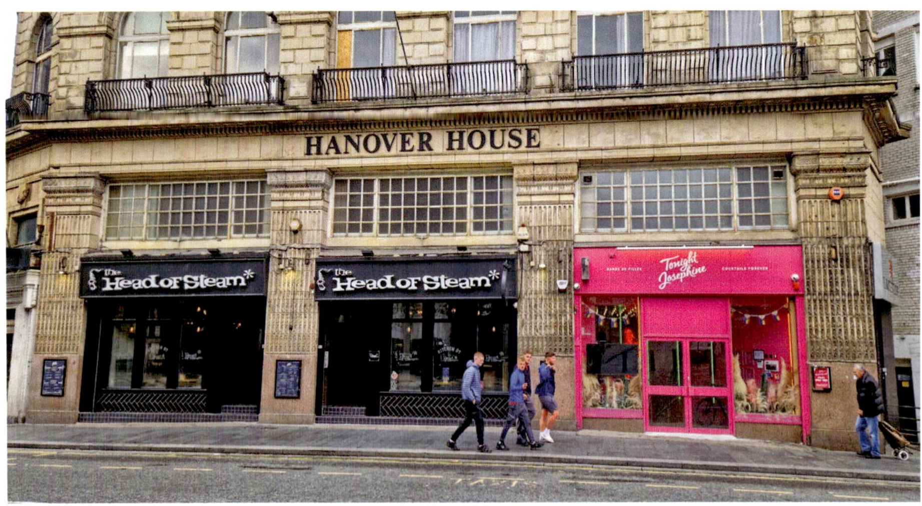

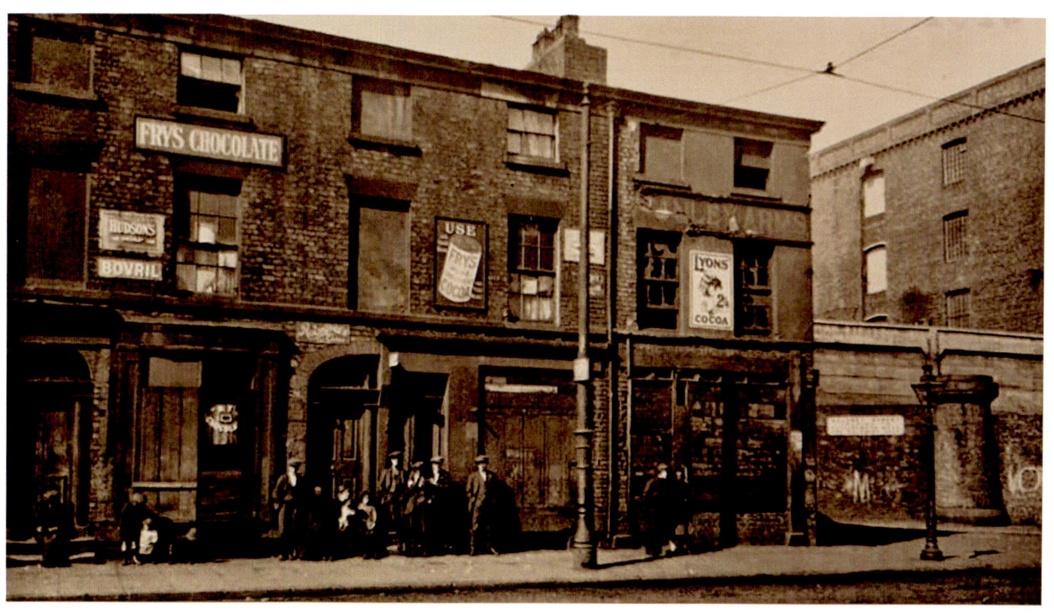

Great Howard Street

Above: By the 1920s poverty had befallen this stretch of Great Howard Street, as shown by the poor condition of the skeletal buildings. These properties had been constructed almost a century earlier to serve the growing neighbourhoods north of the town with limited embellishment or frills. Simple neoclassical columns had survived to doorways joined by haunting reminders of previous use, such as faded signage and product advertisements.

Below: These decaying buildings were demolished and following a sharp decline in traditional manufacturing, this part of Liverpool stood as evidence of the economic downturn. This section of Great Howard Street remains vacant; however, the vast Tobacco Warehouse nearby is in the process of conversion to residential apartments, with more examples of much-needed regeneration now emerging all around.

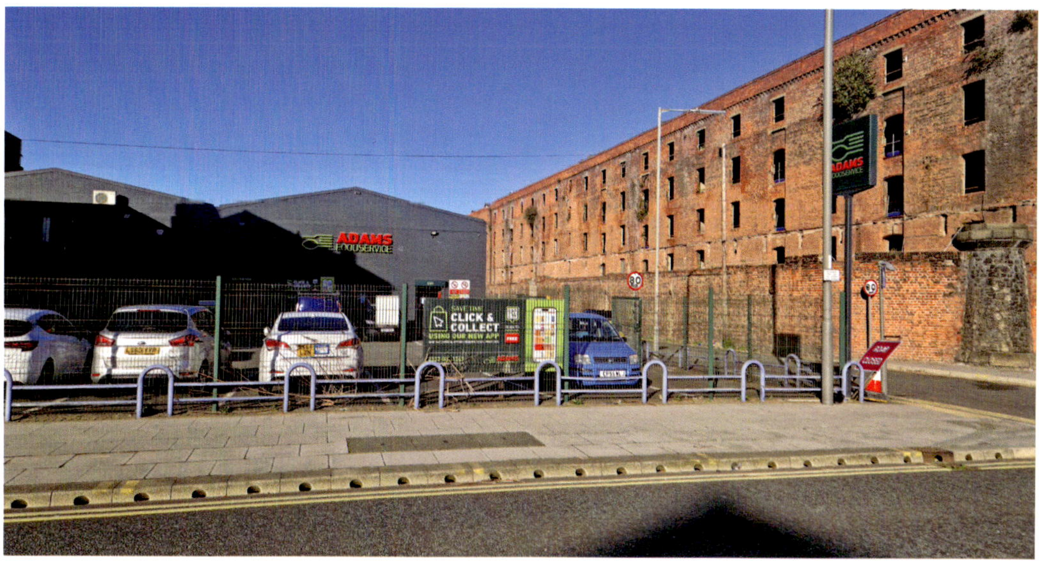

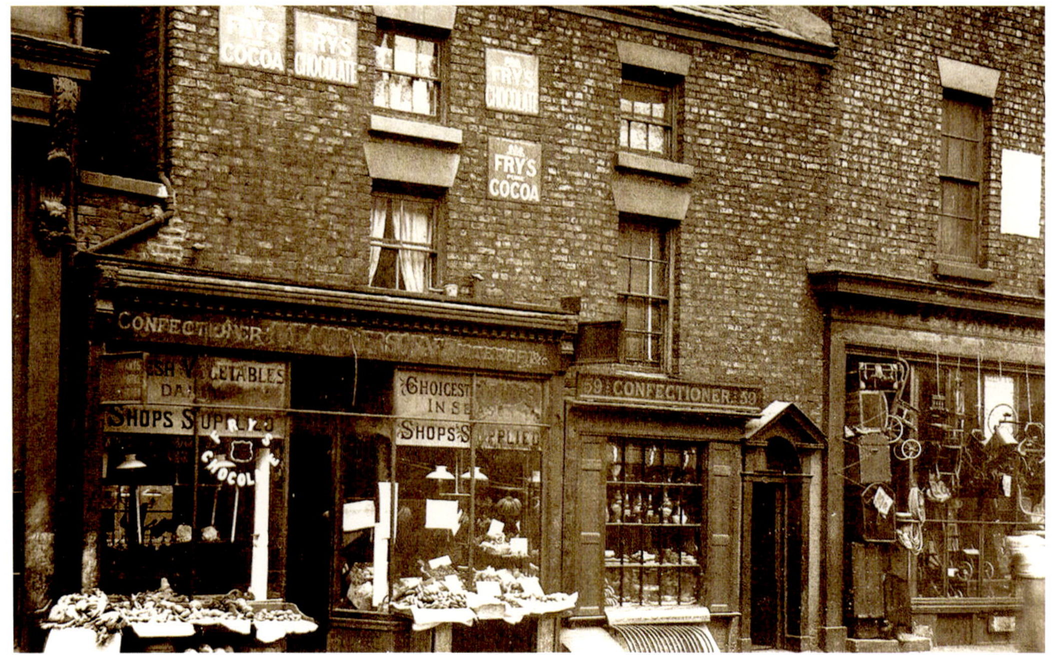

Islington

Above: Confectionary could be purchased by our Edwardian predecessors from No. 59 Islington. This small shop had a classical entrance beneath a pointed pediment with a charming window display. Healthier options could be found next door with a fruit and vegetable merchant whose produce sat out front, whilst a variety of household miscellanea was sold further down along the terrace.

Below: This part of Islington would be unrecognisable to the old retailers who used to live and work around this part of the city. Vast waves of property were cleared away to make way for the rise in vehicular traffic and the endless bid to clear congestion in the city centre. The street now leads to the busy intersection lined by a recent rise in multistorey apartment blocks.

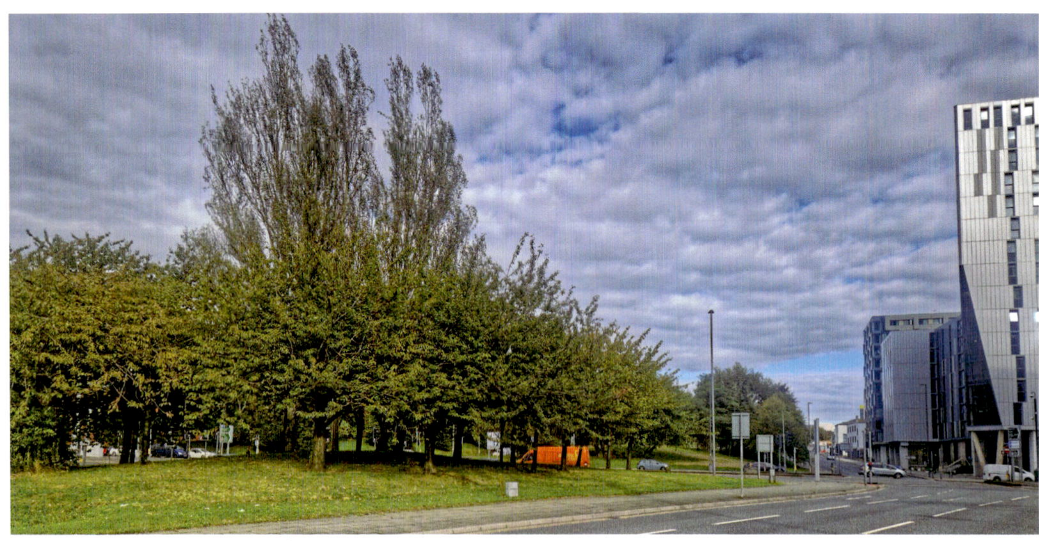

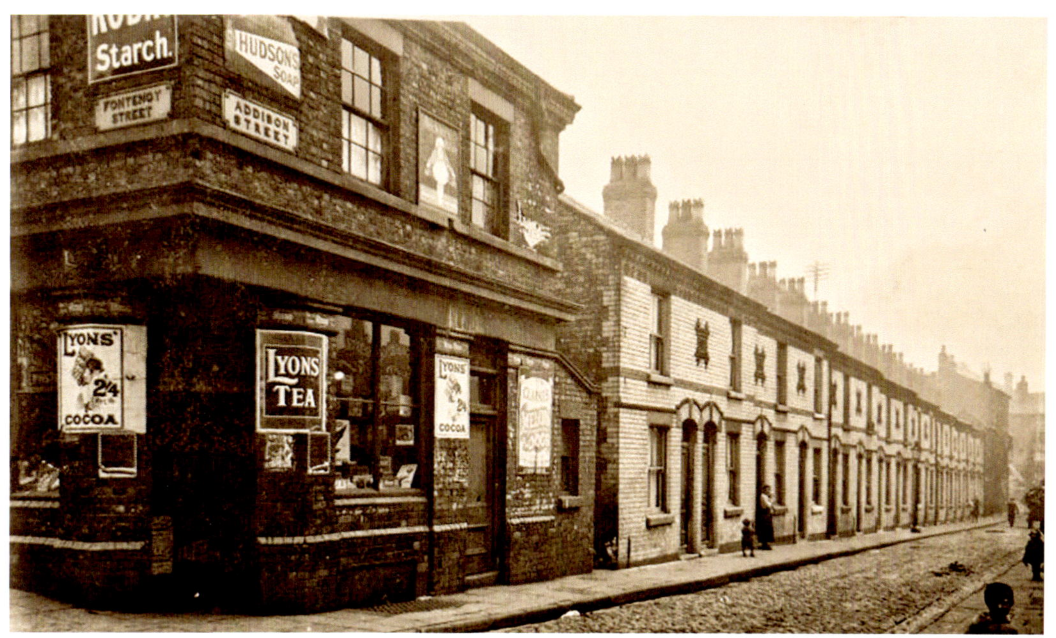

Addison Street

Above: This typical corner shop could be found at the corner of Addison Street and Fontenoy Street. Its simple brick exterior had been covered in advertisements ranging from Lyons Tea to Hudson's Soap. The modest design of the store reflected the humble setting in which it stood, with rudimentary housing and communal courts sprinkled about the locality.

Below: Few clues now of the poverty and strife common to these old streets in the Victorian era, with late twentieth-century housing in place of the unenviable terraces, courts and industries. The neighbourhood today is predominantly residential, with Holy Cross Primary School and the Marybone Youth Association also situated nearby.

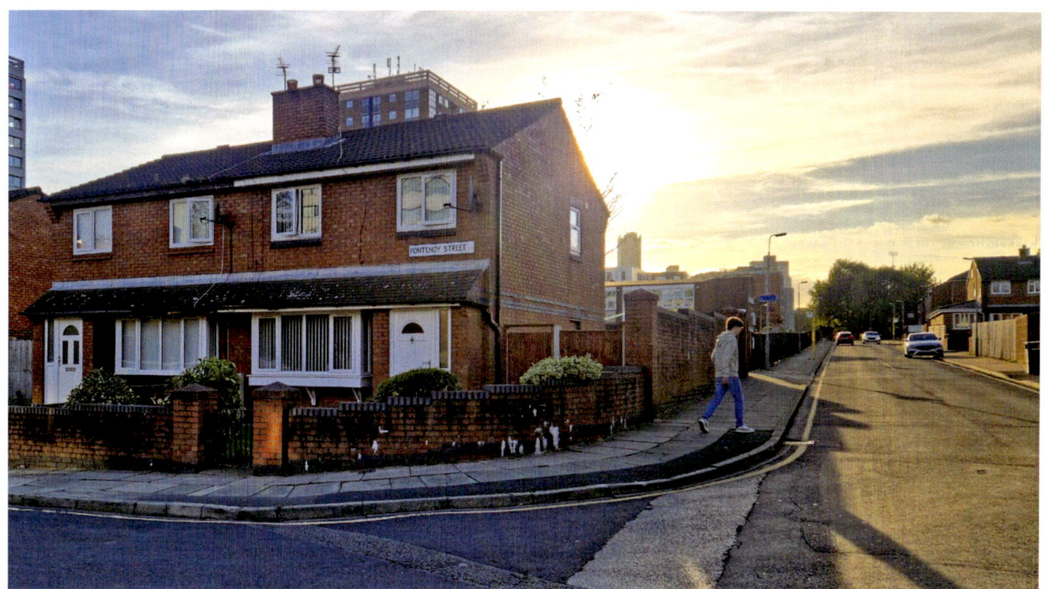

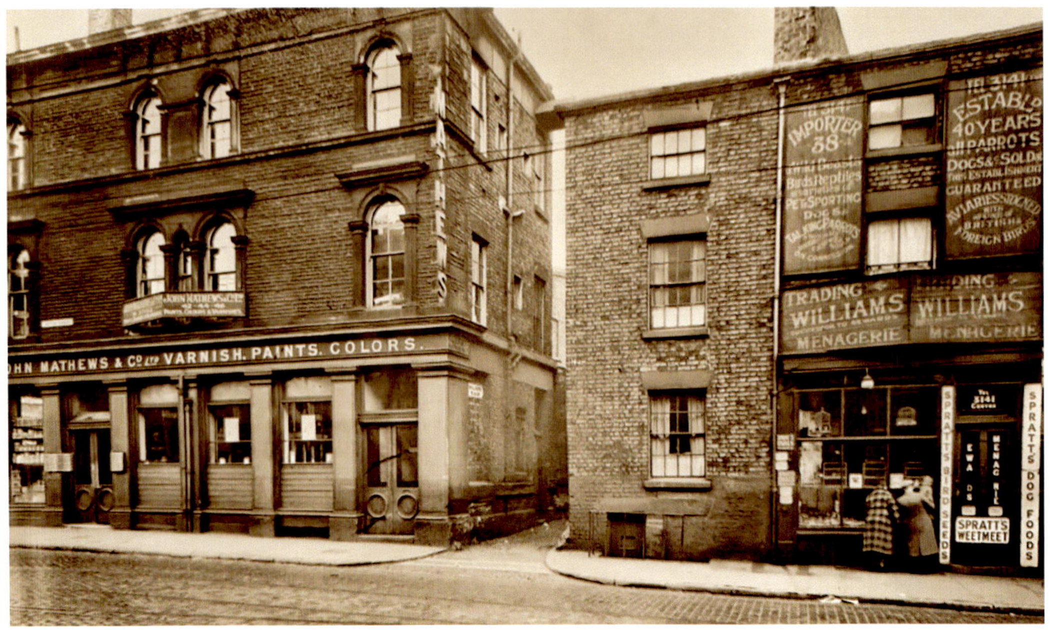

Hatton Garden

Above: A collection of timber advertising panels promoted the labours of James Williams who earned his living dealing in live animals which were frequently admired through the Hatton Garden shop window. The name of a previous owner still haunted the glazing of the doorway of this diminutive property, but extra advertising space for dog and bird food was found in the surround. Across Walker Place, the paint and varnish company of James Mathews stood nearby.

Below: Council offices constructed after the Second World War in a building known as Premier Court stand partly on the site of these old businesses, as well as a more modern tower of student accommodation in the form of Ablett House. Much like London Road, this part of the city has become a popular place to stay for those pursuing courses of study at Liverpool's various universities.

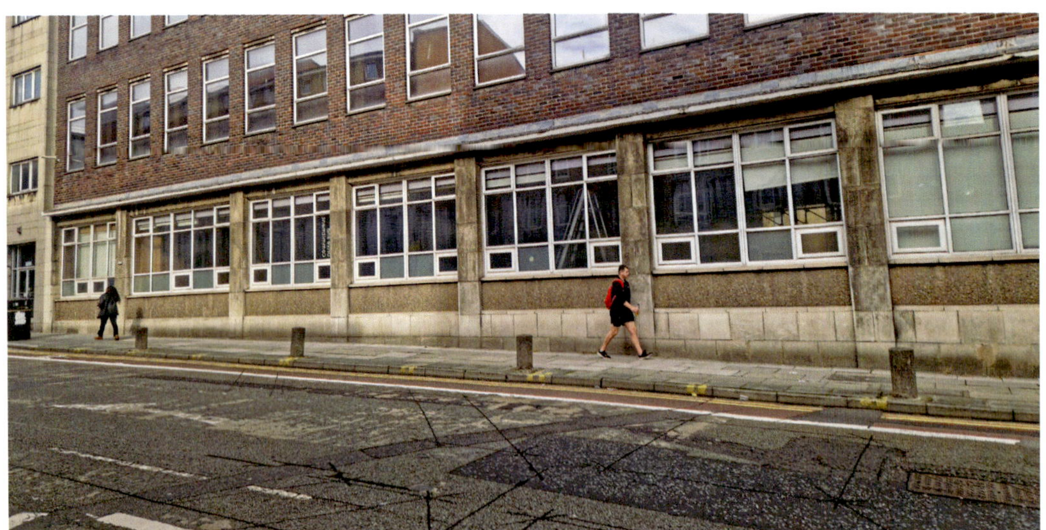

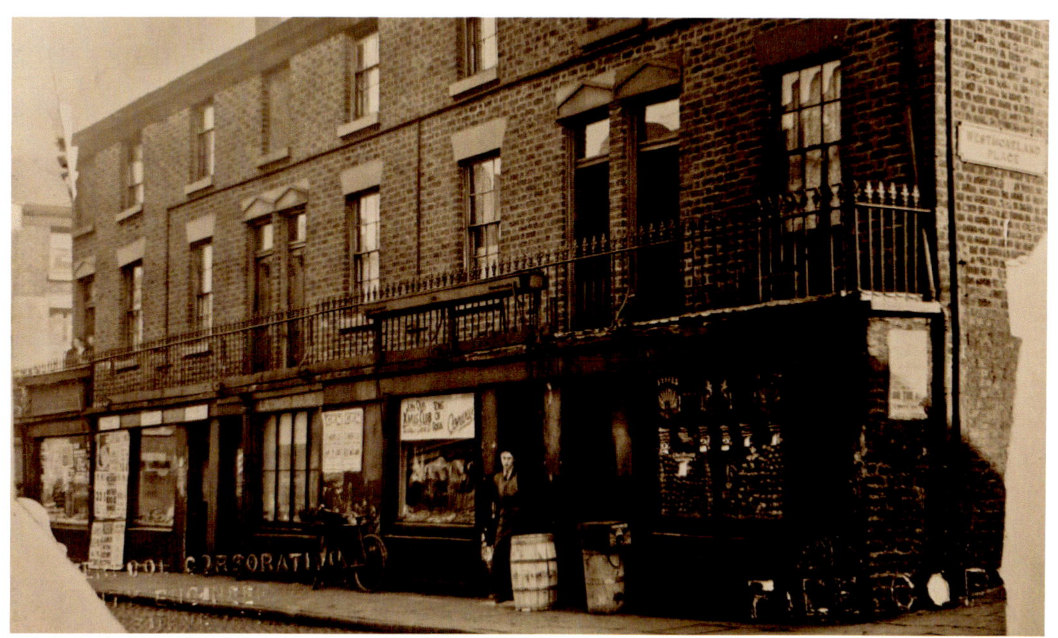

Latimer Street

Above: A greengrocer with his stock piled high within the window could be seen at the end of this Latimer Street terrace at the corner of Westmorland Place, with a butcher's shop next door. This row of shops was near indistinguishable, each designed with simple square glazing and a plain doorway in a largely unremarkable fashion. Housing sat above behind an iron railing offering accommodation, perhaps to shopkeepers and their families, in this underprivileged area of the city.

Below: Several of the streets around these parts have been radically altered with this corner of Westmorland Place now known as Callaghan Close. In a bid to improve living conditions, many of the old properties across Vauxhall were demolished to make way for more adequate housing in the 1970s and 1980s. Today the area features a mix of low-density bungalows, terraces and semi-detached dwellings complete with private gardens and outdoor recreation spaces within the community.

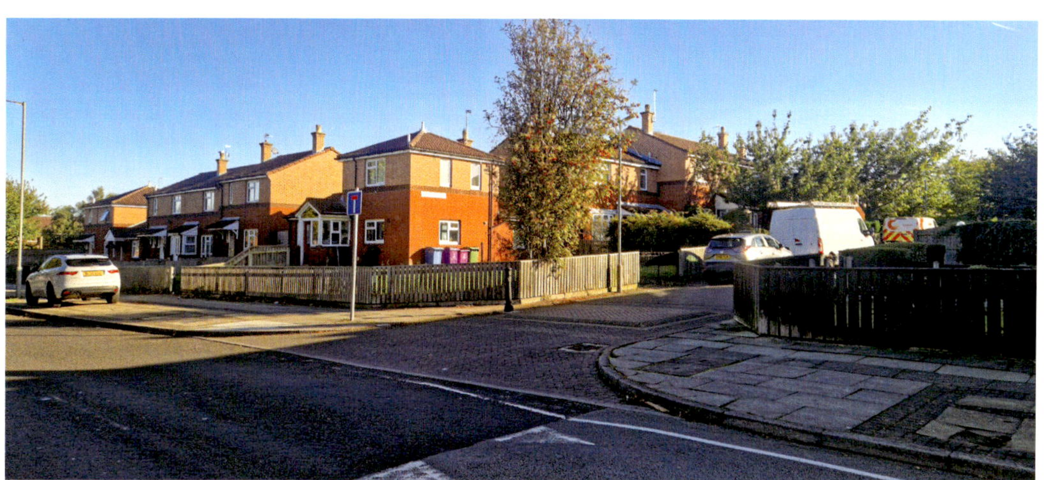

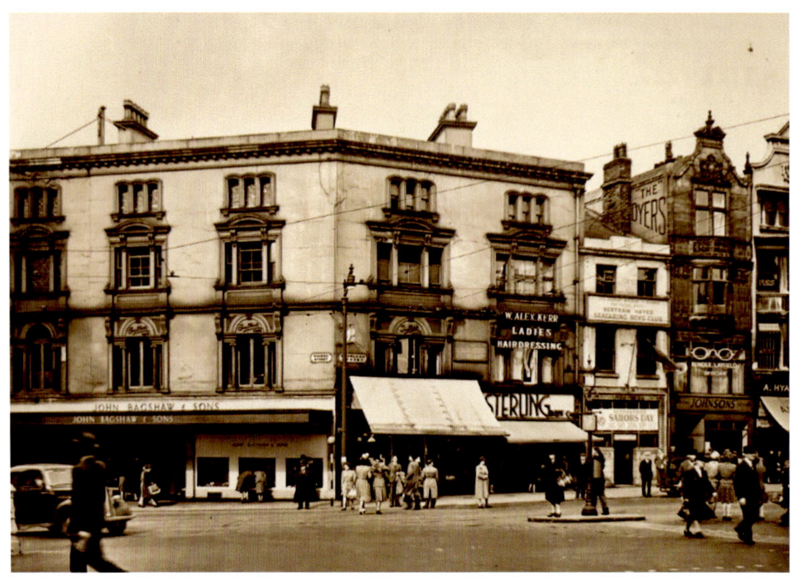

Ranelagh Street and Church Street

Above: This prominent corner property at the junction of Ranelagh Street and Church Street was occupied by the jewellers John Bagshaw & Sons who had a plain and simple tripartite window display beneath a fixed canopy. The awnings of its neighbours, a confectioners and shoe shop respectively, had been drawn across. A large flag fluttered over the door of the smaller building of the Mersey Mission, whilst a pair of giant spectacles graced the premises of a nearby opticians.

Below: Remarkably the building that is now a McDonald's was entirely rebuilt in 1988 as part of the development of Clayton Square Shopping Centre. Its appearance, but for the loss of the top floor, is remarkably similar to that of its much older forerunner. Less dramatic changes can be observed to its neighbouring retailers, but new shopfronts and questionable signage do detract from the otherwise wonderful architecture still to be admired.

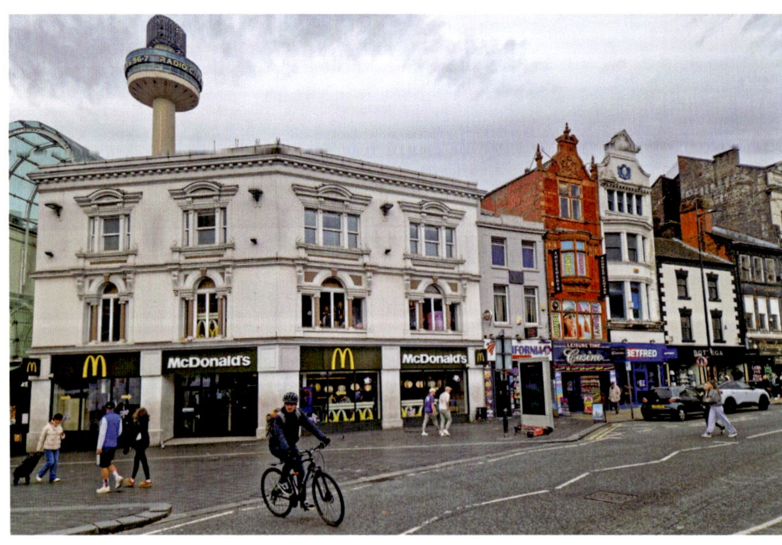

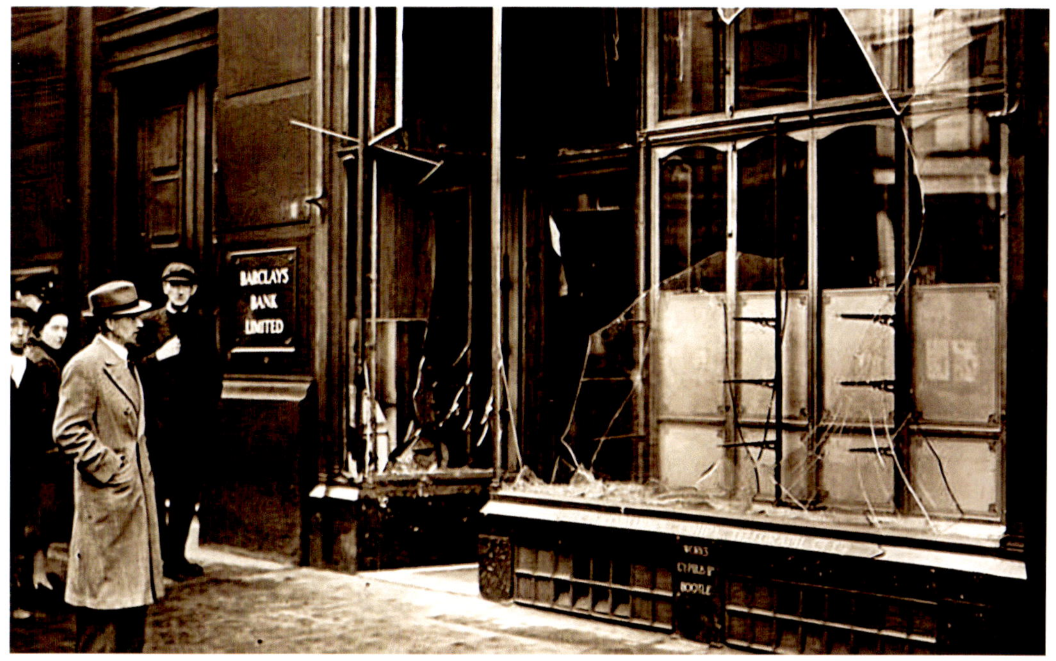

No. 47 Castle Street

Above: In the early hours of 26 April 1939, the Castle Street shopfront of Chadburn's Ship Telegraph Company was shattered when a bomb attributed to the IRA exploded. Its plate-glass window was blown back into the shop shattering into pieces, along with the destruction of a range of valuable nautical instruments which had sat in the window. Despite the grave nature of the incident, the remainder of the property appeared to escape any serious harm.

Below: The site of the explosion is now occupied by the distinctive 1970s structure that is the Equity and Law Building by Quiggin & Gee. This is now a budget hotel, and its upper floors offer an interesting interpretation of the nearby Oriel Chambers building from the previous century. On the ground floor, the space and that within its curtilage has been adapted for restaurant use.

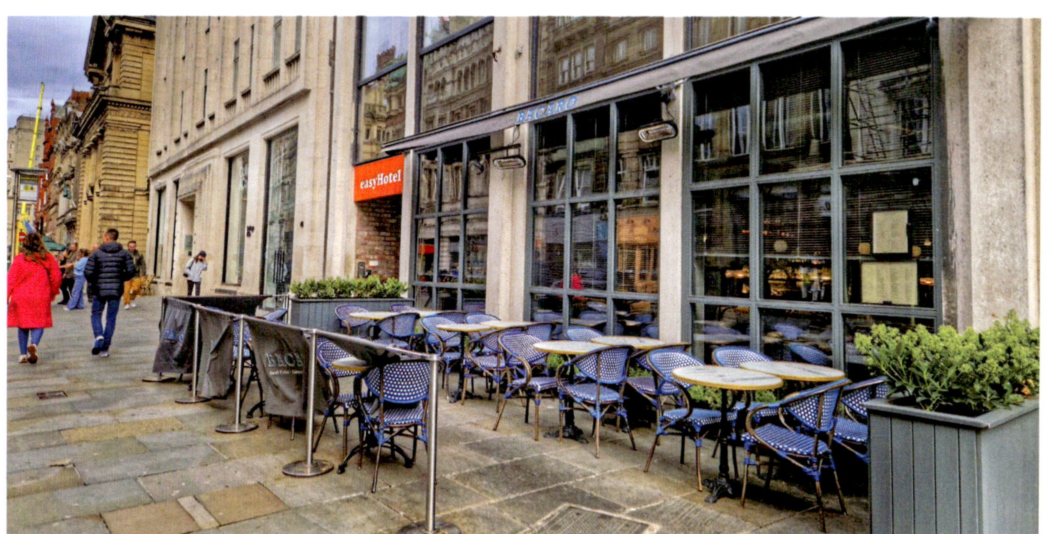

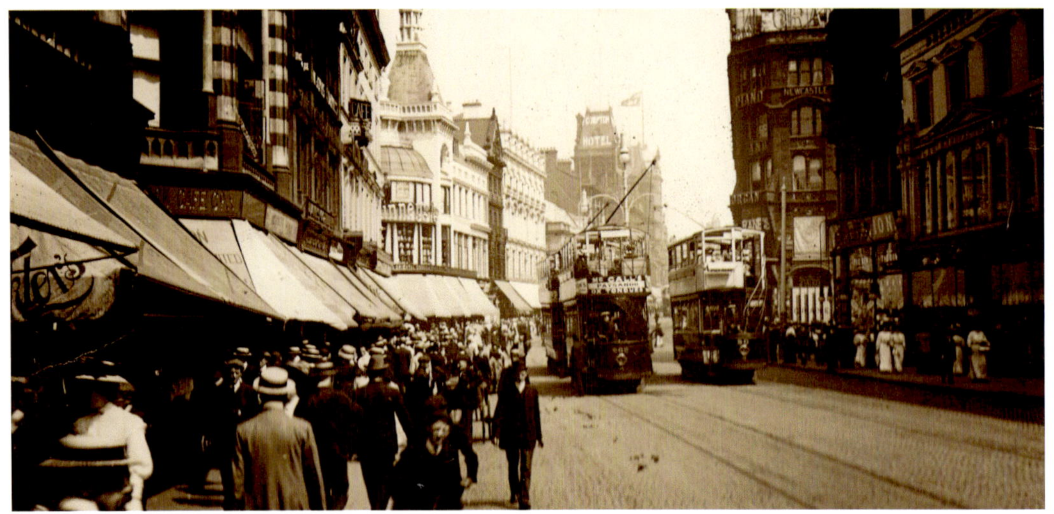

Lord Street

Above: A busy day in Lord Street with its pavements seen full of Liverpudlians enjoying the offers to be found across one of the city's most commercialised streets. Awnings hung over the majority of the stores, including the Arcade which featured bands of red and white stone and more shops within. Across the way stood the exquisite Dresden Rooms which housed a glass and china manufacturer, whilst at the corner of Paradise Street was the Don Association. Their large display windows could be seen full of the latest menswear at this attractive central location.

Below: The Lord Street Arcade building still stands but this Grade II listed structure was modified in 1935 to the designs of British Home Stores. Their plans included the insertion of new shopfronts and the sad loss of the large open interior. Worse fates awaited its neighbours, many of which were destroyed the following decade. The corner building dates from 1954 and forms just a part of the mass regeneration that took place across the ruined city centre. A branch of McDonald's now occupies the site at this frequently frenetic nodal point.

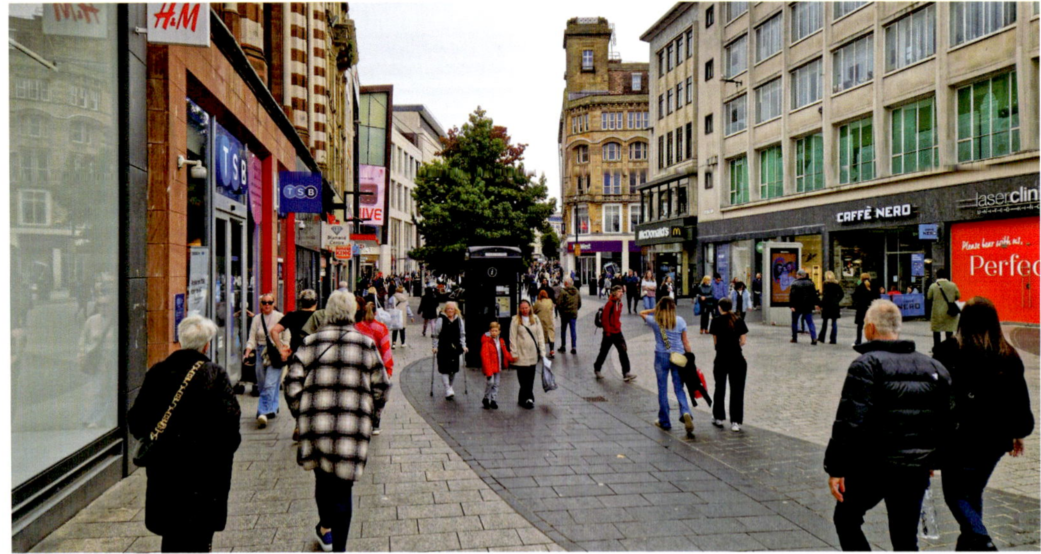